The Cost of Capital

The Cost of Capital

Eva R. Porras

First published 2011 by
PALGRAVE MACMILLAN

Palgrave Macmillan in the UK is an imprint of Macmillan Publishers Limited, registered in England, company number 785998, of Houndmills, Basingstoke, Hampshire RG21 6XS.

Palgrave Macmillan in the US is a division of St Martin's Press LLC, 175 Fifth Avenue, New York, NY 10010.

Palgrave Macmillan is the global academic imprint of the above companies and has companies and representatives throughout the world.

Palgrave® and Macmillan® are registered trademarks in the United States, the United Kingdom, Europe and other countries.

ISBN: 978-0-230-20183-5 hardback

This book is printed on paper suitable for recycling and made from fully managed and sustained forest sources. Logging, pulping and manufacturing processes are expected to conform to the environmental regulations of the country of origin.

A catalogue record for this book is available from the British Library.

A catalog record for this book is available from the Library of Congress.

10 9 8 7 6 5 4 3 2 1
20 19 18 17 16 15 14 13 12 11

Printed and bound in Great Britain by
CPI Antony Rowe, Chippenham and Eastbourne

To my father

Contents

vii

Tables

Figures

Abbreviations

AM	Apparel manufacturing
APBO	Accumulated post-retirement benefit obligations
APT	Arbitrage pricing theory
APV	Adjusted present value
B-S	Black and Scholes
CAPM	Capital asset pricing model
CDO	Collateralized debt obligations
CDS	Credit default swaps
CEO	Chief executive officer
CF	Cash flows
CFO	Chief financial officer
CPI	Consumer price index
CRP	Country risk premium
DCF	Discounted cash flow
DJIA	Dow Jones Industrial Average
DPP	Discounted payback period
EBIT	Earnings before interest and taxes
EBT	Earnings before taxes
ECF	Equity cash flow
EMH	Efficient market hypothesis
EPS	Earnings per share
ERP	Equity risk premium
EU	European Union
FCF	Free cash flows
FCFE	Free cash flow to equity
FCFF	Free cash flow to the firm
Fed	US Federal Reserve System
FV	Future value
GAAP	Generally accepted accounting principles
GDP	Gross domestic product
GLS	Generalized least squares
IMF	International Monetary Fund
IRR	Internal rate of return
IRS	Internal Revenue Service
LBO	Leveraged buyout
LIBOR	London Interbank Offered Rate
M&M	Modigliani and Miller

MBS	Mortgage-backed securities
MICAPM	Modified international capital asset pricing model
MRP	Market risk premium
MSCI	Morgan Stanley Capital International (equity index)
NASDAQ	National Association of Securities Dealers Automated Quotation
NI	Net income
NPV	Net present value
NYSE	New York Stock Exchange
OLS	Ordinary least squares
PBO	Projected benefit obligation for pensions
PI	Profitability index
PP	Payback period
PPP	Purchasing power parity
PV	Present value
ROE	Return on equity
S&P 500	Standard & Poor's 500 Index
SEC	Securities and Exchange Commission
SIC	Standard Industrial Classification
SML	Security market line
WACC	Weighed average cost of capital

Acknowledgements

This book is the product of the efforts and experience of many people who in different ways have contributed towards its development. First, I would like to thank all the professors who donated their energy and time to my education. It was their persistence and dedication which instilled in me a love for the subject of finance.

As a professor myself I have been gratified by the interest my students have shown in the subject of the cost of capital. The sharing of our common business experiences as directors and entrepreneurs helped us recognize the cost of capital as an area where competitive advantages can be achieved by becoming more effective and efficient managers. These advantages can also be gained when making financial decisions in our own private sphere. I therefore want to thank all the students who openly discussed the personal and professional challenges they faced, and who with their questions planted the seeds for this work.

I need to give very special thanks to Renée Takken and Lisa von Fircks of Palgrave Macmillan. They already know the many reasons for my gratitude. I extend this recognition to my family who exercised their patience through the many months it took to finish this work. Finally, I want to thank my very generous colleague Dr. Roderick Martin who read every page of the manuscript and made so many good comments and suggestions. Of course, any mistakes or textual errors are and remain my sole responsibility.

Preface

On the executive programmes in finance that I teach, the cost of capital is one of the subjects that raises the most interest. There are several reasons for this. One is that managers within small and medium size companies dedicate enormous amounts of energy, time and resources to managing the left-hand side of the balance sheet. For example, most people in the business community are aware of models that exist to help them determine the optimal amount of cash or inventory that should be kept in the balance sheet (or warehouse) to reduce unnecessary stocks that consume valuable resources. Nevertheless, for various reasons, fewer managers have equivalent knowledge of how to think about and mix the different sources of capital needed to purchase the assets the company requires to ensure its growth and well-being. In other words, the right-hand side of the balance sheet often remains a mystery or is treated as 'given'. Much the same holds true for personal financial management. I have met very few people outside the finance profession who have a real understanding of how to manage their personal wealth and of the true risks they incur when choosing the composition of their personal investment portfolios.

Since enormous gains are to be achieved from efficiency in managing the costs and risks of financial resources, this book explains the concepts, formulae, theory and thinking related to these 'cost of capital' and 'capital structure' questions, and is designed to serve the following three main purposes:

1. A comprehensive reference for business managers.
2. An introductory text on cost of capital for academic courses and practitioners.
3. A reference for the general reader who wishes to understand the relationship between the return to be obtained from different investments and the risk they take on when they adopt various positions.

Our aim is to give readers the educational and practical background to put them in command of theory, applications and practice in all the issues related to the subjects addressed within these pages.

This work is not written as a textbook, but rather as a 'story book' in which financial terminology, concepts and formulae are explained in simple terms and illustrated with graphs, pictures and examples that a non-expert can easily follow. The chapters treat the subject with different degrees of depth. The 'story' is introduced in a very general way, to provide an intuitive approach to the subject. However, as we move from one chapter to the next, concepts are developed more profoundly, and models are explained in a more detailed manner.

Although some of these subjects appear complex, the problems confronted in modern financial or personal wealth management are equally challenging, so a good knowledge base is therefore required. Also, since consensus has not been reached on many of the subjects developed here, an effort is made to present the issues clearly, reflecting the various points of view, and a range of positions on controversial issues.

The 'story' of the relationship between risk, return and the cost of financial resources to businesses and individuals is put in context by relating it to the needs of investors, the companies with projects to undertake, the requirements of each sector, historical evidence and the theories developed to explain choices and behaviour. In summary, we have attempted to write a text that spans financial theory, the empirical tests of that theory and its applications to real-world financial problems; we hope the book is also entertaining and easy to read.

Introduction

A fundamental dilemma common to individuals, firms, and nations is how to make the best use of their resources. This book is concerned with one of those resources: the financial capital raised to operate and expand a business. The earnings that individuals can expect to receive by making portfolios of investments depend on the returns those nations and firms pay for their savings, which overall are a function of the risk the investors acquire.

To carry out new business, companies require assets such as equipment and offices, or patents and trademarks. These assets need to be paid for, and for this purpose capital has to be raised. Whether the capital is gathered from sources internal to the firm or from others external to the business, the firm's assets need to produce sufficient returns to meet the cost of these claims. This is the cost of capital.

The cost of capital is the rate of return the market requires to commit capital to an investment. Consequently, the cost of capital is tied to the risk of the investment project. The riskier the investment, the higher the reward expected by the investor. Thus, the cost of capital to a firm is the return investors receive from lending their savings. In this sense, the cost of capital to a firm and the return investors receive for lending money are terms which are often used interchangeably.

This book covers a number of topics selected to help the reader get a solid understanding of the main issues related to the cost of capital. For example, what is a country rating? Why are these ratings important? How do they affect the individual investor or corporate investment? How can they affect a country's growth? Can I get an idea of the return I should be earning on a specific investment? Among several options, which is the better financial investment? What are the advantages and disadvantages of acquiring capital from each of the possible different sources? How do these compromise my future growth strategy?

In our current economic system, individuals are faced with many alternatives. For instance, a person might decide to rent a flat rather than purchase

1

a house: this is a financial decision. Making financial choices is continuous and unavoidable, and if these choices are not made explicitly, they are still made implicitly. For example, an individual who chooses not to change her investment portfolio is already making an investment decision by default: she has decided to continue investing in funds according to her previous choices.

As economic beings in a free market system we consume as well as produce, save as well as spend. Our objective as individuals is to maximize the utility of our consumption over our lives as we strive to consume the types of goods and services, in the amounts and at the times that provide us the greatest satisfaction. Thus, each economic unit (whether individual, corporation or nation) needs to develop a set of rules that helps that unit to select optimally among the various choices.

For example, investors seek securities that appreciate in value; businesses search for projects that earn returns larger than the projects' associated costs; financial institutions look for ways to reinvest deposits to earn profits. However, given the number of alternatives, there is not a straightforward answer or an optimal selection tool that works best in all circumstances. The problem of capital allocation – including resources currently at hand plus all additional funds that can be raised one way or another – is universal, and requires good decision-making that is specific to the situation.

Within these pages we present a synthesis that expands financial theory and its applications to real-world daily financial practice. The objective of this text is to ensure that any individual, whether someone with a general interest in the topic, a financial manager or a student will acquire a strong conceptual knowledge-base that will put her in command when she is confronted with financial choices in her private or professional life.

Although some of the subjects treated appear complex at first sight, once we disentangle the vocabulary and explain how to think about these issues, questions related to the cost of capital become surprisingly simple and the answers easy to find. Furthermore, given that most individuals are faced with these types of decision regularly, this book helps to tackle the knowledge gap that needs to be overcome in order to optimize decision-making when dealing with everyday financial decisions about saving and investment, whether for private or business purposes.

The book is organized as follows: Chapter 1 introduces basic ideas, concepts and evidence related to the cost of capital. For instance, it provides an overview of the relationship between risk and return, including historical evidence. The concepts of market efficiency and portfolio risk, the time value of money, the investment criteria to use when selecting the optimal investment from a range of alternatives, and the distinction between free cash flows and equity cash flows are also discussed in this Chapter.

The weighted average cost of capital (WACC) is the average cost of the permanent financial resources of a firm. Managers use the WACC as the basis for evaluating average-risk capital investment projects. The WACC is market-driven, and is a function of the investment under analysis, rather than the particular investor providing the funds. The cost of capital is forward-looking, based on expected returns, measured in nominal terms, and accounted at market value rather than book value. It is the link that equates expected future returns during the life of the investment with the present value of the investment at the time of the analysis. These concepts are introduced in Chapter 1 and expanded in Chapter 2.

Chapter 2 also presents a description of a series of methodologies proposed estimating the cost of capital. Several approaches are reviewed because no one model is the most appropriate under all circumstances. To select the most suitable model, we have to determine why the estimate is being made and the data and information available for this purpose at the time. Furthermore, in practice, each of these methods requires some problem-solving on the part of the analyst, and many compromises.

For instance, a common predicament is that expected returns will be realized in the future, and hence are not observable. Given that it is impossible to predict the future, it is difficult to value upcoming returns. Inflation rates can change, economic crises might arise, and companies may change their risk portfolio. Therefore, the best we can do is to make 'educated predictions' and use current information together with historical data to approximate our future cash flows. Selecting the current and historical data to feed into our models presents a number of additional challenges to the individual doing the analysis. Consequently, Chapter 3 presents some solutions to the most common problems that might arise when using the models to estimate the cost of capital, such as choosing the risk-free rate or calculating the beta.

In addition, Chapter 4 reviews a series of caveats that affect our estimates of the cost of capital. For example, not all the projects or divisions within a firm carry the same amount of risk. When this is the case, different cost of capital estimates should be used to value the investment proposals. A second example refers to flotation costs. This refers to the case when external rather than internal sources of funds are used to finance a project. When a firm chooses to raise external capital, it incurs flotation costs: the costs of floating or issuing new securities. If the issue is sold through underwriters, these costs can be quite significant. To reflect flotation costs, the cost of capital is sometimes increased. However, it has been proposed that these expenses should be taken into account in a different way, given that the cost of capital must reflect the use of the capital, not its origin.

Other caveats are discussed in this Chapter, including risk premiums for non-traded stocks, inflation adjustments, stock options, convertible stock, the effects of taxation and specific concerns for regulated industries.

When investments in foreign territories bring additional exposure to risk, a supplementary risk premium should also be added to the cost of capital. Our discount rate for the cash flows derived from a project should include compensation for all the risks of the cash flows of the project. If those risks are not reflected in the operative cash flows estimated, then they should be reflected in the financial cash flows.

An important issue is then how to quantify the additional risks, and how to incorporate these estimates into the cash flow analysis of our foreign project. Understanding country ratings is key to adjusting the cost of capital in these circumstances. Chapter 5 presents different approaches to adjusting the cost of capital to account for the additional risk of investing in markets other than the home country of the investor. The list presented is by no means exhaustive as numerous authors and practitioners have contributed to this area in an attempt to find refinements that work better in the various scenarios. However, Chapter 5 discusses the approaches used most frequently, as well as the problems managers and analysts encounter most frequently when using these methods. Analyzing why the different models have been devised will help to understand the complications and trade-offs a manager or investor has to face when finding an adequate assessment of the country risk premium, and more generally on how to think about the cost of capital in multinational contexts.

Throughout the first five chapters we also examine how each source of financial capital constrains the individuals and corporations that acquire it. There are advantages and disadvantages to the use of internal and external financial resources as well as to the use of debt or equity financing. Leverage is appropriate if servicing the debt does not result in financial distress and if there are profits from which the firm can deduct the interest expense, which de facto acts as a shield from taxation. Companies whose cash flows can be predicted to a large extent will be better able to use debt, whereas those in high growth sectors may want to keep their debt levels low in order to keep the flexibility the need to take advantage of growth opportunities.

The optimal capital structure is the mix of debt and equity which maximizes the value of the corporation. It is clear that the optimal capital structure strategy is not the same for all companies, not even for those in the same sector. This is the topic treated in Chapter 6.

Through time, economists and scholars have attempted to explain how managers select their capital structures. Currently, two schools of thought prevail. On the one hand, there are those who see the capital structure as the result of a trade off between the benefits and constraints of acquiring additional debt. On the other hand, there are those who believe a hierarchical order does exist, which starts with internal funding as the most preferred method, followed by debt and hybrid securities, and finally, external equity as the least preferred resource of additional funds.

The most advantageous capital mix will depend on the firm's assets, where the company is in its life cycle, the investment opportunities, the specific company strategy, the firm's investors, clientele and management preferences. Finding an optimum requires a serious analysis of the trade-offs given the characteristics of each source of funding, how these features can benefit the firm, and the competitive environment.

In addition to a succinct review of the different schools of thought that attempt to explain how managers go about selecting their optimal capital structure, in Chapter 6 a numerical example is provided, giving step-by-step guidance on how to estimate the optimal cost of capital. Furthermore, once this numerical optimum is found, we present an analysis of considerations that will have to be reviewed before implementing any optimal capital structure strategy.

It is appropriate to mention that 'pre-packaged' proposals do not work under all circumstances. Strategies which might be perfectly appropriate during a period of low inflation will strangle the firm in a high inflation scenario. Moreover, money occasionally floods the market, or – as at present – it might suddenly dry up, making it difficult to access any funding. Hence, before implementing any approach it is advisable to review how a selected strategy might work under different scenarios. This analysis is also covered in Chapter 6.

1
A General Introduction to Risk, Return, and the Cost of Capital

The relevance of the cost of capital

The cost of capital to a firm is the return[1] investors receive on their investments. Therefore, in this context, an investor is anyone who lends money to a firm or agency in exchange for some 'profit'. The providing of funds to the firm could be done by purchasing some of the company's common stock, bonds,[2] or in a number of additional ways we shall comment on later. The higher the profit desired by the investor, the greater the cost to the firm or paying agency.

One reason why firms calculate their cost of capital is to determine a minimum discount rate[3] to use when evaluating proposed capital expenditure projects. The purpose of capital expenditure analysis is to decide which, if any, of a list of planned projects, the firm should actually undertake. It is then logical that the cost of capital to be estimated and compared with the expected benefits from the proposed projects is equated with the marginal cost of capital the firm raises (the price of acquiring the next dollar, pound, yen or euro ...), not a historical-cost estimate. This is because firms must incorporate the real costs into their calculations when capital is going to be raised, and past historical information is of no use for this purpose.

If the marginal cost of capital is too high, the firm might find out none of its list of proposed projects is capable of returning sufficient profit to cover that cost. For example, let us say you want to open a photocopying business. This project is going to be financed exclusively with equity[4] and, considering the return that could be made on equivalent investments, your shareholders want a 35 per cent return. If all you can expect to make with this project is 10 per cent on each dollar invested, you could not afford to repay what your investors demand. And, if similar conditions were to affect all your hypothetical projects, none of them could be undertaken. On the other hand, if the cost of capital is low, other things being equal, many projects could be considered.

So, what determines this cost? The first of a series of variables that come to mind is inflation.[5] The current inflation rate is the least one would need to pay in order to compensate investors for postponing consumption and lending you, or your company, their savings. The reason why current inflation could be considered a minimum return is that, should nothing else happen to that money, a year after lending it to you the owners would be that much less wealthy. If the person saves $1,000 and the inflation rate that year is 3 per cent, 12 months later one could only use it to buy goods for an equivalent of $970, given that prices would have increased by 3 per cent. Other variables that might impact the investor's decision would be volatility in the financial markets and issues such as alternative uses for the savings.

Let us review some of these options while clarifying the idea with an example. Think of a hard working person who, through sacrifice, is able to save $10,000 over one year. By the end of that period, this person will probably ask herself two questions: a) *what do I do with this money now?* And b) *was it worth the effort?* In order to answer these questions, she would have to start reviewing the alternative uses for these savings. These options would probably include to invest in: a) stocks or shares, b) bonds, and or c) notes,[6] d) some kind of tax-deductible product, e) the down payment for a home, or f) a trip to congratulate herself for all the hard work done, or perhaps a good piece of furniture or work of art.

How could she make up her mind? It seems rather obvious that she would need to analyze the conditions of each of her options before making a choice. Hence, she would have to know the answer to the following questions: 'what am I giving up?' and 'in exchange for what?' In addition, a number of personality traits such as risk aversion, and issues related to her own condition, such as other sources of emergency income or her period within the life cycle would play a key role in determining her choice. Apart from anything else, she would be giving up the immediate consumption of the $10,000 and all the pleasure derived from it. According to which of the above options she selects, saving the money would be an alternative to either some future return yet to be determined, or the immediate enjoyment of a trip, furniture or work of art.

Making up her mind would also require giving up all the options other than the one selected. There is therefore an 'opportunity cost' involved. The opportunity cost is the cost of passing up the next best choice when making a decision. For example, if an asset such as capital is used for one purpose, the opportunity cost is the value of the next best purpose the asset could have been used for. In her case, if she spends the money on a trip, she will have to give up the hypothetical work of art she could have bought and the pleasure derived from looking at it.

Going back to our saver's dilemma, her age, health and family status are data to be considered. If she had no family, and did not expect to live for more than a year, it would probably make no sense to think of any investment whose returns would extend beyond that point in time. On the other hand, if our investor were young and adventurous, had no fear of losing her job, and had never been outside her city of birth, a trip might sound like a very attractive opportunity. Therefore, in the light of the circumstances outlined above, she would have to think in terms of 'utility' (the pleasure derived from the choice) rather than just dollar-quantifiable returns.

The first objective of this chapter is to clarify that should our investor decide to invest the money rather than expend it, the return she receives is paid by someone else; hence it is a cost for this second party. The second point to highlight is that many variables enter into the decision-making process. Investment options is one of them, the others are related to personal traits and circumstances. A third relevant consideration is that users of money, such as governments and corporations, need to offer attractive deals so that households decide to reduce their consumption and lend them their savings for some period of time. Lastly, a fourth issue to consider is that the economy is financed by these savers. If potential investors were not attracted to the returns different corporations and institutions offer at any time, the economy overall would be halted. For any given level of risk, other things being equal, the larger the returns offered, the greater the amount of savings net investors would be willing to lend. However, larger returns would increase the cost of financing and thus affect the number of projects corporations and or institutions were able to take on.

It is also useful to remember that, in this context, users compete for funds. Furthermore, we need to highlight that for-profit and non-for-profit organizations are both in competition for funds, and at both a local and an international level. Economies need cash to foster their growth, and given that most restrictions for the international flow of funds have been lifted, monies come from wherever savings are collected. Some countries, for example China, are net savers, while others, such as the USA are net spenders. Hence, money flows from the first to the second to finance the consumption-led economic model of the USA. An illustrative example of the relevance of the cost of capital can be found in some of the global saving/investing mechanisms that have been operating, especially since 2000, and that have contributed in large part to the current global crises.

Between the years 2000 and 2006, the global pool of money available for savings in fixed-income securities grew from about 36 to 70 trillion dollars. This money came from savings accumulated around the world, including the contributions of some newly developing economies such as China and India. Given that the investors' motto is to obtain the maximum return possible for any specified level of risk, these savings needed to be invested in low volatility products that offered as high a return as possible. Traditionally, treasuries and municipal bonds would have been the financial assets of choice. However, at the time our story begins, the rate offered by US Federal Funds (the Fed) was so unusually low (approximately one per cent), that purchasing these funds became prohibitive. A return of one per cent would not cover the inflation rate, let alone the costs associated with saving and investing money. Therefore, in searching for alternatives, fund managers became interested in USA residential mortgages, because these mortgages paid between four and eight percentage points above the Fed's rate, while sharing many of the characteristics of traditional fixed-income securities. Mortgages were long-term low-risk investments promising investors fixed returns. However, on this occasion the returns were considerably higher, making the risk–return ratio particularly appealing to investors. Hence, by the early 2000s, several trillion dollars looking for low to moderate risk investments with returns above the average inflation rate found the interesting 'promise' of a growing mortgage market...and the rest is history.

The cost of capital is important for many reasons. First, it is a determining factor for economic growth, as it enlarges or shrinks the pool of investors and the number of projects an economy can embark on. However, this effect is felt through different mechanisms. For example, if cost of capital is too low, as in the above example, investors would not feel sufficiently rewarded to save. On the other hand, if the cost of capital is too high, a decline in stock prices and shareholder wealth might result because of the higher discount on future earnings, and a reduction in the number of capital investment projects undertaken. Further distortions can be introduced into an economy by the relative cost of capital in different sectors, for example by taking funds from productive assets into more speculative ones. Second, an important aspect of cost of capital is that it conveys information (about, for example, competitiveness or capital structure) which is transmitted and assimilated within financial markets to establish market-clearing prices.

The relationship between risk and return

In the previous section we outlined some of the events that led to the current crises. However, this brief account of those events is not sufficient by itself to help us predict a financial catastrophe or the future cost of capital. For that purpose we would need to understand the mechanisms created to ensure that the underlying risk of the residential mortgage assets matched the returns offered to the investors. By the early 2000s, when several trillion dollars were looking for low to moderate risk investments with returns above the average inflation rate, several innovations had to be introduced so that investors could take advantage of the growing mortgage market. This is because mortgages were produced in a retail market while the fund market was wholesale. That is, mortgages were produced one at a time by any number of banks and mortgage brokers, while the money from investment funds came in bundles of millions. Consequently, mechanisms had to be put in place in order to facilitate the massive transfer of funds from the net savers to the net users.

There was therefore a need to create forms of retail funds so that a wholesale demand for investments could be satisfied. The way this gap was bridged and the transfer of funds accomplished was through a process in which mortgages originated by local brokers and banks negotiating with individual home owners were sold to big investment firms. These investment firms bundled thousands of such mortgages into 'packages' and then sold shares of the expected monthly cash flows, derived from the payments of the mortgages within each of those packages, to the investors. These shares are called mortgage-backed securities (MBS): asset-backed securities whose cash flows are secured by the principal and interest payments of a group of mortgage loans.

This mechanism allowed the re-packaging of the original retail operation so that it could be managed as a wholesale activity. However, an additional adjustment was necessary to ensure investors with different risk–return requirements would get what they wanted. This additional feature meant slicing or 'tranching' the whole bundle of mortgages to generate different investment classes. Within this package, tranches with a first claim on the assets are 'senior tranches', the safer investments. Tranches with either a second lien on assets or that are unsecured are the 'junior notes'. The more senior rated tranches usually have higher ratings than the lower rated tranches and tranches are generally paid sequentially from the most senior to most subordinate. This means that the investors holding the lowest rated tranches would feel the effects first should any of the mortgages bundled in the package stop making payments, thereby protecting those who purchased the higher rated portions of the package. Another innovation that spread around the markets was the extensive use of Collateralized Debt Obligations (CDO), an investment in the pool of tranches resulting from the MBS we just described.

Unfortunately, structurally well-designed houses can end up being built on swamps…through no fault of the architect or engineer who drew the floor plans and whose specifications were ignored. This is more or less what happened here. Even though the original intent of the fund managers was to invest in safe assets, as time went on, the value of the cash flows generated by the mortgage payments diminished, because the quality of the underlying holder – their ability to repay – deteriorated. That is, the proportion of mortgages held by unqualified households grew. This fact has been explained in two ways: first, the separation of the mortgage originator from the cash flow collector (who are no longer one and the same, which would have protected the originator from any risk arising from default), and second, demand for the product was so great that the guidelines for providing mortgages were loosened. The reasons behind the problems that generated the real estate bubble would take us outside our theme, but the results were that investors who had purchased (and paid for) high quality investments (almost default-free) found themselves with low-rated, high-risk ones.

If we now go back to our example in the previous section, we can imagine a 'Jane Doe' investor who through effort and sacrifice had saved enough to ask herself the question: *what do I do with this money?* Other things being equal, the logical objective of an investor is to get the maximum return possible for a given level of risk. That is, a trade-off has to be made between the rewards granted for postponing consumption and the sacrifices and risks of doing so.

So what would be a good starting point? What kind of analysis can our investor carry out to help herself make the right choices? Well, she could start by considering what would happen to her wealth should she decide not to spend nor invest any money. Given the fact that she had $10,000 and that we are working with an 'imaginary' expected inflation rate for that year of 3 per cent, if she were to put the money in a drawer for 12 months, at the end of that time period her wealth would diminish by $500 to $9,700. This is because the 'purchasing power' of her savings would have shrunk in proportion to the increase in the cost of living. Money has value because it allows us to buy goods and services. The more we can buy, the greater the value of our money; the opposite is also true, and the less we can buy with a given 'pot of money' the smaller will be the value of our wealth. Since Jane Doe wants to increase the value of her savings, doing nothing is very probably not acceptable to her. Hence she might start investigating the alternatives listed before: to purchase shares of stock, bonds or notes, to make a down payment on a home, and to find a good piece of furniture or work of art. We discounted the choices of spending the money on a trip or investing in a tax-deductible product, since we want to keep our example simple for now, but we will keep the other options, including that of purchasing a good piece of furniture or work of art in the hope that its value will increased in the future.

It has already been mentioned that the *raison d'être* of saving is to generate wealth that might be used for various purposes. Consequently, Jane could begin calculating what she could expect to make should she embark on each of the choices above. In order to make the options comparable, each should be analyzed on two equal bases: *if I put my money here, what can I get?* (return), and *what are the chances that I will get that return?* (risk). The answers to these questions would facilitate her decision-making process as she is the one most familiar with her level of risk tolerance and with what, in her view, is a sufficient return, given the sacrifices she made to put aside this money in addition to her other needs.

In the next chapter we will give a detailed description of the most common financial investment vehicles. However, for the time being we will focus on the overall characteristics of these instruments as that gives us sufficient information to understand the relationship between risks and return that Jane would have to assess. In this respect, looking at the options above we can immediately see one characteristic that separates the opportunities into two groups: some alternatives promise a predetermined return, while others do not. Within the first category – that is the group which promises a predetermined return – we include notes and bonds. In both instances, the issuing institution promises to pay a specified return at a precise point of time in the future. These instruments will usually pay a recurrent interest, called the coupon, twice a year. In addition, they will repay the amount originally invested – the principal or face value of the instrument – at maturity: the expiration date. For example, we could purchase a 20-year bond that has a 3.5 per cent coupon rate. The coupon rate indicates the interest that the investment returns on an annual basis, $35 in our example. This is not all, as in estimating the returns from such an investment Jane would have to consider both sources of income: the annual interest, paid in the form of a 3.5 per cent coupon, and the return of the principal in 20 years. We will complicate the example by adding details and information as we progress through the book. However, for now we will be patient and simplify the example by saying that should Jane buy this bond, she would have no doubt about the amount she would get back and the timing of these returns.

On the other hand, what would happen if Jane decides to go for any of the other options? Well, although they are all alike in that none promises a return in the sense specified, each has its own characteristics. For this reason they will need to be examined separately. If we focus on the first option, a share of common stock is known as a 'variable-income security', indicating the fact that the actual returns will vary with any number of factors. The main determinant of whether this investment produces a positive return is the market's expectations of its future performance. If the corporation is expected to increase its market share, other things being equal, it is quite likely that the price of the share will increase. However, expectations are not promises. Jane would be taking the chance that the share price does in fact not increase, and should she go for this option she would have to accept this risk. Furthermore, however remote it seems, she would also have to accept the possibility that the price of the share may decrease a little, or even all the way to virtually nothing. Consequently, the question she needs to ask is: what return would be sufficient to lead me to take the risk of losing any possible expected gains on the investment as well as the principal? Well, we already know part of the answer. Given that with the 'fixed income' security we just described she could get 3.5 per cent with no risk, a pricing estimate would have to be set up by which additional compensation is given for the additional risk of purchasing the share instead of the bond.

It is not only Jane who has to consider such matters. The CFO of each corporation would have to concern herself with the following question: considering alternative investments of similar risk in the market, how do I have to compensate prospective investors? Once more, we need to remember that 'users of funds' compete for these savings. As a result, they can pay no less than the next corporation with an equivalent risk profile. Otherwise, informed investors would select a different option.

The last two alternatives we suggested – to make the down payment on a home, or purchase a good piece of furniture or work of art – share three traits: their returns are uncertain, their returns cannot be completely measured in terms of monetary rewards, and however low their market values go there is a residual value of the physical asset itself, unlike in the example of the bond, where the 'paper' has no value. Let us briefly develop these ideas.

When a person purchases a home this asset provides a range of valuable services to the owner. Some of these services have a clear economic value and some have an emotional value which one might or might not be able to convert into countable units. In the first place, purchasing a home is a savings mechanism as equity can be built up, in contrast to expenditure on monthly rent. In addition, tax savings can usually be made, as governments frequently use this tool to incentivize home ownership. If the dwellings are not for personal use, they can also be rented out, generating income for the owner. In addition, owning a home can give a sense of pride, safety and economic security. Safety can be derived from the idea that no-one can expel you from your home, in contrast to the situation where the landlord can decide to regain possession of the rented apartment. Economic security can also be derived from the fact that if necessary, the owner can sell the house and capture the equity. However, even if one does not sell the asset, in many instances the expenditure one would need to make would be less than those needed to cover the rent, other things being equal and if one kept the same lifestyle. Consequently, even if the investor finds herself at the bottom of a real estate cycle and her equity savings seem to have disappeared, other benefits remain. Furthermore, as real estate prices usually either increase at least with inflation or follow cycles, one can expect that in the medium term those savings will be recovered.

As a matter of fact, home purchase has been called 'the largest pension plan' available since retirees can use it as a 'piggy bank' from which to draw money via additional loans or sales in case of need. The attractiveness of home ownership also increases during periods when interest rates are low and equity markets volatile making it a more appealing option at such times that the returns on debt or stock ownership.

Our last alternative, purchasing a valuable piece of furniture or work of art, shares some of the characteristics of acquiring a home, in that the value derived from the investment is not exclusively measured in economic units since, in this instance, an individual might put a value on the enjoyment of the object. In terms of financial returns, the art world has its own markets and trading mechanisms and, like the housing and stock markets, is also affected by economic cycles.

Several researchers have compared the returns generated in the stock market and those in art markets. In one such study published in 2006 by Worthington and Higgs, the authors looked at the Australian stock exchange and the art market for well-known modern and contemporary Australian artists. Their study included 50 artists and more than 30,000 paintings which were sold at auctions between 1973 and 2003. Their results showed the average returns of these investments to be approximately five per cent, with a standard deviation (the measure for risk) of 16 per cent. Interestingly enough, their findings also confirm no statistically significant difference in the relation between risk and return in the art market as compared to that of the Australian stock market over the same period. The authors also found that the returns of the art market followed a random walk, like the returns on the stock exchange, and that an increase of ten per cent in the latter market was correlated with an increase of approximately three and a half in the former. These results seem to suggest close similarities between the stock market and the art market in Australia, at least for the fifty artists in the study and the chosen time period. It also identifies a correlation in the cycles of both markets. That is, when the stock market is up, so is the art market and vice versa.

So how should Jane feel about this alternative investment? First, she could analyze the relationship between risk and return and compare it to those of her other plausible choices, including taking a close look at the lower portion of the returns curve. As already suggested, Jane will have to determine how much risk she can handle, that is how much volatility in the expected returns is acceptable to her, as well as her liquidity needs, as some of these markets are less liquid than others.[7] With these requirements on the one hand and the alternative choices on the other, she can determine what makes more sense at this stage of her life, given all her needs.

At the beginning of this chapter we indicated that the cost of capital and the return an investor obtains for deferring consumption are one and the same thing. The lender is the net saver of money and the borrower is the user. For this service, the borrower will pay a return to the saver. Given that demand for funds is global, and given the many alternatives the potential investor has, the relationship between risk and return is standard in the sense that for any given unit of risk, a specific return will be demanded. The corporation or institution which does not compensate sufficiently for the risk they transfer to the investor will face difficulties in raising the necessary funds. However, those who pay more than they have to will put themselves at a competitive disadvantage, because the cost of every dollar, euro or yen they borrow is greater than what their competitors pay.

Historical evidence

A few months ago one of my favourite bloggers[8] (and I don't have many favourites), wrote as the heading of an article about a totally unrelated subject: 'I am shocked that you are shocked'. I think there can be no better sentence to introduce the subject of the relationship between risk and return, and particularly what history tells us about that relationship. So far we have provided a brief introduction to the issue. However, though by now we do have a for the subject, the relevance of my blogger's sentence can be better understood when looking at what specific investments have returned historically.

In order to analyze the relationship between risk and return in the historical context, we first have to define formally the meaning of these words from the point of view of a financial investor. In this sense, the percentage return of an investment can be calculated with this simple formula: (Selling price of the asset – Purchase price of the asset + dividends or any other distributions received while holding the asset) / Purchase price of the asset. Let's put some figures into the formula and check whether we have properly understood it. Suppose that a year ago we purchased a share for $40. During the year we have received a dividend payment of $1, and now we plan to sell it at the current market price of $42. Using the formula, our return on the investment is (42 – 40 + 1) / 40 or 7.5 per cent. If the current market price were below the purchase price by more than the dividend payment, our return would be negative. For example, if the current market value were $38, we would have had a negative return of 2.5 per cent. To check this, just substitute 42 by 38 in the formula.

If we are comparing returns different financial assets can provide to a specific holder, we might want to calculate those returns on an after-tax basis since the earnings produced by different investments can receive different tax treatments. To estimate the return on an after-tax basis we just have to multiply the result of the formula above by $(1 - T)$, where T is the tax rate.

Suppose Jane Doe has inherited a portfolio of financial investments from her mother and she is trying to determine the expected return on this portfolio for the coming year. She knows what returns this investment has produced over the last five years, namely: 0.06, 0.09, 0.02, 0.39 and 0.21 respectively. If we add the yearly returns and divide by five we get an average of 0.1540. Hence, over the last five years Jane Doe's mother's portfolio of financial investments has produced an average return of 15.40 per cent per year. However, in looking at the returns themselves, it is clear that during none of these five periods has she obtained a return close to the 15.40 per cent average. There is an obvious difference between the average just estimated and the actual returns obtained.

If Jane was trying to predict what the likely returns for the next period should be, she could use this average. Nevertheless, looking at the past, it is clear that 15.40 per cent would only give a partial idea of what she could expect. A more complete description would include the probability that she would not obtain this average, but a return somewhat above or below it, just as during the prior years. For example, if we take a look at the stated return for the first year, 6 per cent, we see that in reality it is 9.4 per cent below the average of 15.40 per cent. If instead we examine last year's realized return of 21 per cent, we observe that the average falls short of the actual return by 5.6 per cent. Consequently, in assessing future expectations Jane could estimate that during the next year she would receive 15.40 per cent plus or minus an amount to be determined. This amount indicates the likely deviations from the average and is calculated as a standard deviation of the returns from the mean.

In this context, the standard deviation is a measure of risk describing the likelihood of getting an amount different from that predicted from the mean of past returns. Hence, the possibility that our real returns are more or less than the expected returns is the volatility or risk of the investment. Using the numbers above, Jane would calculate this risk using the standard deviation[9] of the portfolio as follows:

$$\sigma = \sqrt{\frac{\Sigma(RR - ER)^2}{n° \text{ observations}}} \qquad\qquad \textit{Formula 1.1}$$

where σ is the standard deviation of the portfolio of investments, $\sqrt{}$ is the square root of the sum of the differences between the average return estimated and each of the real returns obtained, Σ is the summation symbol, RR are the real returns obtained each year, ER is the expected return (the average which has been estimated), and n° of observations is the number of years for which we have returns.

The formula might look cumbersome but the estimate turns out to be quite simple when done step by step:

$(0.06-0.1540)^2 + (0.09-0.1540)^2 + (0.02-0.1540)^2 + (0.39-0.1540)^2 + (0.21-0.1540)^2 = 0.089$. We divide this number by 5 and obtain 0.017. Then, we take the square root of 0.017 and get 0.13.

We would interpret this result as follows. On average, during the past five years Jane's mother received a return of 15.40 per cent. Nevertheless one cannot ignore the fact that this average is associated with a volatility of returns of 13 per cent. This means that if these returns follow a normal distribution in future with 68 per cent probability (one standard deviation), the earnings would be anywhere between 2.40 per cent and 28.40 per cent. Those numbers are the result of adding the average return obtained, 15.40

per cent, to the estimated standard deviation of 13 per cent. Since the deviation can be positive or negative, the range of our likely returns is 2.40 per cent to 28.40 per cent.

The normal curve drawn below describes a probability distribution. The shape of this curve implies that the majority of the observations cluster around a central value (the mean), and the higher and lower values taper off smoothly according to their probability of occurring.[9] Accordingly, the area below the curve describes the probability of each event happening. The first line below shows the number of standard deviations above and below the mean. The second line provides the numbers estimated for Jane's portfolio. Inside the curve the percentages describe the area or probabilities explained by each standard deviation. For example, one standard deviation (plus and minus) explains 68 per cent of the events under the normal distribution (Figure 1.1).

Hence, if Jane were to calculate what she could obtain with a probability greater than 68 per cent, she would have to multiply the standard deviation by 2 or 3 and add and subtract this number from the estimated mean of returns. For a 95 per cent probability she would use two standard deviations, obtaining returns somewhere between –10.6 per cent and 41.4 per cent, whereas for 99 per cent probability she will use three standard deviations, with results between –23.6 per cent and 54.4 per cent. This issue will be revisited later to ensure we gain a better understanding of the implications, since this is a key aspect of the cost of capital.

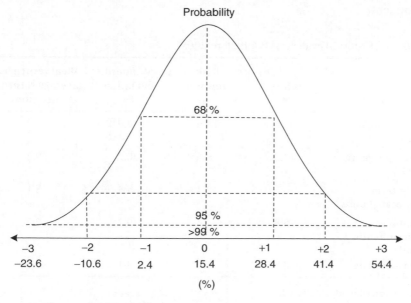

Figure 1.1   The normal distribution

A portfolio of investments is a group of assets (such as a set of shares) in which we invest. As we saw above, the return on a portfolio of investments depends upon the amount invested and the characteristics of the assets which have been purchased. That is, as in our example above where we were trying to determine Jane's options for her savings, should the portfolio be made up of very risky assets, the overall return expected would be larger and the volatility would be greater than if the portfolio were to be made up of something less risky, such as Treasury Bonds.

For several years, on an annual basis, Ibbotson and Sinquefield have published the results of a study which shows the growth that $1 would have achieved if it had been invested in each of five different portfolios over a period of time. The example below is the one published in the SBBI 2006 Yearbook. This shows the historical relationship between risk and return by investigating the average returns and volatilities on five different portfolios of investments created between the years 1926 and 2005. The report answered the following question: had we invested $1 in each portfolio in the year 1926, how much would we have by 2005? Table 1.1 shows their findings. From left to right, the columns show a description of the portfolio, the average return associated with each of these assets, the risk premium, the risk or volatility of these returns, and the 'real return' – the difference between the average return and average inflation. The rows provide the information for each of the portfolios: small company shares, large company shares, corporate long-term debt, government long-term bonds and government short-term debt.

Table 1.1   Historical evidence, USA 1926 to 2005

Investment	Average return %	Risk premium %	Standard deviation %	Real return % (average return – inflation)
Small company stocks	17.4	13.6	32.9	14.3
Large company stocks	12.3	8.5	20.2	9.2
Long-term corporate bonds	6.2	2.4	8.5	3.1
Long-term government bonds	5.8	2	9.2	2.7
Treasury bills	3.8	0	3.1	0.7

Note: Average inflation 3.1%, 4.3.

Source: SBBI 2006 Yearbook.

Immediately below the table we can also see the average inflation (Consumer Price Index) for that period and its associated standard deviation.

To understand these results fully, you also need to know that they assume the reinvestment of dividends on stocks and of coupons on bonds, and no personal taxes. The companies which have been used for the figures in the table for both stocks and bonds are in the S&P500 index. The S&P500 index includes 500 of the largest stocks (in terms of stock market value) in the US. Within those, the small company stocks are the fifth capitalization quintile of stocks whereas the large ones are those in the S&P500 Stock Composite Index.

Moving through the rows from the bottom to the top of the table, we go from lower to higher returns as well as risk. To understand this better, let us describe very briefly the characteristics of the assets within each portfolio which, as mentioned earlier, will be further described in Chapter 2.

US Treasury notes are understood to be 'risk free' securities. This is because they represent debt with short-term maturities (usually less than one year, although sometimes up to three years). Given that the interest rate is contractually agreed before purchasing the financial asset and that, at the current time, the probability that the US government will default is zero for all practical purposes, these securities provide 'known returns'. Consequently, the probability of obtaining returns different from those expected is null. If we focus on the cell which is in the first row and column, we see that the average return for the US Treasury Bills during the specified period is 3.8 per cent. In the third column we observe that the risk premium obtained for holding such assets is zero. Logically, since these are 'risk-free' securities the government does not have to compensate for risk, so the risk premium is zero. The last two columns show the difference between expected and received returns (risk as measured by the standard deviation of returns), and the real rate of return calculated by deducting the average historical inflation for the period in question from the obtained return.

The next row of investments refers to long-term US government bonds. Longer term government bonds have maturities up to 20 or 30 years, and normally command higher returns than shorter term debt. This is because for equal changes in interest rates, their prices vary more than those of shorter term debt securities. For example, if interest rates rise, then prices of long-term bonds fall, resulting in losses for any investor who must sell the security prior to maturity. The explanation is that since these instruments offer a 'fixed return', when interest rates change investors who already hold the security will either be earning more (if interest rates decrease) or less (if interest rates raise) for a given level of risk than those who are purchasing the newly issued securities. These deviations from the expected path will accumulate through the period up to the maturity of the instrument. Therefore, investors normally require a premium to compensate for this interest rate risk: the risk that interest rates will change before the maturity of the instrument.

Again, let us remember that risk in this context is uncertainty, meaning deviation from expectations. For example, the Treasury bond rate for 1 January 1999 was 5.15 per cent, for February of the same year 5.37 per cent, for March 5.57 per cent and for April 5.54 per cent. We can easily infer that some volatility of returns is involved, even if it is minimal compared to changes in the prices of shares for the same period. However, if the expectation for each of those periods was exactly what the realized rate turned out to be, then the deviation from expectations would be zero.

However, returns cannot, unfortunately, be estimated ex-ante in real markets. There is always some deviation from expectations. This is represented in the table in the column showing standard deviation, which shows that the risk premium investors have commanded on average over the 79-year period to compensate for the additional risk incurred by purchasing bonds instead of shorter term debt is 2 per cent. The premium is calculated as the difference between what the government has paid investors in Treasury bills and what it has also paid in the form of returns to those investors purchasing long-term government bonds. The interpretation is that over time, in order to encourage lenders to purchase the more risky security, the government has had to pay them, on average, a 2 per cent higher return than that paid for the shorter term instrument.

Long-term debt securities from a government are usually (but not always!) less risky than those of corporations established in the same country. The reason for this is that governments control the money supply and they can always print more money to fulfil their financial obligations. Thus, moving from the less risky investments to more volatile options the next row up shows the returns obtained when investing in corporate debt.

If capital markets are to clear (that is, if supply is to equal demand), firms must offer returns consistent with investors' expectations. A firm would find no buyers if it offers a security for sale at a return below what investors' require. In this instance, the security will not find buyers unless the firm increases the return by decreasing the price of the instrument, raising the interest paid, increasing the dividend rate, or other means. The securities will remain mostly unsold, and the firm will not be able to raise capital needed to realize its projects.

The cost of capital to the firm is therefore equal to the equilibrium rate of return demanded by investors in the capital markets for securities with a specific degree of risk. That is, for each level of risk, investors demand a specific return. Companies with a high default risk must offer high coupon interest rates in order to sell their debt issues because the market recognizes that such companies are more likely to have difficulty meeting their obligations. For example, the yield in late 1999 on B-rated bonds was over 10.5 per cent.

Because investors need to be able to easily compare issues carrying different levels of risk, debt is usually rated. Therefore, debt issues are identified by their probability of default. The example below uses Moody's terminology, where AAA is the highest quality (least probability of default) instrument and BAA is the lowest quality.

Tables 1.2a and 1.2b the actual difference in returns or yields between government debt and corporate debt by comparing the long-term government rates with those for corporations with ratings AAA, AA, A and BAA for the same period, and with the return offered by the B-rated bond mentioned above:

Table 1.2a shows returns for corporate long-term debt with various ratings for the first four months of 1999. Table 1.2b displays the risk premium that each of those instruments has to pay over the long-term government bond return given in the first column of the second table.

The most remarkable aspects of the information in the tables are that: a) interest rates change constantly, b) as the probability of default indicated by the rating increases, so does the return required to induce investors to buy the asset, c) there is a standardization in the risk–return relationship across instruments and markets, and d) prices provide information that is readily available to all market participants.

If we compare these data with the means estimated by Ibbotson and Sinquefield we see that over these years the average-risk premium demanded to invest in long-term corporate debt instead of government bonds is merely 0.4 per cent and the premium over the risk-free rate 2.4 per cent. The relatively

Table 1.2a   Long-term debt yields and spreads over Treasury

	Corporate long-term debt			
	AAA	AA	A	BAA
Jan/1/99	6.24	6.68	6.84	7.29
Feb/1/99	6.40	6.79	6.97	7.39
March/1/99	6.62	6.98	7.14	7.53
April/1/99	6.64	6.96	7.13	7.48

Table 1.2b   Corporate long-term debt yields and spreads over Treasury

	Spreads over long-term treasury (LTGD)				
	LTGD	AAA	AA	A	BAA
Jan/1/99	5.15	1.09	1.53	1.69	2.14
Feb/1/99	5.37	1.03	1.42	1.60	2.02
March/1/99	5.57	1.05	1.40	1.57	1.96

Source: Moody's Long-Term Corporate Yield Averages 1999.

small difference between what investors command for government and corporate debt can give an overall idea of the traditional average investor confidence level on the whole corporate bond market. The uncertainty created by news related to the current crises is therefore not surprising.

Common stocks differ from fixed-income securities in that equity is called 'variable income'. This type of security is riskier because the returns demanded by investors are not guaranteed by any contract. The greater degree of uncertainty associated with investing in common stock is due to the fact that the pricing of these instruments reflects the market's expectations of the future performance of the specific firm. Because shareholders have a residual claim on the assets of the firm, different variables such as earnings and dividend policy will affect the share price and, in comparison, the payment of common stock dividends is riskier than that of the interest on debt, or preferred stock[10] dividends. Dividends paid to common stockholders are made from cash remaining after interest and preferred dividends have been paid. Thus the former are the first to be cut when the firm encounters difficulties.

In the table summarizing Ibbotson and Sinquefield's findings, the returns from common stock investments are divided by company size into large and small. In each case, we see that corporations have to pay a larger premium overall to attract investors to variable-income securities instead of the fixed-income securities issued by the same corporations.

In summary, Ibbotson and Sinquefield's study shows the historical relationship between portfolios containing assets subject to different risks and the return they obtained over 79 years. It is easy to see that as we move from low-risk securities into higher risk, both the return and the volatility of those returns increases. Knowledge of the historical results helps us form more realistic expectations about the future performance of these financial instruments.

Market efficiency and return

The efficient-market hypothesis (EMH) was developed by Professor Eugene Fama while writing his dissertation in the early 1960s at the University of Chicago, Booth School of Business. This hypothesis states that in 'well-behaved' markets, prices on traded assets reflect all existing information, adjusting rapidly to innovations. The basic idea is that competition will ensure all information is instantaneously incorporated in the prices of financial securities. Given that the maximum price an investor is willing to pay for a security is the current value of the expected future payments derived from the investment, agents are actually trading on the degree of certainty of the information available about the variables that will affect these cash flows.

A market is 'efficient' when prices adjust immediately to new information. Hence in an efficient market the prices of securities reflect all the available relevant information and represent an unbiased estimate of the worth of the investment. The main implication of the hypothesis is that no one can, on a regular basis, outperform the market. Some of the underlying assumptions of the theory are that: traders are utility-maximizing agents, traders update expectations with news, and, overall, the market is correct, even if no one single trader is herself correct. The EMH accepts the fact that some agents may over-price or under-price securities as they over-react or under-react to new information. All that is required by the EMH is that investors' reactions be random and follow a normal distribution pattern so that the net effect on market prices cannot be reliably exploited to make an abnormal profit, especially when considering transaction costs including commissions and spreads.

During the 1970s, Professor Fama reviewed the theory and the evidence for the hypothesis and extended his work to include three forms of financial market efficiency that differ according to the level of information available in the market: weak, semi-strong and strong. In the weak form of market efficiency, current prices incorporate historical price and volume information. Because this information is public and readily available, no single trader is comparatively better prepared than anyone else in the market to make accurate assessments about the security's future performance. This form of market efficiency concludes that market participants cannot take advantage of 'inefficiencies' in a systematic manner. Consequently, in these markets future prices follow a random walk and price movements are determined by information extraneous to the price series.

In the semi-strong form of market efficiency, prices reflect and incorporate instantaneously all public information. The set of data in this instance is larger than in the weak form of market efficiency, as in addition to historical volumes and prices, other company-relevant information such as financial statements, announcements and economic factors of interest are incorporated. Because everyone in the market has immediate access to this information, no-one can use it to earn additional returns in a systematic manner independently of the type of analysis – technical or fundamental – used by the traders.

In the strong form of market efficiency, prices are said to reflect all information, private and public. Hence there is no privileged information on which people could trade to outperform the market. The rationale is that the expectations formed based on this information will ensure the market correctly anticipates any future developments. The idea that prices cannot be consistently anticipated by any trader to realize returns superior to those of the market overall is an extension of the EMH.

There are many reasons why the EMH is a foundation stone of financial theory. To start with, it helps the price discovery process, as the behaviour of traders under the theory will ensure all pertinent information is embedded in prices. These prices turn out to be an educated consensus of the expectations of corporate performance under specific scenarios. To make an estimate of the price a financial asset might command in the market, there first needs to be an approximation of the likely returns an investment in that asset might provide. This estimate will encompass an assessment of future revenues and costs the corporation might incur, including both operational and financial cash flows. The cost of financing the corporate operations will be the discount rate used to calculate the present value of the future cash flows.

Since the price of an asset is estimated by bringing to present value any future cash flows the asset might distribute, these future cash flows need to be estimated under different scenarios, that is, the probability of different states of the economy will need to be quantified. In this process, rational agents will incorporate any new information that provides an opportunity for maximizing their returns, given the level of risk they are willing to accept. Let us again remember that in this context, risk is a deviation over expectations and that the market estimates both returns and risk on the basis of a consensus of expectations.

Even though the EMH is well accepted there are several price-related events that cannot be explained under the theory. These include the fact that stock markets follow trends over some periods, anomalies such as the fact that stocks with low price-to-earnings ratios outperform other stocks, the 'January effect', or that the only way in which no privileged information could exist is by making all private information public. Although exceptions to the EMH are acknowledged to exist, practitioners and academics continue to agree that it is an insightful and useful model which works overall. It is believed that the most developed markets function under a semi-strong form of market efficiency. Nevertheless, not all markets are empirically efficient, especially some emerging economies where lack of information, transparency and/or liquidity prevail.

Portfolio risk and return

Following our comment about the estimation of future returns under various likely economic scenarios, let us imagine that we want to invest in two shares, A and B, and that next year we think there is a 60 per cent probability of a recession and a 40 per cent probability of economic expansion. Under normal circumstances this might seem strange, but at the time this book is being written it is not unrealistic. If the expansion occurs we will make a 30 per cent return on share A, and lose five per cent with our investment in share B. On the other hand, if the recession happens we are bound to lose ten per cent with A, and make 25 per cent with B. Hence our average yield for A (R_A) and B (R_B), considering the likelihood of each scenario, will be calculated as follows: $R_A = 0.40 * 30\% + 0.60 * -10\% = 6\%$. $R_B = 0.40 * -5\% + 0.60 * 25\% = 13\%$. Thus with A we expect a 6 per cent return on average and with B a 13 per cent. In order to estimate the risk, we calculate the standard deviation (SD) of each of the investments in the following manner: VAR $(R_A) = 0.40 * (30\% - 6\%)^2 + 0.60 * (-10\% - 6\%)^2 = 0.0384$, and VAR $(R_B) = 0.40* (-5\% - 13\%)^2 + 0.60*(25\% - 13\%)^2 = 0.0216$. The standard deviation of each would be SD $(R_A) = \sqrt{0.0384} = 19.6$ per cent, and SD $(R_B) = \sqrt{0.0216} = 14.7$ per cent.

As we want to smooth our earnings under each of the two plausible economic scenarios we have hypothesized, we form a portfolio by purchasing one unit of each of these two shares A and B. For the sake of our example, we decide to invest 50 per cent of our fortune in A and the other 50 per cent in B. The average returns under each of the two possible scenarios, economic boom and recession, would be estimated as follows. If an economic expansion happens we would obtain (0.5) 30% + (0.5) −5% = 12.5%. However, if the economy moves into a recession we would have (0.5) −10% + (0.5) 25% = 7.5%. The average expected return on the portfolio would be 0.40*12.5% + 0.60*7.5% = 9.5%, and the average risk $0.40* (12.5\% - 9.5\%)^2 + 0.60* (7.5\% - 9.5\%)^2 = \sqrt{0.0006} = 2.45$ per cent.

As we see, the immediate effect of combining these two shares in a portfolio is that the standard deviation of the portfolio is not equal to the addition of the standard deviation of the individual shares. That is, the SD($R_{PORTFOLIO}$) ≠ 50% * SD(R_A) + 50% * SD(R_B). By investing in A and B at the same time, we have been able to reduce the overall risk of our investments. Why does this happen? Apparently, the companies in this example benefit from the different states of the economy. Company A obtains greater benefits at times of economic expansion, whereas Company B does so during recession. The effect of smoothing out risks by investing in more than one financial asset is called diversification.

Diversification is the reason why investors purchase different assets to create portfolios. The extent to which we are able to diversify a portfolio depends on the correlation between the returns of the investments we bundle together. Would purchasing any two shares achieve the same diversification effect as that shown with A and B in our example? Not necessarily. The key is the correlation coefficient between the investments.

The correlation between two variables is a relative measure that shows their tendency to move together. For example, a perfect positive correlation would be indicated by a correlation coefficient of 1.0. This would indicate that the two investments move in the same direction by the same proportion. If A and B were to have perfect correlation we would not achieve any diversification benefits, because when A's value increases by 30 per cent, so would that of B. Perfect negative correlation would be indicated by − 1.0. In this scenario the values of both shares would move in opposite directions but in the same proportions. For example, if A were to gain 20 per cent in value, B would lose 20 per cent. A coefficient of 0.0 would indicate there is no correlation. The implication is that the value of both shares moves independently of one another and the price change of one gives no information about the price change of the other.

Thus, by combining shares that react differently from one another under various economic scenarios we are able to diversify away, meaning to reduce, the specific company risk within our portfolio of investments.

For example, Alcoa is one of the largest aluminium producers in the world. If we were interested in purchasing shares in this firm, we could reduce the impact of the variability of the returns on those shares by simultaneously investing in the shares of another industry whose movements are uncorrelated to those of the aluminium industry. For example, we could purchase shares in a gold mining company. Why? Because during economic expansion aluminium is sold for infrastructure projects such as highways and bridges, while during recessions, gold sales increase because people see gold as having value as a refuge.

The specific risk of each company that can be smoothed out by building portfolios of financial assets is called 'unsystematic' risk. This type of risk can be eliminated or diversified because the returns of different companies are not perfectly correlated. The amount of risk reduction obtained depends on the degree of correlation between the returns of the shares included in the investment portfolios.

Let us provide a numerical example of the shares of two firms, A and B, for which we shall assume different levels of correlation with an index. Once more, the statistic we use to estimate risk is the standard deviation of the returns of a portfolio of shares. Again, the formula looks cumbersome. However, with a little practice and a calculator, we can easily compute the standard deviation of the portfolio's return, as follows:

$$\sigma_{\text{PORTFOLIO}} = \sqrt{W_A^2 \sigma_A^2 + W_B^2 \sigma_B^2 + 2W_A W_B \rho_{AB} \sigma_A \sigma_B} \qquad \qquad \textit{Formula 1.2}$$

where W is the proportion of the total investment (100 per cent) that we use to purchase each of the shares, σ^2 is the variance, σ is the standard deviation, and ρ_{AB} is the coefficient of correlation between the portfolio's shares, in this case A and B.

In our example we distribute our investment capital between the two shares A and B in the following proportions: $W_A = 0.75$, $W_B = 0.25$. The standard deviation of A by itself (σ_A) is 10 per cent, and that of B (σ_B) is 20 per cent. The correlation coefficient between the two investments (ρ_{AB}) is positive at 0.50. These two shares move in the same direction (either both go up or down) but only by half the magnitude.

Replacing these values by the symbols in the above formula, the standard deviation ($\sigma_{\text{PORTFOLIO}}$) or risk of the portfolio is given by:

$$\sqrt{(0.75)^2 (10)^2 + (0.25)^2 (20)^2 + 2(0.75)(0.25)(+0.5)(10)(20)} = 10.90\%$$

Given the normal distribution drawn before, the interpretation of this standard deviation is that with 68 per cent probability we can expect to earn the average return of the portfolio, plus or minus 10.9 per cent. As mentioned, if we want to associate our predictions of the return with a greater probability we will have to calculate the two and three standard deviations. In that way we shall be able to predict the range of likely earnings with 100 per cent certainty. If we repeat our example giving the correlation coefficient (ρ_{AB}) different values (0.75 and 0.10), we obtain a range of values for the standard deviation or risk of the portfolio ($\sigma_{PORTFOLIO}$), namely:

$$\rho_{AB} + 0.50 = 10.90\%$$
$$\rho_{AB} + 0.75 = 11.72\%$$
$$\rho_{AB} + 0.10 = 9.42\%$$

It is obvious from this example that as the correlation coefficient among the investments within the portfolio is reduced, the standard deviation of the return (or risk) diminishes, and vice versa. This relationship between risk and return can be extended to analyze portfolios with more than two shares.

Because agents are rational, they to obtain the maximum possible return for any given level of risk. All of the portfolios that fulfil that condition are said to be 'efficient'. Thus a portfolio is efficient if for a standard deviation (a given level of risk) there is no other portfolio with greater return. The standard deviation is a measure of total risk.

Figure 1.2 depicts the expected returns from all portfolios on the vertical axis, and the associated risks as measured by the standard deviation on the horizontal axis. All the possible portfolios of investments result from different combinations of risk and return and they are contained within the outline of the drawing somewhat resembling the upper portion of an umbrella. The efficient frontier is where all efficient portfolios fit. This is the smooth line that starts near the bottom left-hand corner of the drawing and goes from the 'Low risk', to the 'High risk' points. Portfolios that fall on this line compensate investors fairly for the risk they have accepted. All other feasible portfolios are not efficient because they do not compensate investors fairly since, as we can see, at any point away from the line but within the umbrella there is always an investment that provides a higher return for any given level of risk.

Later in the text we shall expand further on how this idea is relevant to the cost of capital. However, the discussion here will allow us to start developing some intuition for this subject if we remember that any risk has to be compensated for and it is the user of funds who has to pay according to the risk investors accept. Consequently, any borrower will have a cost of capital that can translate to the equivalent of an efficient scenario for the lender.

Previously we discussed how investing in a combination of shares with different correlation coefficients can help us reduce company-specific or

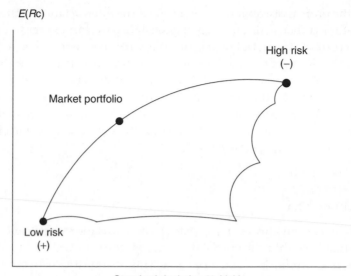

Figure 1.2   Efficient frontier

unsystematic risk. Table 1.3 provides some numbers that illustrate how this risk reduction is achieved.

The table shows the number of shares in the portfolio and the annual standard deviation of that portfolio. The 'portfolio' of one share will have a risk or standard deviation of 49.24 per cent associated with its expected return. The other rows show that as shares are added to our portfolio, the risk of our overall investment diminishes to 19.69 per cent, which is still a lot of risk. Figure 1.3 shows how risk reduces as the number of shares in the portfolio is increased.

In Figure 1.3, the vertical axis shows the risk as measured by the standard deviation of the returns, and the horizontal axis shows the change in the portfolio composition from one share to one thousand shares. From the graph it becomes obvious that risk can be diversified away quite speedily as we start adding shares. However, if we assume that an equal economic unit is invested in each one of the shares, once we have approximately 38 shares, further risk diversification is achieved at a much slower rate. Moreover, we can also see from the graph that beyond a certain limit, risk cannot be reduced any further by including additional shares in the portfolio. The risk that is 'left over' after we have achieved complete diversification is called 'systematic risk'. This risk cannot be diversified away, so it is the only risk for which investors are rewarded.

In summary, the expected return from our financial investments rarely translates into reality. As we have seen from Ibbotson and Sinquefield's historical example, in hindsight there is always a deviation from the market's

Table 1.3   Diversification and risk

As the number of shares within the portfolio increases	The portfolio's annual standard deviation decreases (%)
1 share	49.24
10 shares	23.93
50 shares	20.20
100 shares	19.69

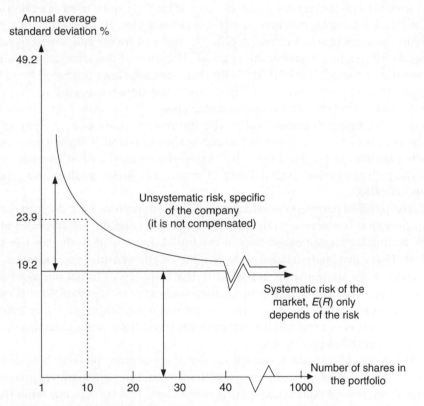

Figure 1.3   Portfolio diversification

expectations. This deviation from expectations is the risk which lenders incur by investing and it has two sources: the specific risk of particular firms (unsystematic risk), and that of the overall economy (systematic risk). Because the unsystematic portion can be diversified away, markets do not reward investors for incurring this kind of risk. Hence, the only risk for which investors are rewarded is the systematic risk that cannot be eliminated.

The time value of money and investment criteria

We have already mentioned that a dollar today is preferable to a dollar in the future. With time, money loses value because the purchasing power of its holder diminishes as prices increase. However, once a lender commits her resources, she would need to worry, not only about inflation, but about the danger of losing her savings and the alternative uses of the money she is forgoing when selecting a specific investment. Therefore, because investors are rational and aim to maximize economic utility, it is important to determine both the adequate return for an investment and the best allocation of resources.

Given that resources are finite, the cost of capital can be used as a criterion for choosing among potential funds sources and uses. In this sense, a corporation or individual faces two decisions: where to invest and where to raise funds. Hence, to determine the optimal allocation of the savings alternative investments should be ranked. To do this, the cash flows produced by these alternative options must be set up on the same time framework so that the different opportunities are comparable. This is accomplished by 'discounting' or 'bringing to present value' the future cash flows and by comparing the results of the analysis to some acceptance criterion. We shall provide a few examples to illustrate how this is done by using the most common criteria: payback period, internal rate of return, net present value, and profitability ratio.

The payback period (PP) rule answers the question 'how long does it take to recover an investment with the cash flows the outlay produces?' It is calculated by adding the negative cash flow of the initial investment to the positive net cash flows that materialize during the life of the venture. For example, let us say we are analyzing an opportunity that requires an initial outlay of five hundred dollars and produces two hundred a year over five years. In this case, it would take us two and a half years to recover our investment. If our criteria were to recover our original investment within this time frame, then this could be an acceptable opportunity.

Using the PP criteria to accept or reject investment projects has several advantages. It is simple, and many decisions do not merit exhaustive analysis. It is biased toward liquidity, favouring investments that free up cash faster than others. If we judge that later cash flows are more uncertain than those to be obtained early in the life of the project, this method corrects for uncertainty.

However, notice also that we have not made any provision for the 'economic loss of value' that is associated with time. Furthermore, we do not know the percentage returned per dollar invested – a figure we need if we are to compare the investment with other choices. That is, which is a superior deal, one that returns the original investment in three months, or one that does so in three years? Would it not depend on which makes you wealthiest? The payback period criterion does not answer this question. It is clear, then, that using this method alone as the only basis for an investment decision has major flaws. For example, the time value of money is ignored; it does not consider risk differences among alternatives; there is no objective rule for selecting a payback threshold within which the project is acceptable, and it ignores any cash flows received after the point when our investment has been covered. In fact, it ignores all cash flows other than those necessary to make up for the initial outlay. It consequently results in a bias towards accepting short-term investments rather than long-term investments that may be more profitable.

We can use a modified version of the PP, the discounted payback period (DPP) criterion, to correct the problem of ignoring the time value of money. The DPP works in the same way as the PP except that all the cash flows that occur after the initial outlay are discounted to reflect the time value of money of the cash flows that occur through time.

Following our previous example, we have the opportunity of investing $500 in exchange for five equal cash flows of $200 that occur at 12 months intervals over the five year period. Since we are introducing the DPP, we need to convert these future cash flows to their present value. To discount these cash flows we need to use a rate, let us say 10 per cent, which is the one we would obtain from alternative uses of money for the same risk class (see Table 1.4).

The formula we use to calculate the present value of our investment by estimating discounted cash flows (CF) is:

$$PV = \frac{FV}{(1+r)^t} \qquad\qquad\qquad \textit{Formula 1.3}$$

where PV is the present value of all the amounts, FV is the future cash flow expected at point in time t ($200 for each of the periods in our example), r is the cost of capital (whether debt, equity or a mixture) in this case 10 per cent, and t the period when the monies are received (in the example, t goes from 1 to 5).

Table 1.4   Discounted payback period

Year	CF $	Discounted CF $	Net accumulated CF $
0	−500		−500.00
1	200	$200 / (1 + 0.10)^1 = 181.8$	−318.18
2	200	$200 / (1 + 0.10)^2 = 165.3$	−152.89
3	200	$200 / (1 + 0.10)^3 = 150.3$	−2.62
4	200	$200 / (1 + 0.10)^4 = 136.6$	133.97
5	200	$200 / (1 + 0.10)^5 = 124.2$	258.15

Understanding the above formula and the concept is easier if we rearrange the terms on both sides of the equation by moving the divisor to multiply the present value of our investment:

$$FV = PV * (1+r)_t \qquad\qquad\qquad \textit{Formula 1.4}$$

Let us say we have $500. We deposit this amount in the bank during one period (in this case a year) and we get an interest rate of ten per cent. After 12 months we shall have the $500 of principal plus $50 more of interest, adding up to $550. If we leave both the principal and interest in the account, after five periods our savings will come to $500 $(1.10)^5$ = $805.25. Equally, we might want to know what is the value today of receiving $805.25 in five years. Since this is the future amount, we would use the first formula where we would substitute FV. We would obtain the PV by $805.25 / $(1.10)^5$ = $500. So, as we can see, we can bring the value of money back and forth in time by multiplying or dividing by the cost of capital while adjusting for the time frame when the cash flows occur. This technique allows us to compare alternative investments.

We said that one of the criticisms of both the PP and DPP is that these criteria give no information as to the rate of return obtained by an investment. For example, let us say someone proposes to us a deal 'a' in which we make an initial outlay of $100 and which within one year will return $10 in addition to our principal. Should we take it? Is this opportunity better than an alternative 'b' in which we also invest $100 but get three back in six months, and two more during months seven, ten and eleven?

In this situation we would use the internal rate of return to determine which is the better investment. The internal rate of return (IRR) is also called the rate of return, effective yield, or marginal efficiency of capital and it tells us what rate we are obtaining when making an investment with cash outflows and inflows. For example, in the case of the proposed deal 'a', and in terms of the formulas above, we should set the problem and solve it as follows:

$$PV = \frac{FV}{(1+r)^t};$$

$$100 = \frac{110}{(1+r)^1};$$

$$100(1+r)^1 = 110;$$

$$1+r = \frac{110}{100} = 1.1;$$

$$r = 10\%$$

Hence the return offered by opportunity 'a' is 10 per cent. We would accept the project 'a' if 10 per cent, the IRR of the investment, were equal to or higher than the rate of return we require. Otherwise the project should be rejected.

The main advantage of the IRR method is that it provides an intuitive answer that can be used to compare different investment alternatives. However, it has some problems, such as the fact that it cannot be used in situations when cash flows change sign more than once, as it would provide more than one rate of return. In addition, a rate of return cannot be confused with an 'amount' of money. For example, you could have a 10 per cent return but, as in our example, only make $10, whereas another project could return a 6 per cent and enrich you with several millions. Hence we have to realize that the IRR is scalable.

A very important rule we need to introduce at this time is the net present value (NPV). The main idea behind this criterion is that an investment is worth undertaking if it creates value for its owners. The rule is that an investment should be accepted if its NPV is positive and rejected if it is negative.

The way to determine the NPV of a project is by calculating the present value of its future cash flows and subtracting from this amount the expenditures incurred in undertaking the project. Going back to our prior example, let us say that the investment proposed requires an initial outlay of $500, the life of the investment is five years during which we obtain cash flows of $200 each, and the rate of return we desire from such an investment is 10 per cent. Should we accept the offer?

$$NPV = -\$500 + \frac{200}{(1+0.10)^1} + \frac{200}{(1+0.10)^2} + \frac{200}{(1+0.10)^3} + \frac{200}{(1+0.10)^4} + \frac{200}{(1+0.10)^5} =$$

$$-\$500 + 181.81 + 165.29 + 150.26 + 136.60 + 124.18 = 258.14$$

We can see that the NPV of this investment is a positive 258.14. The interpretation of the result is that we do get our 10 per cent desired return and, in addition, we are $258.14 richer. Hence the IRR of this investment is higher than 10 per cent.

The general formula utilized to estimate the NPV is:

$$NPV = -Investment + \sum \frac{NCF}{(1+r)^n},$$

We extended this in our example as follows, to include each period's net cash flows:

$$NPV = -Investment + \frac{NCF_1}{(1+r)^1} + \frac{NCF_2}{(1+r)^2} + ... + \frac{NCF_n}{(1+r)^n} \qquad \textit{Formula 1.5}$$

In our example, the result was positive and we accepted the project, as it met our requirements. Should the result be negative the implication would be that accepting the project would make us poorer. In general, the NPV represents the difference between what an investment is worth and what it costs. So a negative NPV tells us that an investment costs more than it is worth and warns us against undertaking the project. A positive NPV implies the investment is worth more than it costs and hence should be undertaken. A zero NPV means that the investment is worth what it costs, in other words, it produces the same return as the hypothetical investment at 10 per cent.

Finally, we also want to mention the Profitability Index (PI), which is a criterion closely related to the NPV. The PI, also called 'benefit to cost ratio', is estimated as the present value of the future cash flows (FCF) of the project, divided by the initial investment. Using the numbers above, Initial investment = $500, PV of FCF = $758.14, PI = $758.14 / 500 = $1.516. The interpretation is that we generate $1.516 or create $0.516 of net present value per dollar invested. The rule is that if the PI is greater than one, the project is acceptable, whereas if it is less than one it would be rejected as the project has a negative net present value.

Some of the advantages of this criterion are that it is easy to estimate, it is closely related to the NPV, and it is intuitively understandable. The main disadvantage is that when comparing mutually exclusive investments it may lead to the wrong decision. For example, let us say we are comparing Projects A and B. A requires an investment of 3 and has a NPV of 6, whereas B requires an investment of 10 and has a NPV of 15. The PI ratios are 2 and 1.5 respectively. Based upon the PI criterion one would select project A, as it has a larger ratio than project B. However, it is the second project that adds more wealth to the company (compare 3 with 5). The profitability index was designed to favour projects which return the most per dollar invested. Nonetheless, this does not translate into the most *profitable* projects. We have to realize that if we use this index as our sole criterion we might bias our choices towards projects with smaller investments.

Cash flows: Free cash flows, Equity cash flows

At this point, we need to make a brief digression to explain a concept that is very useful in thinking about the cost of capital and evaluating the various sources of financing. If we look at the typical balance sheet of a non-banking institution we recognize that the items on the left-hand side and those on the right-hand side add up to the same value. The value of all the assets on the left-hand side equals the value of all liabilities and owner's equity on the right. Let us recall that in non-banking organizations the left-hand side of the balance sheet lists the assets needed by the business to run its normal operations and the right-hand side lists the sources of capital used to purchase those productive assets. Any lender to the firm has a claim on the assets of the firm. Therefore, securities such as stocks and bonds derive their value from the assets on which the owner has a claim. For example, a share has no value as a physical asset. but derives its value from the fact that it represents a percentage ownership of a business giving the holder a claim on the output of the firm. If a bond-holder does not receive his coupon payments, the corporation will be forced to sell its assets and pay the bond-holder the monies due out of the cash flows that are realized after the sale. Consequently, just as in the case of the share, the bond derives its value from the productive capacity of the assets of the firm, and if the worst comes to the worst, from the ability of those in charge of bankruptcy procedures to liquidate its assets. That is why there is a direct relationship between the risk of the operations (the productive assets) and the risk of the financial instruments used to finance those operations. Thus, all of the risks on the left-hand side of the balance sheet are supported by all the investors who, through different instruments, lend their money to the firm. If the business environment changes and operations become riskier, so does holding the financial assets. If there is just one type of capital, that kind of lender will have to support all the firm's risks.

When a firm raises additional capital to finance a project, there is an exchange between the physical assets purchased by the corporation to ensure the firm's productive activities and the financial assets brought in by the different investors. If the new assets purchased by the firm have the same risk as the assets they already had, the investors would require the historical average rate of return. Nonetheless, if these new assets change the risk structure of the firm, the compensation paid to the investors will have to be adjusted. As we have seen in our examples, in discounting, the cash flows resulting from the investment in the assets are expressed in the numerator of the ratio, whereas the cash flows representing the payment for the cost of the financing are represented in the denominator.

Hence, we have already established that the return investors demand is related to the risks they undertake. The discount rate will account for these differences. However, we also mentioned that the discount rate would be determined in accordance with the risks the project adds to the balance sheet of the corporation.

In talking about the time value of money, we reviewed a series of criteria to help us determine which projects add value to our business. Nonetheless, as has become clear in the process of estimating these criteria, we first have to correctly forecast the relevant cash flows for the project under examination. This is true for any kind of investment project, whether the purchase is of a business, the development of a new product, or the acquisition of a financial asset. For example, if we are looking into the acquisition of a new photocopier for industrial purposes, in addition to the cost of the equipment itself, we shall have to consider any other cash flows that change with the purchase decision: does the new machine need a different type of maintenance? Does it require the acquisition of special parts or components? Does it photocopy at a different speed? How much will it help increase our sales, and at what price? What is the life expectancy of the equipment? What will happen at the end of that time? For each of these questions we must estimate both the level and the timing of the project's cash flows.

There is a series of principles that can assist us find the answers. First, the relevant cash flows are defined as those which are incremental with the decision to invest in a project. Hence these relevant cash flows will be any and all the cash flows that change with the decision to invest. Next, we are interested in after-tax cash flows, which is different from accounting profit and net income. The reason for this is that investments are made with after-tax cash flows, so all cash flows should be put on an equal basis. If for some reason it is decided that in a specific case it is more appropriate to use pre-tax cash flows, then these should be discounted at the pre-tax discount rate instead of the usual after-tax basis. Also, since most prices (including interest rates) are quoted in nominal terms, except in very specific instances, we will use nominal cash flows. Inflation applies to labour costs, materials and supplies purchased or sold, so consistency requires that cash flows are also in nominal terms.

The evaluation of a project based on the project's incremental cash flows is called the 'stand-alone principle'. The following are some examples that help us to recognize whether a cash flow is incremental. For example, sunk costs are costs that have already been incurred, so will not change with the decision to invest. However, one might have a natural tendency to include them in the analysis of a project when the expense seems 'operationally' related to it. Any cash flows that occur as a side-effect of the investment decision should be included. Within this category we could think of reducing sales of one product as a consequence of launching a second product, or changes in net working capital, such as those mentioned in our photocopier example. In addition, financing costs (such as interest or dividend payments) will generally not be considered in the numerator, because at this point in the analysis one is interested in the cash flows generated by the project: how these are later shared by owners and creditors is irrelevant to the investment decision.

Before reviewing the different definitions of cash flows, it is necessary to clarify a few issues. First, we need to ensure we discount cash flows and not accounting profits. It is important to stress this point because quite often people use income statements or changes in balance sheets to assess cash flows. However, these documents do not track cash flows. Depreciation is a typical example. If one purchases a piece of machinery, such as our photocopier, the cash used to pay for it is disbursed the time of the purchase. However, accounting rules allow the firm to depreciate the asset over a number of years. We should realize that the only cash flow related to the depreciation is the tax saving generated, not the depreciated amount itself. Someone using the income statement might not recognize the actual cash payment at the time of the purchase and might not correct for depreciation. A second observation is that the income statement reflects revenues when sales take place and not when the bills are collected. Finally, projects are attractive because they generate cash above and beyond the costs they entail. This cash can be distributed among the owners of the business or reinvested in the firm.

When we think of costs, we should incorporate both operating and financing costs. In discounting, the operating costs are most often included in the numerator whereas the financial costs are usually expressed in the denominator. If our investment criterion is the Net Present Value, the project will be acceptable to the firm if at least all such costs are covered (NPV = 0). Hence the project's present value depends on the cash flows (inflows and outflows) it creates that are incremental to those already generated by the firm. This goes back to our stand-alone principle.

Again, one would think it is quite easy to identify which cash flows should be included, but let us provide two examples which will prove otherwise. Let's say we lease an office for a monthly cost of $50 per square metre. We currently have spare capacity and we have been asked to rent a couple of rooms, which will not be utilized otherwise, with a total of 50 metres, to a teacher for $700 a month. In order to determine whether this is a good deal, the natural tendency of an analyst would be to multiply the 50 metres by the f$50 per square metre and conclude that $700 does not cover one third of the monthly cost of the lease. However, we have to pay for the lease whether or not we sublease some of the space. Hence our costs would be irrelevant in this instance. In our second example, suppose we consider purchasing the services of a consultancy firm to help us analyze the practicality of launching a new product. The temptation would be to include the payment of the consultant as part of the cash flows of the project. However, these costs will have to be paid whether or not the project is launched. Hence, again, these should not be included in the analysis of the project.

Look again at the last paragraph. In the teacher example it said 'we have been asked to rent a couple of rooms, *which will not be utilized otherwise*'. This part is important because it means there are no opportunity costs to take into consideration. Otherwise, irrespective of whether actual cash changes hands, these opportunity costs would have to be considered. Suppose I own a building which I can either keep empty, use for a new product I want to launch, or sell for the current market price of half a million dollars. The estimation of the net present value of keeping the building empty would have to start by accounting for the 'no cash flow' of $500,000, which is what would be lost as a consequence of the decision not to act. Hence 'not to do anything' is a decision which has differential cash flows equivalent to the opportunity cost of the 'next best alternative' we are giving up. Half a million dollars, not the historical cost of the building, is the differential cash flow associated with the current market value of the asset. Given the fact that there is a real alternative use for the building (its sale), if we were to analyze the second alternative, even if we do own the building and no cash changes hands, we would still have to account for the fact that $500,000 is the investment we are making for the use of the facilities. This will therefore be a cost associated with the decision to launch the new product: cash forgone as a result of an action.

In our photocopier example we mentioned that attention should be paid to changes in net working capital. Net working capital is the difference between the short-term assets and short-term liabilities of the firm, which usually change with the decision to take on a new project. In accounting for net working capital cash flows, the three most typical mistakes are ignoring changes in net working capital, assuming they will remain constant through the life of the project, and forgetting to recover them after the liquidation of the project.

Finally let us go back to our teacher example. It is very likely that if we were to propose such deal, in addition to being blamed for not covering the 'rental fee' someone would probably suggest adding overheads (electricity, cleaning, heating, etc) to such costs. The principle of incremental cash flows will allow us to determine whether such charges are necessary, since only the marginal expenses incurred from renting the rooms should be included.

When we calculate cash flows from a project we ignore how the project is going to be financed. Nevertheless, once we have established the cash flows we need to ensure that the discount rate matches the cash flows to be discounted both in its riskiness and its type. Errors in asset and project valuation as a consequence of the mismatch between cash flows and the discount rates are quite common and lead to serious mistakes in appraisals. In instances such as valuing a bond, a share or a company we need to ensure the cash flow estimate is made on the same basis as the discount rate. For example, the value of the share could be determined by setting the cash flow in the numerator equal to the dividend payments and the discount rate in the denominator equal to that appropriate for the level of risk of that firm's equity. In the case of a bond, the cash flows would be the interest and principal payments made by the bond through its life, whereas the discount rate would be the one returned by investments of equal risk. In the case of valuing a privately held business we would need to decide whether to assess the value of the firm for the shareholders or the value of the firm itself. The answer will help us set the right ratio of cash flows to discount rate. If we choose shareholder value, the denominator should be the cost of equity discount rate and the numerator the free cash flows to equity holders. However, if we want to know the overall

value of the business, then we should set the weighted av
as the discount rate and the free cash flows in the num
review these concepts.

Equity cash flows (ECF) are the cash flows available to be distributed to shareholders or reinvested in the firm once all the funds needed to secure the corporation's growth have been allocated. Free cash flows (FCF) are the cash flows available to be distributed among both creditors and shareholders or reinvested in the firm, again, once all the funds needed to secure the corporation's growth have been allocated. Given that each of these two definitions account for financial expenditures in a different way – for example, ECF includes both short-term and long-term interest costs while FCF does not – care should be exercised when selecting the appropriate discount rate, to ensure we do not include the same costs twice. This is because in a discounted cash flow evaluation the discount rate consists of the financing not included in the cash flow projections and incorporates all the funding sources on the balance sheet below the point at which the cash flow calculation stops.

As mentioned in the last paragraph, the discount rate used to calculate the present value of the cash flows produced by a business should conceptually match the cash flow. For example, in determining the value of an ongoing concern we can use the discounted cash flow method in a number of ways. The two most common are (1) to estimate the expected FCF over the life of the business and discount them at the weighted average cost of capital and (2) to estimate the expected ECF and discount them at the cost of equity.

Since most of the discounted cash flow appraisals project accrual basis financial statements, the indirect method is frequently utilized by making the following adjustments. In order to estimate the FCF we start with net income (NI) and add the interest expenditures that have been subtracted to reach the NI estimate. We also add back depreciation and any other non-cash charges that were previously deducted. Then, we net out expected changes in working capital requirements and include those as well. This figure could be positive or negative depending upon whether we need to increase or decrease our investment. Lastly, all capital investments (or disinvestments) should also be accounted for. That is, we should add any capital expenditures that are forecasted or reflect a positive cash flow, should any capital asset sales be planned.

There are two major differences between NI and FCF: the accounting for capital assets and for net working capital. In the first case, NI uses depreciation while the FCF applies the last period's net capital purchases, or an estimate of those expenditures in the future, which means spending is in current dollars. In the second, FCF accounts for increases in net working capital rather than current working capital. In addition, one has to ensure extraordinary items, such as income from discontinued operations, do not appear as part of the FCF.

Using this definition of FCF we are including all short-term debt (with and without cost, plus announced dividend payments) in the numerator, thus when structuring the weighted average cost of capital one should double-check that the cost of this short-term debt is not in the denominator as well. On the other hand, if we are interested in the ECF, we should adjust the FCF by adding the payment of after-tax interest expenses on short- and long-term debt, any principal debt repayments, and preferred dividend payments (in fact all these are negative amounts, since they are payments). Finally we should add the proceeds from new debt issues. Since the cost of debt is recorded in the numerator when estimating the cash flows, the discount rate that is appropriate to account for all other sources of financing is the cost of equity.

As mentioned earlier, the discount rate in both these two cases (other definitions of cash flow exist) accounts for financing not taken into account in the cash flow projections and includes all financing sources on the balance sheet below the point at which the cash flow calculation stops. Hence, the discount rate, or weighted average cost of capital (WACC), that applies to any cash flow should include the remaining sources of finance not included in the cash flow stream. If the models used for the estimates are consistent, the values calculated with both methods should be the same. In practice it is quite difficult to be one hundred per cent consistent, therefore the results are approximate and not exactly the same.

FCFF (Free Cash Flow to Firm), calculated as:

Earnings before interest and taxes (EBIT)

− Taxes

+ Depreciation, amortization and depletion

+/− Changes in working capital

+/− Capital expenditures

However, we can also use FCFE as defined below. The only additional consideration is that, in this case, we discount the cash flows by the cost of equity, and not the weighted average cost of capital.

FCFE (Free cash flow to equity holders), calculated as:

Net Income

+ Depreciation, amortization and depletion

+/− Changes in working capital

+/− Additional capital expenditures

− Principal repayments

+ New debt issues

Summary

A basic economic dilemma common to individuals, firms and nations is how to allocate available resources so as to make the best use of them. The one resource that concerns this text is the financial capital raised to operate and expand a business.

The problem of capital allocation is universal, requires good decision-making and is specific to the situation. In this context, the objective of individuals is to optimize their consumption over their lives as they strive to consume goods and services, of the type, in the amounts and at the times that provide them the greatest satisfaction.

For example, investors seek securities that appreciate in value; businesses search for projects that earn returns larger than the projects' associated costs; financial institutions look for ways to reinvest deposits to earn profits. Thus each economic unit (whether individual, corporation or nation) needs to develop a set of rules to enable them to make the right choice.

However, making such choices is not simple. Given the number of alternatives, there is not a straightforward answer or an optimal selection tool. To carry out new businesses, companies require assets such as equipment and offices, or patents and trademarks. These assets need to be paid for, and for this purpose capital has to be raised. Whether the capital is gathered from internal or external sources, the firm's real assets have to produce sufficient returns to satisfy the cost of these claims.

The cost of capital to a firm is the return investors receive from lending their savings. Thus, independently of the source of funds, the cost of capital is tied to the risk of the investment project. The riskier the investment, the higher the reward expected by the investor.

The main application of the concept of the cost of capital has been as a criterion for choosing among potential uses and sources of funds. Managers use the weighted average cost of capital to evaluate average-risk capital investment projects. Any deviations from this average are recognized by adjusting the cost of capital. That is, a project which is less/more risky than the firm's average project should carry a smaller/higher financial cost than those of average risk.

The key concepts developed in this chapter include:

Total risk: in this context, the difference between the returns expected and the actual returns a financial asset produces at a given time. The standard deviation is used to measure this type of risk.

Total return: the result of adding the return expected from the investment to any positive or negative deviations from that expectation.

Systematic risk: risk that affects the whole economy. One example is inflation. Beta is used to measure the amount of systematic risk in an asset with respect to a benchmark. For example, we can assess the beta of the returns on a company such as MACMA with respect to an index such as the S&P500.

Unsystematic risk: risk which only affects a specific asset or small group of assets. An example of unsystematic risk would be the probability that the CEO of MACMA becomes seriously ill. Unsystematic risks can therefore be diversified away.

Diversification: the elimination of systematic risk through the creation of a portfolio (a basket of investments) which combines assets whose returns are uncorrelated with each other.

Correlation: the tendency of two assets to change their price together. For example, if through time we observe that two different shares respond equally to events in the market we might conclude they are correlated.

Risk premium: the reward investors obtain for accepting risk when they lend money. The risk-to-reward ratio shows the relation between the premium offered by a specific investment and the risk of this investment.

Payback period, internal rate of return, net present value and profitability index: tools used as criteria to help assess whether an investment is acceptable, given the investors' requirements.

Time value of money: the idea that a dollar (or euro, or yen) today has a higher value than a similar amount to be received in the future, since over time money loses value because of inflation.

2
The Components of the Cost of Capital and Alternative Models

Risk, return, and the cost of capital

In our Chapter 1 example, Jane Doe was trying to optimize her investment decision about what to do with her savings. This was by no means an easy task given that, to optimize results, she first needed to determine what criterion would help her measure realistically the expected performance of her options. Hence she was forced to examine the utility she could derive from each investment alternative available to her at the time of her analysis.

Every consumer has a characteristic that defines her sets of preferences, such as age, life style, liquidity needs and risk aversion. These sets of preferences are 'givens', exogenous to the theory. On the other hand, there are organizations and institutions which exist to ensure the optimization of 'consumer wealth fare' The criterion used by such organizations for determining optimal performance will be endogenous to the system.

Had Jane decided to purchase equity (shares) with her savings, her role within the economy would be that of a consumer as well as that of a shareholder. Given that the owners of firms are households like that of Jane, who with their savings purchase the company's shares, proper management will ensure their decisions serve the interests of these owners. However, given the size of the economy, management cannot attempt to understand the personal wants and preferences of each of the shareholders of a medium or large firm. Therefore, these agents use other means, such as gathering information from the financial markets, to determine which investment and financing decisions will help them maximize the value of the firm for the shareholders they represent. To act in the best interest of these equity holders, management will have to use tools that help them work out which assets to purchase and in which amounts, how to finance the selected projects, and what type of capital structure to hold.

The cost of capital to the borrowers is the return lenders demand in exchange for postponing consumption and accepting risk. The amount of risk is determined by the alternative investment chosen by the saver. It is for this reason that the cost of capital is linked to the use of money – the source of the risk – and not to the supply of money. That is, the lender can, among others, be a bank, a foundation, a fund or a private individual. Nevertheless, this would not be relevant when assessing the right level of compensation in return for capital lent, even if, from the lender's point of view, their 'persona' places restrictions on their needs or lending ability.

Because the cost of capital is linked to the risk of the investment, and because the returns on that investment happen in the future time with respect to the moment in which the investment decision has been made, a bridge has to be built to put current and future cash flows on an equal basis. For that purpose, we introduced the concept of the time value of money in the first chapter. This technique of putting cash flows on an equal temporal basis allowed us to compare investment alternatives which produce return streams at different points in time.

In the simplified examples we provided to estimate the internal rate of return or the net present value, our explanation stopped short of arguing which would be the acceptable return for each level of risk. We just said, for example, 'our desired rate of return on this investment is 10 per cent'. However, before discussing how to estimate the cost of capital according to different models, we need to understand that both corporations and individuals hold sets of investments, each of which adds its portion of risk and return to their overall portfolios. In this sense, the word 'portfolio' is defined as a collection of investments held by an investor. Given that the return investors demand depends upon the risks they accept, each of the investment choices made will command different levels of return in accordance with their own characteristics. This is relevant because the overall risk of the portfolio is the weighted average of the risk of the individual investment or borrowing decisions. Consequently, the weighted average cost of capital to a firm, or the average return on a portfolio of investments, can be, and typically is, different from the risk/return ratio of each of the individual financial assets bought or sold.

Beta

So far we have been measuring risk as the standard deviation of the expected returns from our investments. However, we have already mentioned that some of this volatility can be reduced by creating portfolios of assets that are less than perfectly correlated with one another.

By definition, a diversified portfolio is one which returns closely resemble those of the market overall. High returns on some shares (high volatility of returns) will be offset by low returns (low volatility of returns) on others. Thus, it is obvious that the highest returns do not accrue to those who diversify. Instead, it would be much better to invest all our savings in the one share which produces the highest earnings. However, given that we cannot identify which that one share with the maximum returns will be, ex-ante an undiversified investment strategy represents a bad risk–reward trade-off for the investor.

Suppose an investor employs all her funds to purchase a share, believing that the value of that share is going to increase dramatically. In fact, our investor is expecting to be rewarded for the firm-specific or unsystematic risk she is incurring, in addition to the risk of the system. Other investors in the market will purchase this share as well, but for them it will just be one of the many investments used to diversify their portfolios. Consequently, because these investors only expect rewards for the systematic risk in the stock, the returns paid by the firm will match this expectation. If, on the other hand, this stock were somehow to produce higher than expected returns, more investors would purchase its shares. The excess demand would drive its price up and thus reduce the return on the investment.

Our investor does not think of this investment as part of a portfolio because she is not diversified. Nevertheless, given that most people in the market behave rationally and hold diversified portfolios, the prices and returns of this one share will behave accordingly. Market clearing prices will happen at the levels of return required by the majority. In this situation, ex-ante our investor's choice of purchasing a single stock will be a very shaky strategy, given that she will be taking on all of the risks (both systematic and unsystematic), while she can only expect the returns linked to the systematic risk. Of course, ex-post returns could turn out to be very high. However, unless the investor had information which is not embedded in the market price of the share, this investment strategy is not sensible.

In Chapter 1 we used the standard deviation as a measure of total risk.' However, since the market will not reward us for the unsystematic or firm-specific risk, we cannot use this measure to determine the additional compensation investors require from investing in a specific corporate share. What we need is an estimate of the systematic risk, and this is what beta (β) produces.

A share's beta (β) accounts for the systematic risk of that share with respect to a market proxy. Betas belong to the common 'financial lingo' and are published regularly by specialized sources. For example, in 1996 the Value Line Investment Survey published a beta for Exxon of 0.65. In February 2010, Yahoo Finance reported a beta for the same company of 0.78. To fully understand how to use a beta we need to analyze how this measure is calculated.

The beta measures the historical correlation of changes in the returns on the firm's equity (share price and dividend income) and those on an overall market proxy (e.g. S&P500). Correlation indicates that the movements of both variables are linearly related in the proportion indicated by the coefficient. This coefficient does not explore the causes for this relation, whether these are direct, indirect or unknown. For example, we might observe a correlation between

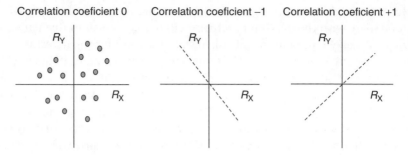

Figure 2.1   Correlation

storks migrating south and newborn babies arriving nine months later, but there is no causal relationship between these two events, and we should not conclude that there is.

The correlation coefficient has a range of values from a maximum of 1, attained when there is a perfect positive correlation between the variables, to a minimum of –1, when there is perfect negative correlation, with a coefficient of zero indicating no relation. Figure 2.1 shows an example of how a correlation coefficient of +1, –1 and zero would be graphed to express the relationship between the returns on shares X and Y.

The formula of the correlation coefficient is simple:

$$\rho_{xy} = \frac{\sigma_{xy}}{\sigma_x \sigma_y} \qquad \qquad \textit{Formula 2.1}$$

In this notation (ρ), rho, is the correlation coefficient, and the suffixes x and y stand for the two variables whose linear integration we are attempting to determine. The sigma with two suffixes in the numerator (σ_{xy}) is the covariance between the two variables, and the sigmas in the denominator (σ_x and σ_y) are the standard deviations of each of these variables.

The covariance (σ_{xy}) indicates the direction of the common variation in the variables. We estimate it as follows:

$$\text{Cov}[x,y] = \sigma_{xy} = E\{(x - \mu_x)(y - \mu_y)\} \qquad \qquad \textit{Formula 2.1}$$

where (μ_x) (μ_y) are the means of all X and Ys.

Suppose we have a time series of returns for the companies x and y (see Table 2.1) and we are considering the purchase of both stocks. Before buying them we would like to ascertain the co-movement of these two shares, in order to ensure we shall increase our diversification when incorporating them into

Table 2.1   Average return estimation

Observations	Return X	Return Y
1	0.0667	0.0897
2	0.0899	0.1099
3	0.0132	0.1131
4	0.3693	0.3277
5	0.2299	0.2523
Total	0.7690	0.8927
/ 5		
Average return or Mean expected return	0.15380 (µx)	0.17854 (µy)

Table 2.2   Covariance estimation

Observations	$(x - \mu_x)$	$(y - \mu_y)$	$(x - \mu_x)(y - \mu_y)$
1	−0.0871	−0.0888	0.0077
2	−0.0639	−0.0686	0.0043
3	−0.1406	−0.0654	0.0092
4	0.2155	0.1491	0.0321
5	0.0761	0.0737	0.0056
Total			0.0590
/ 5			
σ_{xy}			0.0118

our portfolio. For this purpose we estimate their correlation coefficient using formulas 2.1 and 2.2.

The first step is to get the means of each of the series of returns. The second and third columns in Table 2.1 indicate the returns for both x and y which can be used for this purpose.

Tables 2.2. and 2.3. take us through the steps needed to obtain the correlation coefficient between the returns of the shares of the firms x and y:

$$\rho_{xy} = \frac{0.0118}{(0.01293)(0.0944)} = 0.9674 \qquad \textit{Formula 2.1}$$

The results of our example above show a correlation coefficient of 0.9674. By investing in both the shares of companies X and Y we would therefore not achieve any additional diversification, as the returns of these stocks seem to move together. That is, as far as we are concerned, purchasing x is equivalent to purchasing y.

Table 2.3 Standard deviation estimation

Observations	$(x - \mu_x)$	$(y - \mu_y)$	$(x - \mu_x)^2$	$(y - \mu_y)^2$
1	−0.0871	−0.0888	0.0075	0.0078
2	−0.0639	−0.0686	0.0040	0.0047
3	−0.1406	−0.0654	0.0197	0.0042
4	0.2155	0.1491	0.0464	0.0222
5	0.0761	0.0737	0.0057	0.0054
Total			0.0836	0.0445
Average			0.0167	0.0089
Square root			0.1293	0.0944
			(σ_x) 0.1293	(σ_y) 0.0944

The concept of correlation is the basis for understanding beta. It is important to realize that even though we shall propose two general ways for calculating it, practitioners and theoreticians introduce adjustments to these formulas in order to correct for different types of effects. In practice, however, given that they are made available to the general public by reputable companies, we may never need to calculate them ourselves. Nevertheless, we need to understand how betas are estimated in order to use them properly.

The first way we can estimate beta is by using the ratio of the covariance between the returns of the market and the firm to the variance of the market:

$$\beta_J = \frac{\rho_{JM}\sigma_J\sigma_M}{\sigma_M^2} \qquad\qquad \textit{Formula 2.3}$$

where,

ρ_{JM} is the correlation coefficient between the rents of J and those of the market portfolio M

σ is the standard deviation of each of the variables of either J or M, and σ_M^2 is the variance of the returns of the market portfolio.

With the following data we can produce a numerical example:

$$\rho_{JM} = +0.5$$

$$\sigma_J = 10 \ \sigma_M = 20 \quad \sigma_M^2 = 400$$

$$\beta_J = \frac{\rho_{JM}\sigma_J\sigma_M}{\sigma_M^2} = \frac{0.5(10)(20)}{400} = \beta_J = 0.25$$

If the beta coefficient is close to +1, both the returns on the market and the J share move in the same direction and by the same magnitude. If the beta coefficient is −1, then the returns on J move in the opposite direction but by the same magnitude as M, whereas if the beta were to be zero, movements in one variable would give us no information about the movements of the other.

A second way of estimating beta is by running a regression analysis. With this method beta is calculated as the slope of a regression line between the periodic (annual, quarterly, monthly, weekly or daily) returns of the market (we need a proxy such as the S&P500) and those of the firm. The formula which summarizes the linear regression will look something like:

$$R = \alpha + \beta R_{\mathrm{M}} + \varepsilon \qquad\qquad\qquad \textit{Formula 2.4}$$

where,

R are the periodic returns,

α is a constant term determined by the regression (the value taken by the dependent variable if the independent variable were to be zero);

β is the historical beta estimated for the corporation with respect to the market proxy;

R_{M} is the periodic return of the market portfolio (e.g. S&P500);

and ε is an error term treated as a random variable. This last term represents the part of the variation in the returns of the corporation which is unexplained by the proposed explanatory variable 'returns of the S&P500'.

Figure 2.2 gives a graphical representation of the relationship between the returns of Itty Corporation and those of a market proxy. The slope of the line is the ratio of the changes in the Y-axis with respect to the changes in the X-axis. In this case, the slope indicates that the changes in the Y-axis are less pronounced than those in the X-axis. That is, given Itty's beta, a change of one in the market returns is associated with a change of 0.78 Itty's in returns. Both are positive, meaning that if the returns of one of the variables go up, so do the returns of the other (and vice versa). However, the magnitude of Itty's changes is less than that of the market.

If we were to draw a regression line of the market proxy with the market proxy, the line would cut the 90 degree angle in half: if the returns in the market go up by one, so do the returns on the market. Thus, the slope of the market returns (its beta) is one. We can infer that companies with less volatility than the market will have shallower slopes, while firms with slopes steeper than that of the market will have more volatile returns.

In 1996, Value Line reported a beta for America Online of 2.40. This coefficient implies high volatility: when the market moves in one direction by one unit of magnitude, the returns of America Online move in the same direction by 2.4 units. Holding these shares would be considered much more risky than holding the market portfolio. Table 2.4 shows how to interpret different betas:

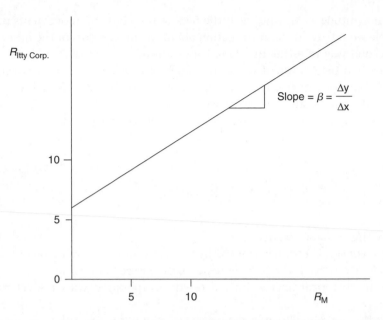

Figure 2.2   Regression line between the returns of the market and Itty Corporation

Table 2.4   Beta examples and their meaning

β	Return shifts	Meaning
2.0	Same as the market	Double risk
1.0	Same as the market	Risk = market
0.5	Same as the market	½ risk
0	No relation	No relation
−0.5	Opposite to the market	½ movement

Risk premium

Going back to Ibbotson and Sinquefield's historical analysis of the relationship between risk and return, let us recall that one of the objectives of their publication was to clarify the risk premium that had been associated historically with different portfolios of financial assets. For example, in the case of the portfolio of shares from large companies, their estimates showed that over time corporations had paid an 8.5 per cent average risk premium to attract investors who could otherwise invest in risk-free securities. Likewise, using betas we can estimate the risk premium individual shares have to offer to compensate investors fairly for taking risks that deviate from that of the overall equity market.

The market risk premium is estimated as the difference between the return required by the investors from the overall equity market as proxied by an

Weighted yield of the assets

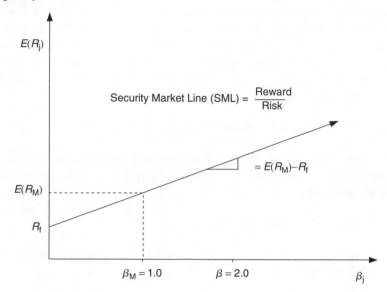

Figure 2.3 Reward–risk ratio

index, and the risk-free rate. If the Dow Jones Industrial Average (DJIA) annual return is 16 per cent and the risk-free rate for the same period seven per cent, then the risk premium estimated using this index is nine per cent. Nine per cent is the compensation that the market provides investors for investing in risky variable-return instead of risk-free fixed-return financial assets.

If the share in which we plan to invest has a risk equal to the market average, represented by a beta of one, then it should compensate investors by the same amount as the market. However, as in the case of Itty, the firm has less risk than the market average (R_M), then the compensation this company needs to offer would be less than that of the market. Given that the beta of the market is 1.0, and that of Itty 0.78, for each 100 points of compensation the market gives, Itty needs to offer only 78. Conversely if the share has a beta of 2.4, such as in the 1996 America Online case, then logically the risk premium granted has to be 240 points rather than the 100 offered by the market.

The Security Market Line (SML) shows the relation between the expected return and the risk of the security (see Figure 2.3).

The Y-axis of the figure shows the returns offered by the financial assets, while the X-axis shows the risk represented by the beta of the investment. The slope of the line reflects the reward that has to be offered for accepting a specific level of risk. This slope is estimated as the ratio of the changes in the y-axis to the changes in the x-axis.

We can illustrate this relation with an example. Suppose the beta of A is one, the risk-free rate (R_f) commands a return of 5.5 per cent, and the market's return on variable income securities (R_M) is 12.9 per cent. With this information we can estimate the risk premium of the overall market simply by subtracting the risk-free rate from the market return. This difference or 'market risk premium' comes to 7.4 per cent. Given that A's beta is the same as that of the market, the return of A is that of the average,

$$R_A = 5.5 + 1(7.4) = 12.9 \text{ per cent}$$

Company B, on the other hand, has a beta of 2. Given that B contains exactly twice the risk of the market, as indicated by its beta, the return of this share should amount to

$$R_B = 5.5 + 2 \ (7.4) = 20.3 \text{ per cent}$$

We can use formula 2.5 to judge if A or B investment opportunities are sufficiently attractive:

$$R_J = R_f + \beta_J \ (R_M - R_f) \hspace{4cm} \textit{Formula 2.5}$$

In this example, we have two projects with different risk and return characteristics. Company A has a beta of one and offers a return of 17 per cent, while company B has a beta of two, and offers a 20 per cent return. If we just pay attention to the returns, clearly the second project seems more rewarding than the first. However, in Figure 2.4 we can see clearly that once we adjust these returns to incorporate the systematic risk contained in each option as measured by the respective betas of the investments, things change. When we do this, alternative A is the more attractive option as it over-compensates by the difference between 17 per cent, the return it offers, and 12.9 per cent, the return that would be necessary considering the market's idiosyncrasy. Alternative B, on the other hand, does not provide sufficient reward to match the additional risk of the project (20 per cent versus 20.3 per cent).

The reward–risk ratio is constant across assets, as the risk premium is calculated by dividing the reward (the market risk premium) by the beta of the asset.

$$(R_M - R_f)/ \beta_J \hspace{4cm} \textit{Formula 2.6}$$

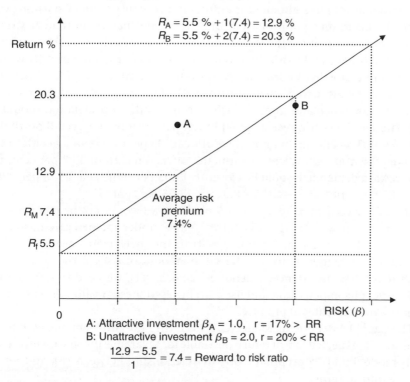

Example of two investments a and b

$R_A = 5.5\% + 1(7.4) = 12.9\%$
$R_B = 5.5\% + 2(7.4) = 20.3\%$

A: Attractive investment $\beta_A = 1.0$, r = 17% > RR
B: Unattractive investment $\beta_B = 2.0$, r = 20% < RR
$$\frac{12.9 - 5.5}{1} = 7.4 = \text{Reward to risk ratio}$$

Figure 2.4 Reward–risk ratio for two investments

The capital asset pricing model (CAPM)

Risk is defined as the degree of uncertainty regarding expected future net cash flows and discount rate. In the CAPM, the discount rate or cost of equity capital is the combination of two factors: the risk-free rate and the premium for risk which compensates for interest rate, systematic risk and unsystematic risk. Interest rate risk (also known as maturity or horizon risk) is the risk that the value of the investment may increase or decrease because of changes in the general level of interest rates. The longer the term of an investment, the greater the interest rate risk. The systematic risk (also called market or undiversifiable risk) is the uncertainty due to the sensitivity of the firm's return to variability in returns of the market as whole, while the unsystematic risk (also called diversifiable or unique risk), is company-specific risk. It is the uncertainty arising from factors unique to the firm of concern. Since the risk measure utilized in the model is the beta (β), it suffices to say that the only reward the investor receives under this model is that related to the amount of systematic risk within the assessed asset.

No rational person would accept the same return for purchasing a Treasury bill with maturity in eight months as for lending equity to an IT start-up. And, from the borrower's point of view, one would not pay more than is strictly necessary to compensate the lender on the same basis as he would be compensated with other equally risky investments. Consequently, if historically we had a portfolio consisting of Treasury Notes returning an average of 5.5 per cent and we start considering the opportunity of supporting an IT start-up, the return we should demand from the new venture under consideration should be unrelated to the returns we obtained in the past. Before, our overall portfolio's return was 5.5 per cent, but now if we allocate 25 per cent of our wealth to risk capital which for equivalent investments offers a return of 35.7 per cent, the new reward demanded would be closer to 13.05 per cent. That is: 75 per cent * 5.5 + 25 per cent * 35.7 = 4.125 + 8.925 = 13.05 per cent.

Should we continued to accept 5.5 per cent we would not be compensated fairly for the new risks we are acquiring since, under the new circumstances, there would be many opportunities within the investments available which would offer a higher return for the same amount of risk, or the same return with much less risk. Hence, as lenders or borrowers, we need to estimate the right level of compensation and use it to bring to present value the cash flows that the investment will produce.

The Capital Asset Pricing Model (CAPM) is the best-known model used to determine the expected rate of return desirable for a 'variable income investment'.[1] This model builds conceptually on the relationship between risk and return taking into account:

(R_f) the minimum level of expected return required from a risk-free asset,

($R_M - R_f$): the expected market risk premium used to encourage investors to move from risk-free to variable income investments, and

(β): the systematic risk in the share under consideration represented by its beta at the time the investment is assessed.

Thus, according to the CAPM, the desired or expected return for share J at any point in time would be estimated as follows:

$$E(R_J) = E(R_f) + \beta_J (R_M - R_f) \hspace{3cm} \textit{Formula 2.7}$$

The most relevant underlying assumptions of the CAPM are:

- Investors hold well-diversified portfolios
- Investors want to maximize their economic utility (more return is preferable to less)
- Investors are risk-averse
- Investors cannot influence prices

- Investors can lend and borrow at the risk-free rate
- There are no transaction costs or taxes
- All of the necessary information is free and easily accessible by all participants at the same time, and
- The traded securities are divisible into small parcels.

The underlying assumptions of investment theory, and specifically of the CAPM, are that investors are rational, that they aim to maximize economic utility, and that they are risk-averse.

As shown in the prior Treasury bill versus IT start-up example, we need to differentiate between the average cost of capital of our operations, and the specific cost of capital of the investment for which we are seeking funds at a precise point in time. If we look at the composition of the right-hand side of the balance sheet of a non-banking institution, we will see different sources of funds. However, because money is 'fungible' once it gets into the firm, any additional unit of currency raised will be destined to support the general asset structure of the firm, not just one of the corporate assets. In this sense, the capital structure is determined at the level of the firm. Since companies maintain a specific debt to equity ratio, it is reasonable to assume that this ratio will also stay constant at the project funding level. On the other hand, the specific way a project is financed will depend on a number of factors. Thus it is over multiple funding decisions that a company will tend towards its optimal capital structure or desired debt to equity ratio, but this does not imply that each individual financing decision will bring the firm close to that optimum.

The weighted average cost of capital (WACC) refers to the cost of all the financial resources a corporation uses. For the fund user, it would be the equivalent of the portfolio of returns we just mentioned for the lender. Either way, for a borrower or as a lender, each project accepted adds a specific level of risk to the portfolio of investments. Hence, in discounting the cash flows from the proposed project, this forward-looking risk must be taken into consideration.

The weighted average cost of capital (WACC)

The weighted average cost of capital (WACC) is the average cost of the permanent financial resources of a firm. The formula for the WACC reaches the average by performing a 'weighted addition' of the capital structure components multiplied by their costs. The model is concerned with determining the components of the capital structure of the firm, their relative weights and the cost of each of the sources of funds.

Given that each firm's capital structure is different, a firm's WACC might have any number of terms, each representing a source of funds. However, it will always have two: debt and common equity. A starting point for understanding these costs would be to use the right-hand side of the balance sheet of the firm to identify the components of its capital structure. An overall guideline is to consider all components used for the long-term financing of the operations and, in addition, any significant amounts of short-term debt that are renewed annually, which de facto would be a permanent part of the capital structure of the company.

A company known to me has the following types of debt in their balance sheet: long-term non-convertible bonds, hedged long-term debts, long-term payables to credit entities, long-term lease payments, long-term financial debt, other short-term financial debts, short-term loans, short-term lease payments payables, other short-term debts under securitization agreements, bank overdrafts, derivatives (no hedging liabilities), derivatives (currency hedging liabilities), derivatives (currency with no hedging liability). Should we be looking for other sources of financing in addition to those mentioned? Should all of these items be included in our estimate of the weighted average cost of capital? Before getting into our computations, let us give a general description of the most usual funding options we might find in a balance sheet and their risk and return characteristics. We need to do this in order to evaluate correctly which items to include in our estimates and how to think about them.

The capital structure of most companies includes two or more sources of financing, each of which has its own cost. In general, the most common way to value these costs is through an analysis of the future cash flows that will arise as a consequence of making the funding decision. Thus, in estimating the weighted cost of capital of a firm one needs to first identify all the components of its capital structure and then their associated cash flows to be able to value them correctly. If we are interested in the cost of the next source of financing, further attention ought to be paid to determining whether the historical components of the capital structure are to be maintained in the future.

The most common categories of funds for companies are grouped as debt, preferred equity and common equity. However, within each of these categories, as we said at the beginning of this chapter, there might be different items, each with its own characteristics and risk levels. In addition, there may be hybrid securities such as convertible debt, warrants or options.

To start with we need to distinguish two closely related concepts: capital structure and financial structure. The capital structure refers to the amount of permanent short-term debt (e.g. not including seasonal peaks), long-term debt, preferred stock, and common equity used to finance a firm. In contrast, the financial structure refers to the amount of current liabilities, long-term debt preferred stock, and common equity. The capital structure is part of the financial structure, representing the permanent sources of the firms' financing: the is our subject of concern.

Because we are interested in the structure of the funds used to finance projects with lives of several years, conceptually only long-term resources are incorporated in the capital structure. Consequently, when deciding which sources of financing to include, we first exclude any sources used to finance temporary increases on net working capital and the like. For example, in the case of debt, we should consider only debt that remains permanently in the structure. In the next few pages we look at eight types of liabilities.

1. When looking into the liabilities of the firm, we should ensure we consider both long-term debt and its current portion, as well as short-term debt when used as if it were long-term debt.

If any debt listed as short term in fact never disappears from the books, we can consider it as long-term debt.

2. Lease financing is considered a form of debt; one which is used extensively in some sectors.

When leasing an asset in exchange for rental payments, the lessee acquires all or a portion of the asset's use value. The lessor retains the title to the asset and the right to sell or dispose of it for its salvage value. Leasing distributes the right of ownership by separating the asset's use value from its salvage value.

The key issue that arises in the accounting treatment of leases is whether or not the lease must be included in the firm's balance sheet. Here we shall be referring to the US generally accepted accounting principles (GAAP), but other accounting standards have also gone through the same 'trials and tribulations'.

Prior to January 1977 most financial lease payment liabilities were documented in footnotes to the balance sheet and current lease payments recorded as expenses in the firm's current period income statement. The Statement of Financial Accounting Standard No. 13 changed the way financial lease obligations were to be recorded, and differentiated between capital leases, which should be recorded in the balance sheet and operating leases, which did not need to be recorded. Because capitalized leases are included within the reported Balance Sheet's reported debt, they are part of the capital structure. However, because operating leases are often not included, they are disregarded.

For the purposes of estimating the weighted average cost of capital, the distinction between capital leases and operating leases is artificial. In either case, the lessee enters into a debt obligation to make periodic payments, so operating leases are a substitute for debt. Therefore, both in-balance and off-balance sheet leases should be included when valuing the debt capital of the company. The same concept is extendable to any country where the reporting standards treat leases differently. The intuition is that de facto a leasing agreement conveys duties and rights similar to those of other debt. Hence, independently of any current accounting standards, these obligations should be recognized and treated as debt.

3. In looking through the statements of a closely held company, one might find that some debt is secured by personal guarantees. When this is the case, there is a distortion in the reported value, since by reducing the risk of the lender a guarantee de facto lowers the cost of the debt.

Some insurance companies offer insurance which guarantees notes payable to a seller. Credit is sometimes not available without personal guarantees and the cost of equity capital would be the only discount rate available. Hence, one is interested in finding the higher cost of debt the firm would incur without this guarantee. We would need to estimate this cost by, for example, looking at the credit rating of the debt.

4. A big item in many balance sheets is the obligations firms maintain with former employees derived from provisions in the employees' original contracts.

For example, post-retirement obligations have currently become a topic of discussion in the financial press. This has been the case recently in reference to the automotive industry. Unfunded liabilities related to pension plans, such as defined-benefit pension plans and retiree medical plans, are debts firms need to honour because they were negotiated as deferred compensation in the original contracts with their employees.

A defined-benefit plan is a retirement plan where the employee is guaranteed certain benefits. Because the benefits are defined, the responsibility of ensuring that they are provided falls on the firm's management. Hence, the company is obliged to honour these agreements, and bears all the risks. If the investments set aside for these payments do not cover the expenditure, employers will need to look for other sources of funding, such as the firm's current earnings.

Defined-benefit plans are different from 'defined contribution plans' because in the latter the firm is only obliged to make specific contributions to the plan rather than ensure a specific fund performance. Thus, in this case the firm does not bear the risk of the performance of the funds selected to meet their obligation.

One must understand post-retirement obligations are treated for accounting purposes in order to measure them properly. This involves the assessment of the current value of the firm's plan assets and a comparison between those assets and the projected benefit obligation for pensions (PBO) and the accumulated post-retirement benefit obligations for retiree medical obligations (APBO). However, the PBO may not show the full economic liability of the firm because it does not include future benefit improvements.

Unfunded pension liabilities or any other types of deferred compensation are equivalent in nature to debt. However, care should be exercised when making any adjustments, given that in the case of pension liabilities and the like, the full amount of the expense incurred in meeting these obligations will result in tax deductions. Therefore, one needs to state the accounts on an after-tax-basis.

If we were able to expense both debt interest and principal, then the treatment would be equivalent.

Attention needs to be paid to any changes made to cover unfunded obligations, since this will affect the capital structure of the firm. For example, if the debt is increased to cover the unfunded projected benefit obligations, it will reduce equity. This affects the capital structure by changing the capitalization, possibly affecting the firm's debt rating and consequently increasing the cost of debt and equity capital.

5. Some companies fund themselves through preferred equity. This source of capital has components of both debt and equity, in that although the return is in the form of a dividend, this payment is considered fixed. In other words, it is treated the same as the coupon payment on a bond and, as with bonds, it often merits a rating.

In trying to determine the cost of preferred equity, analysts will have to adjust for the characteristics of the particular issue, such as if the stock is callable or if the holders have any voting or liquidating rights.

6. Convertible debt is also considered a hybrid instrument in that, like the convertible preferred, it combines the characteristics of two instruments in one. Both types act as either regular debt or preferred equity, but in addition they have a warrant. This warrant is a benefit to the issuer, since it is usually the firm which calls the issue, forcing the conversion of the security. The cost of capital of these funds will have to account for the sum of the costs of the two elements.

7. In addition to preferred, another form of equity is stock options. Stock options are part of the compensation scheme used by firms to attract and retain employees. Issuing these options is a cost to the company and this should be recognized.

8. Finally, there is equity, which could have characteristics that merit special attention. Like debt and preferred it has two components: the dividend distributions and the changes in the market value of the securities. Because

their value is affected by expectations which cannot be observed, valuing these securities is far more complex than valuing other funding alternatives which promise a fixed income.

The weighted average cost of capital (WACC) is the average cost of the financial resources to a firm or individual. This definition allows us to gain an intuitive idea of what we are trying to measure. However, in order to use the model correctly, we have to determine the purpose of our estimate. If the idea is to analyze the average cost of the resources utilized in the past, then we can gather historical information for the period under review and put that into the model.

However, because the typical use of the formula is for discounting future cash flows for the purpose of firm or project evaluation, the data should be forward-looking. In other words, we calculate the WACC to determine how much the next dollar, yen or euro used in the acquisition of productive assets would cost. Hence, historical or accounting information is deemed inappropriate and we will have to assess the components of the pro-forma balance sheet that will exist in the future.

When calculating the weighted average cost of capital we should carefully analyze the different items that make up the capital structure of the company. Keeping in mind that any permanent component of the capital structure should be considered, we work with market values, not accounting values; the analysis is forward-looking and we work on an after-tax basis. In addition, we must take care not to overlook any characteristic of the sources of funds that could affect their value.

Newcomers to the financial field often have the misconception that with a good spreadsheet, optimal decision-making takes about as long as it takes to input the necessary data into the computer program. A rude awakening is about to start in the coming pages, as it will soon become clear that to be a financial manager is quite a bit more complicated than that. Finance is part of the social sciences, and even though at present it relies heavily on mathematical models, the value of the output of such models depends on the quality of the values we input for each variable.

Because models are simplifications of reality, and because information arrives in nanoseconds, changing the overall scenarios we are trying to represent, much hard thinking has to go into determining the values to assign to the different variables. Furthermore, information is usually incomplete, forcing the manager to make educated guesses.

To take one example, recall that the one of the challenges in the application of the CAPM formula reviewed earlier is that we use historical values to assess future events. Hence, without modifications to our inputs, our assessment of the future will only be as good insofar as the future resembles the past. One can determine the fair value of a bond to be sold today. However, seven days later, unexpected events might change the overall assessment of the likely future, deeming our one-week old valuation unfit to represent the new reality.

At any point in time the best decision can only be made with the information that is available at that moment. As a guide, though, it is good to remember that the return obtained from the investment in a financial asset is correlated with the risk of that financial asset. Keeping in mind Ibbotson and Sinquefield's results for the different portfolios built between 1926 and 1996 gives us an idea of how true this statement is, not just a figure of speech but real, as the future cannot be predicted.

In addition to our lack of adequate data (e.g. the beta is estimated with historical time series), and our inability to predict future events, the WACC is an 'open' formula in the sense that it will extend or contract to include as many terms as necessary so that the sources of funds for the case under consideration are estimated in their relative proportions. However, in reality the WACC does not include all sources of financing or all the costs. For example, we are incapable of agreeing exactly how to value certain instruments, such as swaps and warrants, and some of the costs derived from gathering new funding are accounted for outside the formula (e.g. sometimes flotation costs will be calculated separately and incorporated at a later stage).

Explicit costs of capital

To determine capital costs, future relevant cash flows must be correctly identified. If the future is to the same as the past, a simple glance at the balance sheet will allow us to identify these components. On this basis, we should make the adjustments needed to represent our best assessment of the future.

The financing opportunities available to the firm are varied: bank loans, factoring receivables, bonds of different types, commercial paper and so on. Nonetheless, they can be grouped into two broad categories: increases in liabilities, and decreases in assets. Increasing liabilities allows for the acquisition of liabilities not currently on the balance sheet. It also allows for changes in the owners' equity, defined, for brevity, as a liability. Decreases in assets allow us to remember that funds can come from the sale of the 'stuff' the firm owns. The typical financial control template 'sources and uses of funds' can help us visualize these choices.

The cost of capital consists of different elements. One of these elements can be called the *explicit* cost of capital, which reflects the discount rate that equates the cash inflows generated from the financing opportunity with the investment outflows. Given that the explicit cost of capital is the rate of return of the cash flows generated by the financing opportunity, to estimate it we can use the same formula as that of the IRR example. The second of these elements is the *implicit* cost of capital, essentially, opportunity costs.

A general approach to determining the explicit costs of the various sources of funding is simply to identify the cash flows associated with each of the financing options. These cash flows include the present value of the fund and any subsequent amounts that are disbursed. The pattern of such cash flows will vary depending on the option under scrutiny. For example, it could consist of two cash flows, one in the present and the second some time in the future, or it might be an annuity of equal or growing payments, a perpetuity, or any combination thereof. We reviewed several ways of doing this when looking into the criteria used to evaluate the adequacy of the return of different projects. Let us look at several examples of sources of funds and how these can be analyzed under the explicit costs approach.

Funding through increases in liabilities at no cost

Suppose a governmental agency offers a $100 loan with no interest to be paid and a payback deadline of the principal in three years. To see that the explicit cost of the loan is zero, we just need to substitute the values in the present value formula:

$$PV = \frac{FV_t}{(1+r)^t} \qquad\qquad \textit{Formula 1.3}$$

To prove this we just have to substitute zero for r:

$$100 = \frac{100}{(1+r)^3}$$

Funding through increases in liabilities with cost

If the same dollar amount loan were to require an interest payment of $33 to be paid at the end of the third year together with the repayment of the principal, then the explicit cost of capital of the loan would be:

$$100 = \frac{133}{(1+r)^3}$$

so *r* is equal to 0.10, or 10 per cent.

However, if the $100 loan required combined interest and principal payments of $40 at the end of each of the next three years, to find that the value of *r* is 9.7 per cent we would set the problem as follows:

$$100 = \frac{40}{(1+r)^1} + \frac{40}{(1+r)^2} + \frac{40}{(1+r)^3}$$

Funding through asset decrease

a. The sale of a redundant asset which produces no rents and has no future cash flows:

So far we have given examples of how to calculate explicit costs using funding sources that increase the firm's liabilities. However, at the beginning of the section we also mentioned the possibility of obtaining capital through the sale of assets. One such asset could be cash. If a certain amount of cash has no operative use the firm should not incur the expense of holding it. Excess cash as a financing source has an explicit cost of capital of minus 100 per cent. To see this we use another example where we decrease our cash holdings by $100:

Assume we can take $100 out of our cash account without affecting operations. If we try to set the present value of the cash flow equal to the future value of the payments discounted at the adequate rate we shall see that, transforming our earlier Formula 2.1:

$$PV = \frac{FV}{(1+r)^t},$$ *Formula 2.1*

$$r = \frac{FV}{100^{1/t}} - 1$$ *Formula 2.8*

Given that the future value of the repayment is zero, r equals −1 or −100 per cent. If such a source of financing were to be employed as a hurdle rate for assessing a venture, it could be used to finance a project with a rate of return of −100 per cent. The reason is that the net present value would increase to zero and the cash flows generated by the project would be sufficient to cover the investment amount plus the desired rate of return. The key is to remember we do not use the historical or accounting cost of capital but the replacement cost.

b. The sale of a redundant asset with no future cash flows:

In estimating the explicit cost of capital of funds raised through the sale of assets, it is often difficult to assess which cash flows are incremental to this operation. The inflows are easy to identify as they are just the proceeds of the sale of the asset adjusted for any expenses borne by the firm. However, to determine the future cash flows that change with the sale of the asset is rarely a simple task. The main difficulty lies in identifying all the positive and negative cash flows which would have occurred if the asset had not been sold, such as cash earnings or expenditures that the asset would have incurred.

Suppose that in selling a piece of equipment we obtain $100 for the machine and forgo the opportunity of earning $20 each year for the next ten years. The explicit cost of capital of this financing opportunity is:

$$100 = \frac{20}{(1+r)^1} + \frac{20}{(1+r)^2} + \ldots + \frac{20}{(1+r)^{10}}$$

so $r = 15$ per cent.

There are many situations in which the sale of assets would require estimates with different cash flows, but it is probably clear by now that the evaluation of costs is done through drawing the cash flow pattern derived from the financing opportunity.

Funding through increases in short-term liabilities with no cost

When we get a short-term loan such as accounts payable and accrued taxes with no interest attached to the offer, the cost of capital is zero. However, if penalties are incurred or discounts forgone, these incremental cash outflows must be considered in the estimate of the explicit capital cost.

Funding through increases in long-term liabilities: new equity with cost

There are many ways of measuring the cost of issuing new shares of common stock. Some managers compute this cost in terms of dividends, others prefer to use earnings, while there are also those who prefer to estimate costs in terms of the effects of the issuance upon book value or return on investment, variously defined. We shall review each proposal, but to be consistent with the general definition of the explicit cost of any form of capital, we focus on the differential cash flows that occur as a consequence of issuing the new stock. The inflows would be the price per share times the number of shares sold, and the outflow the dividends that would have to be afforded in the future. Hence the explicit cost of capital of an issuance of new shares is the discount rate that brings to present value the future cash flows from dividend payments.

Funding through increases in liabilities: internally generated funds, equity with cost

Internally generated funds such as retained earnings and those provided by depreciation and other non-cash charges are also exceptionally important as a source of financing. Retained earnings can be defined as net income minus dividends paid, and its cost is often taken to be the same as that of a new issue of common stock. This definition is based upon the principle of opportunity costs. However, if we are concerned solely with the incremental cash flows that occur as the consequence of accepting our financing alternative, no future cash flows to or from the firm are associated with it. Therefore, the explicit cost of capital of retained earnings is –100 per cent, just as in the case of the free of charge government loan discussed earlier.

The second source of internally generated funds comes from depreciation and other non-cash charges such as depletion and amortization. These items are not true cash flows, as those happened at the time the asset was purchased and paid for, but an accounting mechanism that allows expensing a percentage of the value of the asset over its life to achieve some tax savings. These tax savings are the cash flows associated with the non-cash expenditures. In this case, since these sources of financing simply represent an adjustment in the true figure of retained earnings, the explicit cost of capital is –100 per cent. This may be verified by observing that depreciation and other non-cash charges do not impose any future required or contingent cash flows on the firm.

Implicit costs of capital

The second element within the capital structure we introduced is the implicit cost of capital. The explicit costs were defined as the discount rate that equates the initial differential cash flows from the lenders with the future cash flows from the project. In contrast, implicit capital costs arise from foregoing other investment opportunities available to the funds in question.

We covered this concept earlier when we clarified that, given the competition for funds, borrowers must pay as much as the next equal risk investment opportunity available to the lender. Hence, the implicit costs of capital are opportunity costs: the rates of return on other investments available to the firm or investor in addition to that currently being considered.

Jane Doe's dilemma provided an example. The implicit costs include the shareholder's opportunities to invest inside or outside the firm as well as her opportunities for consumption. The implicit cost of capital of funds raised and invested by the firm may, therefore, be defined as the rate of return of the best company project, stockholder investment opportunity, or stockholder consumption opportunity that would be foregone, if the project presently under consideration were accepted. For example, if we realize a firm can always purchase its own shares in the market, this constitutes one such opportunity, with a cost equivalent to the rate of return on the repurchased shares.

The fact that the primary duty of managers is to maximize the value of the company for its owners means they must look for a structure that minimizes the overall cost of the financial resources. Wealth is maximized because valuing future cash flows to the firm or shareholder requires the discounting of those cash flows, and the smaller the divisor, the larger the present value. In addition, the wealth maximization criterion fulfils the objective of disregarding individual preferences, as shareholders can adjust their income streams to their own consumption choices.

How to estimate the weighted average cost of capital (WACC)

A review of a typical balance sheet will provide an example of how to estimate the WACC. However complicated the formula looks, in reality it is just a weighted addition of the capital structure components. The model is concerned with determining the components of the structure, their relative weights and the future cost of each source of capital.

Because the most general case is that of firms financing their operations through debt and equity, the typical formula of the WACC includes these terms as follows:

$$K_A = \frac{E}{V}(K_E) + \frac{D}{V}\big[K_D(1-t)\big],$$

Formula 2.9

where:
$K_A =$ Weighted average cost of capital
$E =$ Equity
$V =$ Total value of the company
$K_E =$ Cost of equity
$D =$ Market value of debt
$K_D =$ Cost of debt
$t =$ Tax rate

In our example, just to make it more interesting, we are including two other sources of capital: preferred stock and leases. Hence our formula will be extended as follows:

$$K_A = \frac{E}{V}(K_E) + \frac{P}{V}(K_P) + \frac{D}{V}\big[K_D(1-t)\big] + \frac{L}{V}K_L,$$

Formula 2.10

where in addition to the above:
$P =$ Market value of preferred shares
$K_P =$ Cost of preferred shares
$L =$ Market value of financial leases
$K_L =$ Cost of leases

The variable V is the market value of the firm. Its calculation is as follows:

$$V = E + D + P + L \qquad\qquad\qquad Formula\ 2.11$$

If other components are identified as relevant in the capital structure of the firm, they should be added. However, if a company does not use more than one or two sources of financing, the value of the other terms is simply zero and they disappear from the equation.

A starting point in this operation could be to use the right-hand side of the balance sheet of the firm to identify the components of its capital structure. An overall guideline is to consider all components used for the long-term financing of the operations and, in addition, any significant amounts of short-term debt that are renewed year after year, which de facto would be a permanent part of the capital structure of the company.

Let us assume that a business is financed with debt, common and preferred equity, and leases, and that in the future, this business intends to preserve the same proportions of each source of financing within the capital structure. How do we calculate the WACC? How do we estimate the cost of each of the sources of financing that make up the WACC? The following section provides a number of suggestions to help us quantify the cost of capital of a firm using different models and sources of funds.

The cost of debt (D)

The variable D in the calculation of the WACC is the total market value of the corporate debt that is part of the capital structure. Usually companies have more than one type of debt. Our task is to identify all of these types, quantify the current market value of all the debt within the capital structure, and then find the cost of issuing additional debt.

Therefore, in the formula, D represents the sum of the values of different bank loans, whether short-term notes, long-term or medium-term. If the firm can access the corporate debt markets, it will also include obligations and bonds. In addition, a firm might have mortgages and other classes of external resources that are used to finance the growth of the company; if so, they should be included as well, unless estimated under leases.

Usually the primary source of borrowed funds is bank loans. With this type of borrowing, short-term loans with a maturity of less than one year are usually self-liquidating and consequently are not part of the permanent capital structure of the firm. This is because firms borrow to build up their working capital requirements and, as goods are sold, the loans are repaid. To ensure the loan is not used to fund long-term investments the lenders may require the firm to be completely out of debt for a specific period of time, such as one month during the year. However, one should check this is the case, as otherwise the short-term commercial paper and loans in the short-term category should be taken as part of the permanent capital structure of the company.

In addition to short-term debt, banks and insurance companies also extend term loans. These are medium- and long-term maturity loans with durations of between one and ten years. These loans are repaid in equal periodic instalments that include an interest charge plus a certain portion of the principal.

An alternative to bank debt is corporate bonds that the firm can issue and sell in the market. Corporate notes have maturities ranging from one to ten years, whereas bonds are long-term securities issued to raise capital over periods ranging usually from ten to thirty years. For the sake of simplicity we just call these corporate debts securities. Bonds offer a coupon payment over the life of the financial asset plus repayment of the principal at maturity.

To find out the proportion of debt (*D*) in the total structure (*V*), we simply multiply the market value of each kind of note, bond and financial instrument held by the firm in this category by the total number of notes, bonds, etc, outstanding. Then we just add the results. Finally, we calculate the ratio of total debt to total company value, the result being the percentage of the current capital structure that is financed with debt.

The main challenge in this analysis is to find the market value of the different issues of debt outstanding as well as that of the cost of debt to be issued. Again, the balance sheet can help us identify these various sources of funds and we can find the pricing information from many sources, such as the financial press or specialized agencies.

Since short-term debt usually has a variable interest rate, it is normally assumed that the coupon rate represents the market value. This is why the accounting value of short-term debt approaches its market value. To value traded debt, one can use prices published in the financial press such as The Wall Street Journal or the Mergent Bond Record (previously Moody's).

Because we are trying to determine today's value of the debt in the company, the price one can expect to receive for bonds is the yield of new corporate bonds with similar risk. For example, if among the debt there is a bond with an eight per cent coupon but, when the estimate is being made, the market pays seven per cent for debt of equal risk and maturity, the discount rate to be used to value the issue correctly is seven per cent.

In addition to the examples already provided on how to value this debt using the cash flow stream, if the structure contains a perpetual bond we can estimate its current value with the perpetuity formula, which calculates the present value of the instrument by discounting the perpetual cash flow by the adequate rate. Rearranging the terms of the equation 2.12 we can clear for the rate or cost of capital as follows:

$$PV_0 = \frac{\$}{r}$$ *Formula 2.12*

$$r = \frac{\$}{PV_0}.$$ *Formula 2.13*

where PV is be the market price, $ the coupon paid, and r the cost we are trying to estimate.

If there are issues of debt which are not traded, the following formula can be used to assess their market values:

$$B = \sum_{j=1}^{m} \left[\frac{interest_j + payment\ of\ principal_j)}{(1+K_D)^j} \right]$$ *Formula 2.14*

where m is the date of maturity date of the debt instrument, interest is the fixed coupon payment, and K_D is the present market cost of debt with similar risk and maturity characteristics.

Be careful to avoid a frequent mistake that comes from treating the coupon and the discount rate as one and the same. K_D is the firm's cost of debt at the current time, while the interest of our coupon was the required rate at the time the bond was issued. It represents a historical cost. Also, it might help to remember that the cost of debt can be estimated by adding the market yield of a government security to an estimated credit risk spread. Hence, another approach is to try to determine the credit risk premium of issues equivalent in risk and maturity to that of our concern.

When reading the notes to financial statements, we sometimes encounter explanations such as: '[ ] to pay $7,000,000 to several money lenders with rates between 6 per cent and 13 per cent and maturity between 4 and 12 years'. If no further clarification can be gained, in these instances creativity and the ability to form educated guesses plays an important role in estimating a reasonable scenario to value this part of the debt.

K_D – The cost of debt
So far we have been trying to determine the current market value of all the debt currently in the capital structure, in order to find out how much of the firm's activities is financed with debt. The second step is to determine the market cost of the new debt we want to acquire. This debt might or might not be similar to that already in our balance sheet.

The estimate of K_D is easy if the company has issued traded debt. For this purpose, we can use the Corporate Bond Yield Averages in the Mergent Bond Record. The average return is an estimate of the cost of capital of the long-term debt, K_D.

If we cannot get average efficiencies for low quality bonds, such as Ca, an acceptable technique is to find 30 bonds with Ca category (and prices near par if possible) and use the average return to maturity of those bonds in order to estimate the cost of debt, K_D.

When debt is not traded and the firm has no rating, one can analyze the description of each rating from Aaa to D, and compare them with the historical financial information of the company (current ratio, debt ratio, ratio of interest coverage, benefits, stability and so on). With this information and some intuition one can make an educated guess of the likely rating.

If we assume that short-term debt is part of the capital structure, we will also have to estimate the cost of that debt. The rate of variable debt is generally relative to the preferred interest rate or the London Interbank Offered Rate (LIBOR). The Mergent Bond Record graphically provides daily rates in the US, but there are other sources of information such as the financial press and the banks.

With respect to debt, the cost will be the interest that is currently being paid in the market for projects of equal risk and maturity. This maturity rate and cost to the company are observable: we can see what is being paid in new issues of equal risk and maturity of current debt outstanding.

The historical cost of debt is irrelevant, but why? Suppose ten years ago we sold a bond with nominal value of $1,000, 20 years' maturity, and promising interest of 12 per cent. At that point both the coupon and the discount rate would be the same, making the present value of the issue equal to its face value. Today, this same bond is being sold in the secondary market for $860. Hence its present yield is 14 per cent, the new going rate for this risk class and not the original 12 per cent. Therefore, if we want to issue similar debt we will have to compensate investors with this 14 per cent.

Finally, estimating the cost of debt must allow for the fact that the interest payment is tax-deductible. Thus, the cost of debt to the company would be the payment made with interest, minus the portion that can be deducted from tax payments. For example, if we are in the 48 per cent tax bracket and issue high quality bonds, for example Aa3, which for the same maturity pay 8.75 per cent before taxes in the market, our cost would be:

$$K_D = R_D(1 - \text{taxes}) \qquad\qquad \textit{Formula 2.15}$$

8.75 (1 – 0.48) = 4.55 after taxes

The cost of permanent leases (L)

The variable L in the WACC equation stands for Leases, a source of funds that is considered equivalent to debt. As we have already mentioned, both operating leases and capital leases are debt, irrespective of their accounting treatment. Lease payments made by the lessee are fully deductible from its income for tax purposes but are taxable income for the lessor. In addition, the depreciation expense associated with the asset is tax-deductible for the lessor, like any other expense associated with ownership of the asset. If the asset qualifies for an investment tax credit, the lessor is entitled to that credit. Thus, in essence, the lessor is the owner of the asset and, as such, is entitled to all the tax benefits and costs associated with ownership.

A problem arises with respect to tax, and that is whether the lease qualifies as a lease for tax purposes. The IRS applies a set of conditions, and if the lease is disallowed, the lessor cannot claim the investment tax credit, nor deduct the depreciation expense associated with the asset, etc. The lessee then must treat the asset as if he owned it.

Leases can therefore be used to sell the tax benefits to a firm that places higher value on those benefits (because it is in a higher tax bracket). Leasing may be advantageous if the lessee firm is in a lower corporate tax bracket than the lessor, or if the lessor has an economic advantage over the lessee's firm in borrowing in that its borrowing costs are lower than the lessee's. Lease financing may then provide a way for the lessee to obtain cheaper finance and the lessor may, due to specialization, have a better idea of the salvage value of a particular piece of equipment than the lessee. Other advantages of lease financing have been suggested, such as the conservation of working capital, ease of obtaining credit, flexibility and convenience.

Financial lease contracts may contain option components. For example, the lessee may have the option to renew the lease at the end of its original term or cancel it before the end of the term. Financial leases may also contain options to purchase the asset upon completion of the lease term. One can think of the value of the purchase option as a European call option (an option allowing the holder to buy *at the end of the term*) with an exercise price equal to the purchase price. However, this raises a problem in that the salvage value of the asset is unknown, since there is generally no secondary market for it. In addition, the lessee can affect the value of the asset through the quality of the care and maintenance given to it over the lease term.

To make a correct estimate of the value of such a lease would require access to the depreciation tables, knowledge of the residual value of the assets at the end of the contract, and so on. Since this information is usually not available, one can estimate the market value using the accounting value.

One way accountants use to estimate the book value of such contracts is by discounting the stream of the lease payments at a cost debt.

$$L = \sum_{j=1}^{m} \left[\frac{\text{lease payment}_j}{(1+K_{D}.)^j} \right]$$

Formula 2.16

A better way to value these leases is:

$$L = \sum_{j=1}^{m} \left[\frac{(\text{lease payment}_j + D_j^t)}{[1+K_{D}(1-t)]^j} \right] + \frac{\text{RV}_M}{(1+K_A)^m}$$

Formula 2.17

Where D is the depreciation of assets, t is the tax rate, and RV is the residual value. As already mentioned, such information is likely to be known only to insiders to the firm. In addition, the circularity problem estimating K_A must be resolved. We might therefore have to use the first option.

The cash flows of a lease are contractually recognized by law as debts like any other, so the non-payment risk in the case of both debt and lease is equivalent. Therefore the marginal cost of leasing financing is:

$K_L = R_D (1 - \text{taxes})$ Formula 2.18
8.75 (1 − 0.48) = 4.55 taxes after taxes
If there is an additional cost, e.g. 1.5 per cent over K_D then:
8.75 + 1.5 (1 − 0.48) = 5.33 per cent after taxes

The cost of preferred stock (P)

The variable P in the WACC equation refers to preferred shares. Given the fact that there are restrictions on the issue of this types of title, a company does not usually have a significant number of nonconvertible preferred shares. In the exceptional case when it does, it can be valued by multiplying the average price of shares or the closing price by the number of shares outstanding (P = price per share * number of shares outstanding). We can find these prices in financial press, such as the Wall Street Journal, Yahoo Finance, or any other public source.

If the preferred shares are not traded, we can value them as follows:

$$P = \frac{\text{Dividend}}{K_P},$$

Formula 2.19

as for a perpetuity, and

$$P = \sum_{j=1}^{m} \left[\frac{(\text{dividend}_j + \text{sinking fund}_j)}{(1+K_P)^j} \right]$$

Formula 2.20

If the preferred shares have PIK or other special attributes, we have to adjust the value in a creative way.

The marginal cost of financing with preferred stock (K_P).
If a company has preferred shares, the marginal cost of these shares, K_P, can be derived from a cash flow estimate such as for long-term debt (K_D). For reference, use the tables that publishing 'Average Preferred Stock Yields', with average returns per rating.

For preferred stock without rating, one can look at the historical financial information of the company and assign a category based on the descriptions of different ratings. When we know the price and dividends paid by a company, we can calculate the return using the same formula as for perpetuities. The reason is that in effect, the dividends of preferred shares are like company debt (except those related to bankruptcy by non-payment). Due to the fact that these dividends, including those in arrears, have to be paid before common share dividends, in this sense preferred stock is considered a debt of the company with respect to this type of shareholders.

To value the cost of preferred equity we use the following formula:

$$K_P = \frac{D}{P_0} \hspace{4cm} \textit{Formula 2.21}$$

The return on preferred shares cost is equal to the dividend paid divided by the current value of the share. For example, suppose that ten years ago we sold preferred stock with an $8 dividend. Today, these shares are sold at $120. The cost or return is:

$$K_P = \frac{D}{P_0}$$

$8 / $120 = 6.67%

The cost of equity (E)
The variable E in the WACC equation stands for the market value of equity. We estimate this is by multiplying the market share price by the number of shares outstanding. Just as in any of the prior sections covering these estimates, caution should be exercised so that accounting values are not used in lieu of market values. If looking at a balance sheet one should not get bogged down in all the ways in which equity can be split. All that is needed is the number of shares outstanding and the last closing price per share. In addition, one should be careful to determine whether there is more than one kind of common stock.

The share market price can be obtained from the financial press or specialized sources such as Standard and Poor's Daily Stock Price Record and Yahoo Finance.

The cost of financing with common stock (K_E) is the return demanded by the investor in exchange for their investment in the company. The marginal cost estimation of equity (K_E) is the most difficult and subjective part of valuing a project – to estimate the weighted average cost of capital involves many subjective estimates. We can approximate this cost in a number of ways, and present seven of them here. The analyst would have to decide which method in each circumstance is more credible, as each (K_E) estimate is likely to offer a different return.

The capital asset pricing model (CAPM)
The CAPM model was introduced earlier in the chapter. This method is still the model most widely used for estimating the cost of equity capital. The CAPM is a 'build-up' method, in the sense that the estimated return on equity is found by adding up different risk premiums for the different sources of risk. Thus it is related to the implicit or opportunity cost of capital. The components of a regular build-up method are: the risk-free rate and the risk premium, including a general equity premium, a small company premium, and the unique company risk premium.

The CAPM approach introduces the market or systematic risk of the share in question to adjust the general equity risk premium. Recall from Chapter 1 that the equity market risk was measured as the difference between the risk-free rate and the market return, measured by the return on a proxy such as the S&P500. The beta was used to adjust the general market risk premium to the systematic risk specific to the company under observation.

Hence, according to the CAPM, the return expected from the shares in a corporation is equal to the risk-free rate plus the market risk premium, multiplied by the company's beta. Thus in the CAPM the required rate of return for a given stock J is composed of only three factors. To obtain the expected return or cost of equity capital of the stock J we need estimates of the risk-free rate (R_f), the market's overall return (K_M or R_M), and the beta of J (β_J), the level of systematic risk associated with the shares of the company.

$$K_J = R_f + \beta_J (K_M - R_f)$$ *Formula 2.22*

The risk-free rate is the return available to the investors on a default risk-free security at the time of the analysis. Practitioners usually use the yield on a 20 year government bond, because these are thought to match the life span of the equivalent investment in the firm's assets better than the alternatives.

The risk-free rate is available in nominal terms, so it includes expectations for inflation in addition to the compensation for postponing consumption and the interest rate risk. Because it includes inflation, when discounting net cash flows at this rate we need to ensure that these are also stated in nominal values.

When analyzing the historical relationship between risk and return we used Ibbotson and Sinquefield's study as an example. The results of their work showed that once we deducted average inflation, the *return on* treasury *bills* barely compensated *for the postponement of* consumption. *Recall that* these average returns stood at approximately of 0.7 per cent. Since different government securities are issued with different maturity dates, the longer the time to maturity, the larger the compensation to make up for interest rate risk. Given that the equity cost is the cost of opportunity, if we analyze a project with a ten-year maturity, we could compare the returns from the project with those from alternative investments of equal maturity, for example a 10-year Treasury Bond. If it is a medium-term project, the risk-free rate Rf could be the actual returns from Medium Term Treasury Bonds. The yields on these securities are available daily in the financial press or specialized publications such as the Mergent Bond Record.

Returning to which estimation method is appropriate for the expected return on the market portfolio (K_M), a common approach is to assume that future returns will be approximately equal to historical returns. The drawback is that historical data for these returns includes inflation. In order to remove the inflation component, a solution proposed by Ross, Westerfield and Jordan (1995) is to use an estimate of the difference between the return on the market and the return on the risk-free rate, (K_M-R_f) instead of (K_M). Ibbotson and Sinquefield provide data with which to estimate this historical difference using the S&P 500 as a proxy for the USA market.

The last variable needed to estimate the CAPM is the beta. Betas are usually available from an array of sources such as the specialized press and investment management services. Beta estimates can be found from, for example, stock exchanges, Bloomberg, Standard & Poor's Stock Reports or the Value Line Investment Survey. However, betas can also be estimated, as discussed earlier.

If the firm is not traded publicly or if we are just trying to estimate the risk of a division of the company, we will not be able to calculate or find estimates for these betas, as the returns will not be readily available. If this is the case, an estimate can be made to see to what extent the net income and cash flows of the company tend to move in parallel with the net income and cash flows of other companies in the economy. Another way to get around this problem is to obtain betas from other firms in the same line of business, and after some adjustments, use these industry betas as a proxy.

Table 2.5 displays betas of companies within three sectors to call attention to the fact that within sectors, betas appear to fall within a range. Companies within a given industry have similar assets, so they share operational risks. However, the capital structure of these companies might differ to the extent that their leveraged betas are very different, even if still within the expected range.

Table 2.5 Betas in three sectors

Oil and gas producing Companies	β	Chemical index companies	β	Electricity companies	β
Alon USA Energy Inc	1.77	Agrium Inc.	1.39	American Electric Power	0.38
Cabot Oil & Gas Corp	1.51	Arch Chemicals Inc	1.59	First Energy Corp	0.58
Devon Energy Corp	1.54	Cabot Corp	1.56	PPL Corp	0.57
Frontier Oil Corp	1.33	Monsanto Co	1.03	TECO Energy Inc	0.91
Murphy Oil Corp	1.40				

Source: http://es.finance.yahoo.com (04/09/2010).

Our three industries have (a) less risk than the market (utilities), (b) risk equal to the market (manufacturing), and (c) more risk than the market (oil and gas Producers). A brief analysis reveals that electrical companies' cash flows and returns fluctuations are small compared with most other companies in the economy. Therefore, electrical companies have low systematic risk level and low betas. On the other side of the spectrum, oil and gas producers' cash flows are very sensitive to changes in the level of economic activity. This volatility is magnified by the use of high levels of leverage. The result is that cash flows and returns are far more volatile than those of most other companies, so these companies have large betas.

Using the data from the previous example and a beta of 1.40 for a company with volatility higher than the market average we can use CAPM in the following manner:

$$K_J = R_f + \beta_J (K_M - R_f)$$
$$K_J = 6 + 1.40 (8) = 17.2\%$$

Gordon's model
The 'Gordon Model' or 'Constant Dividend Growth Model' derives the expected return of the equity in an explicit manner by analyzing the cash flows produced by the investment. The formula departs from the standard security valuation approach of discounting the future cash flows (dividends) that result from the purchase of the share. If the dividends are perpetual and do not carry a growth rate, the formula simplifies to that of the 'perpetuity' scenario, such as was used in the preferred equity case. However, given that dividends on common stock are usually expected to grow with time, this is indicated by adjusting the cash flows and discount rate by the growth rate g:

$$P_0 = \frac{D_1}{(R_E - g)}$$

Formula 2.23

where

$$D_1 = D_0(1+g)$$ Formula 2.24

Thus,

$$R_E = \frac{D_1}{P_0} + g$$ Formula 2.25

In the formula, P_0 is the current market price of the common stock, D_1 is the dividend to be paid in the next period, R_E is the return demanded from the company shares, and g is the expected dividend growth rate. To find the return required, we only have to solve for the R_E term in the equation.

The return required by shareholders, R_E, can be interpreted as the cost of equity capital for the company. Hence, we can re-write the formula using K instead of R:

$$K_E = \frac{D_0(1+g)}{P_0} + g$$ Formula 2.26

The last annual dividend paid by the company D_0 and its share price can be obtained from the financial press and specialized sources. However, the anticipated rate of constant growth, g, is not observable. Given that most of the value of holding the share will come from the dividend payment, the key to obtaining a realistic estimate is to assess accurately the dividend growth rate. Hence, this is one of those instances when the analyst will have to use her judgement and collect the necessary information to make the best possible educated guess.

Dividend payments come out of earnings and are set by management after careful consideration of factors such as expectations of income growth, industry standards and alternative investment projects to be realized in the future. To determine a likely growth rate, relevant sources could be announcements by the firm, reports by industry analysts and historical information. However, for the Gordon model to make sense, the base from which reasonable growth will depart needs to be an estimate of dividends which, for example, might eliminate non-recurring items. That is, the dividend we use might not be the actual cash flow but the result of a normalization process.

In addition, before extrapolating historical growth to anticipated growth, one must realize that this rate needs to be sustainable in the long run. Hence it is important to differentiate short-term or medium-term growth (up to seven or ten years) and constant (perpetual) growth. In general, the expected long-term growth rate cannot be too far away from expected inflation, as a corporation cannot grow for ever at a rate much higher than that of the economy that sustains it. Obviously, though, the right growth rate will depend on the particular case, since it is also possible for a particular company to grow faster than certain economies.

An easy way of producing a dividend growth estimate is by looking at the firm's historical information. One could draw up a time series of earnings per share or dividends paid in the last few years and calculate its growth rate. This rate could then be used to project expectations of future growth. The following example shows how this can be done.

The data in Table 2.6 illustrates a time series of the dividends paid by a company in the recent past. The first two columns show the year and the actual annual dividend paid. The third and fourth columns help us assess the change in dividend payment which is shown in the last column.

Estimating future dividend payments using the historical growth rate makes things easy. However, by doing so we implicitly assume the proportion of net income used for dividend distributions is constant. We can see this relationship with the following formula:

$$g = \text{ROE} * \left[1 - \left(\frac{\text{Dividend}}{\text{Net Income}} \right) \right] \qquad \text{Formula 2.27}$$

Table 2.6   Estimating dividend growth

Year	Dividend	Change in dollars	Divided by	Change in %
2005	$4.00			
2006	$4.40	$0.40	$4.00	10.00
2007	$4.75	$0.35	$4.40	7.95
2008	$5.25	$0.50	$4.75	10.53
2009	$5.65	$0.40	$5.25	7.62

Average growth rate
g = (10.00 + 7.95 + 10.53 + 7.62) / 4 = 9.025%

An example: if the shares of a company are sold for $13.50 and pay at present $1 of dividends that are going to grow to a constant rate of 9.025 per cent, the historical equity risk premium is 8 per cent and the risk-free rate is 6 per cent, the equity cost of capital is:

$P_0 = D_1 / (R_E - g)$, where $D_1 = D_0 (1 + g)$

$$R_E = \frac{D_1}{P_0} + g$$

$R_E = \$1 \, (1.09025) / \$13.50 + 0.09025 = 17.10\%$

where ROE is the return on equity, calculated as the ratio of net income to shareholder equity. If we break down the ROE into its components we can see that essentially the ROE equals the net margin multiplied by the asset turnover multiplied by the financial leverage. Hence any changes in these components will affect the achievable growth rate. In summary, the growth rate is a function of the efficiency with which assets are utilized, operational costs, and capital structure. Thus using the same growth rate implies the assumption that these relationships will stay constant in future.

Although the Gordon model is widely used, it has three major limitations: it can only be used for companies which distribute dividends, it is very sensitive to the estimated growth rate, and it does not consider risk explicitly.

If the firm for which we attempt to estimate the cost of equity pays no dividends, or if it is difficult to assess any likely growth, such as in the cases of companies with no historical information, or if we prefer to consider risk in an explicit manner, we can use other models such as the CAPM or the 'subjective method'. Some of the advantages of the CAPM over the Gordon Model are that it recognizes risk explicitly, and it can be used for all companies. However, as already mentioned, it also has several disadvantages given that educated guesses also need to be made in the estimation of its components.

Relationship between the Gordon and CAPM models

Let us analyze briefly how we can use the expected return (R_E) estimated with one model to determine variables in the second model. In the earlier example, we used the CAPM model and obtained a R_E of 17.2 per cent. This number can be used in the Gordon model to represent the implicit growth of dividends (g) assuming this return. This 'trick' would tell us how logical it is to assume that implicit growth rate in the dividends of the company:

$$R_E = R_f + \beta_E (R_M - R_f)$$

$$R_E = 6\% + 1.40\,(8\%) = 17.2\%$$

If we substitute this 17.2 per cent in the Gordon model (where we obtained a R_E of 17.10 per cent):

$$R_E = \frac{D_1}{P_0} + g \quad 17.2\% = \frac{D_1}{P_0} + g$$

$$17.2\% = \frac{1.09025}{\$13.50} + g$$

$$g = -\left(\frac{1.09025}{\$13.50}\right) + 17.2\%$$

$$g = 9.124\%$$

One would have to compare this implicit nine per cent growth rate to analysts' assessments and our own ideas about the likelihood of its sustainability.

Given the limitations of both the CAPM and Gordon models, we present a third method, which does not require an estimate of dividends, growth, betas or equity risk premiums as defined earlier.

Subjective or risk premium model
The subjective method proposes yet another way of thinking about how the cost of equity capital can be derived without making use of historical time series data. The intuitive idea behind this new model is that if the firm funds itself with both debt and equity, the estimate of the cost of debt for the company must already reflect all the risks the firm assumes. Informed investors are willing to accept a rate k_D from the firm with its accompanying risk. Hence the analyst needs to subjectively estimate ρ, the supplementary premium needed to compensate informed investors for the additional risk that comes from holding a common equity position versus a fixed income position. According to this methodology, the cost of equity capital is:

$$k_E = k_D = \rho \qquad\qquad Formula\ 2.28$$

where K_D is the cost of debt before taxes and ρ is the subjective component. We can use some guidelines to help us assess the ρ estimate. For example, we could look at the premiums that are paid by similar companies. In addition, we could think of anchors for the lower and upper bounds of this premium such as those of regulated utilities or high volatility firms. In this way we can arrive at a range of values in the setting of K_E.

We can also find further guidance by observing the company's beta. For example, if the average premium in the market or the return by a company of average risk is $\rho = 5$, and our beta is 0.8, we might only seek four per cent over the cost of debt, but if our beta were 1.2, we might six per cent more. In this case, the cost of capital would be:

$$R_E = K_D + \rho \qquad\qquad Formula\ 2.29$$

If our beta is 0.8:
$R_E = 8.75 + 4\% = 12.75\%$
If our beta is 1.2:
$R_E = 8.75 + 6\ \% = 14.75\%$

Earnings-to-price approach
Discounting was earlier described as the exercise of bringing to present value some future economic reward. The discount rate was the rate of return obtained by the lender over the life of the investment.

The earnings-to-price approach is similar process, but in this case, the return to the shareholder or cost of equity is defined as the ratio of earnings per share to the current market price per share. That is,

$$P_0 = \frac{EPS_0}{R_{E,E/P}}$$ *Formula 2.30*

$$R_{E,E/P} = \frac{EPS_0}{P_0}$$ *Formula 2.31*

where: $R_{E,E/P}$ is the earnings-to-price definition of the cost of equity, EPS_0 is the current earnings per share ratio, and P_0 is the present value of a share. In this formula, 'earnings' can have different meanings such as accounting earnings, cash flows, dividends or any other measure of income.

The $R_{E,E/P}$ formula describes a process similar to discounting, except that instead of looking at multiple future periods it concentrates on the return offered by the investment over the one period following the valuation date. The single number used in the divisor is called the capitalization rate (c) because it is the rate that capitalizes the current earnings into the value of the firm. Thus, when using the income approach to valuation, the capitalization rate is a function of the discount rate.

Example of perpetuity
Suppose we pay $40 for a share offering a perpetual dividend payment of f$4 per year. We can estimate the cost of equity capital using the capitalization method: EPS-to-price or the Gordon formula used in the perpetuity scenario presented a few pages ago. Either way the result would be ten per cent.

$$R_{E,E/P} = \frac{EPS_0}{P_0} \; ;$$

$$R_{E,E/P} = \frac{4}{40} = 0.10 \quad \text{or 10 per cent}$$

The discount rate equals the capitalization rate because no changes are expected in the perpetual cash flows to the investor, so both methods give us the same result.

Although in this scenario we can use either method, we need to realize that when using a non-cash flow measure of economic earnings, changes in the reporting accounting norms and/or end-of-period adjustments can both affect the estimated rate, regardless of whether cash flow expectations remain unchanged. In addition, the no-growth assumption in scenarios other than preferred stock dividends is not very realistic, given that, investors should at least be compensated for inflation. The critical assumption that the growth in the EPS is relatively constant over the long run therefore needs to be questioned.

Assuming a perpetuity scenario the capitalization rate equals the discount rate (k) minus any expected long-term growth in the earnings measure (g). This relationship can be abbreviated as follows: $c = k - g$, which is actually equivalent to the denominator of the Gordon formula when used for discounting growing perpetuities:

$$P_0 = \frac{D_1}{(R_E - g)}$$

The numerator of this formula is also relevant as it describes the relationship between the cash flows in consecutive time periods. For example, the net cash flow in the next period equals the cash flow in the current period, plus a growth rate. When the growth rate is zero, the cash flows of the current and first periods are equal. Both numerator and denominator simplify into the Gordon formula as:

$$PV = \frac{EPS_1}{k - g} \qquad\qquad Formula\ 2.32$$

Which reduces to

$$PV = \frac{EPS_0}{k} \qquad\qquad Formula\ 2.33$$

when $g = 0$. Thus, as mentioned, in a perpetuity scenario where the growth rate is zero, the capitalization rate is the same as the discount rate.

Incremental earnings are specified differently in both models. When discounting, these marginal changes are explicitly shown in the numerator. However when capitalizing, estimates of changes in economic earnings are aggregated into one annually compounded growth rate, which is then subtracted from the discount rate in the denominator.

Let us provide a couple of numerical examples to show the equivalence of these methods under specific assumptions:

A. We are valuing an investment which provides a $40 annual dividend payment in the next period with a two per cent perpetual growth rate and a desired return of 12 per cent.

$$PV = \frac{EPS_1}{k-g} \; , \qquad PV = \frac{40}{0.12-0.02} = \frac{40}{0.10} = 400$$

B. We are valuing an investment which provides a $40 annual dividend payment with a projected two per cent growth rate and a desired return of 12 per cent.

$$PV = \frac{EPS_1}{k-g} \; , \qquad PV = \frac{40(1+0.02)}{0.12-0.02} = \frac{40.80}{0.10} = 408$$

In the first example, the fair market value of the investment is $400, whereas in the second it is $408. That is because in the latter case we are postponing the receipt of the $40, so our investment increased in value by 2 per cent by earning interest on interest.

If all available cash flows are distributed, the value of the investment grows at the same rate as the cash flows in the constant model. This is because when defining the EPS to capitalize we deduct investments such as capital expenditures and we add the net working capital needed to realize the projected future revenues. Thus the investor earns a total of 12 per cent, 10 per cent current return (the capitalization rate) plus 2 per cent annually compounded growth in the value of the investment. With investment B) we would get the same result if we specified that in the first period the cash flow to be received would be $40.80, with a perpetual growth rate of 2 per cent and a desired return of 12 per cent. In this instance,

$$PV = \frac{EPS_1}{k-g} \; , \qquad PV = \frac{40.80}{0.12-0.02} = \frac{40.80}{0.10} = 408$$

When reviewing the Gordon Model, we called attention to the fact that one needs a normalized amount of cash flow as a base for the investment growth. This might be some time away from the time of the estimate, and in the interval, there might be a few single cash flows that are growing at an unsustainable rate. To get around this problem we need to apply the method in two stages. In the first step we discount the single cash flows, and in the second we take care of the perpetuity portion of the estimate:

$$PV = \frac{EPS_1}{(1+k)^1} + \frac{EPS_2}{(1+k)^2} + \ldots + \frac{EPS_n}{(1+k)^n} + \frac{\frac{EPS_n * (1+g)}{k-g}}{(1+k)^n}$$

$$P_0 = \frac{EPS_0}{R_{E,E/P}}$$ *Formula 2.32*

into

$$R_{E,E/P} = \frac{EPS_1}{k-g}$$ *Formula 2.33*

Sometimes the terminal value of the investment will not be a perpetuity but a single salvage value. In those cases the liquidating value of the asset will be the terminal value. Two important aspects of assessing our inputs or assumptions are that the shorter the projection period, the more impact the terminal value has on the valuation. Also, as the growth rate and the cost of capital get closer to each other, the model becomes more sensitive to changes in the growth rate assumptions.

Exception: when g does not = 0 and B does not equal 1
If all assumptions are met, the discounting and capitalization methods obtain the same results. But when the growth rate does not equal zero and the payback ratio does not equal one, things change. Thus, the example above makes a series of assumptions which allow the above formula to work in the context of the earnings-to-price approach to estimating the cost of equity. We assumed that the EPS in the current period are the same as in future periods, and that EPS equals the dividends paid per share. These two assumptions will only work if the dividend payout ratio (b) is in fact equal to 1. That is, there is no reinvestment, as all the earnings are paid out in the form of dividends. In addition, we would need to assume that the future growth rate of the estimated dividends is zero. That is, the dividend paid per share is the same as the earnings per share, and those amounts do not change over time: the figure is the same this period, or the next, or within five periods. If these assumptions are incorporated we can summarize these relationships as follows:

$$R_{E,E/P} = \frac{EPS_0}{P_0},$$

When the payout ratio is one and the growth rate zero, then earnings per share equals dividend per share and the net cash flow in the current period equals that of the next period:

$$EPS_0 = \frac{Dividend_1}{P_0}$$

Formula 2.34

since:

Dividend$_1$ = Dividend$_0$ * (1 + growth rate on the dividends) and g = 0, then Dividend 1 = Dividend 0.

In addition, because the payout ratio (*b*) is equal to 1, all retained earnings are used for distributions, hence EPS = earnings = dividends.

$$EPS = \frac{D_1}{(1+g)b},$$

Formula 2.35

Then

which holds when $D_1 = D_0 + g$ and g = 0, and when b = 1 and all retained earnings are paid out in dividends.

The functional relationship between the capitalization rate and the discount rate is as follows. C= k–g, where c is the capitalization rate, k is the discount rate or cost of capital for the project and g is the expected long-term sustainable growth rate in the cash flow available to the project.

According to the Gordon Model with growth:

$$R_E = \frac{D_1}{P_0} + g$$

where D_1 is the dividend of the next period and g is the growth rate in dividends. We can set the formula in terms of

$$P_0 = \frac{D_1}{R_E - g}$$

Formula 2.36

where $D_1 = D_0 + g$

The present value of the investment equals the dividends to be received in the next period discounted. If *b* represents the dividend payout ratio, the earnings per share at time 0 can be expressed as a function of the dividend paid at time 1:

$$EPS_0 = \frac{D_1}{(1+g)b}$$

Formula 2.37

If you substitute 2.37 into the equation 2.30:

$$R_{E,E/P} = \frac{EPS_0}{P_0}$$ *Formula 2.30*

$$R_{E,E/P} = \frac{EPS_0}{(1+g)b}$$ *Formula 2.38*

By rearranging the terms algebraically, the earnings/price cost of equity can be represented as a function of the growth model of cost of equity, the growth rate and the payout ratio:

$$R_{E,E/P} = \frac{R_E - g}{(1+g)b}$$ *Formula 2.39*

Try replacing the cost of equity, payout ratio and growth rate by 10 per cent, 30 per cent and 5 per cent respectively. If you substitute these values into the last equation you will get an earnings/price cost of equity of 15.87 per cent. This is inconsistent with the cost of equity derived with the dividend growth model.

The two models rarely agree except when there is no growth and no re-investment, that is, when g equals zero and b equals 1. There are also other combinations of the growth rate, payout ratio and dividend growth model cost of equity that produce no differences between the earnings/price cost of equity and the dividend growth model cost of equity, but these combinations are rare and arise by chance.

If the expected annually compounded rate of growth is stable and sustainable over the long run, then the discount rate can be converted to a capitalization rate, since the capitalization rate is a function of the discount rate. However, in reality, the discount rate and the capitalization rate are two very different things. The discount rate is the rate used to bring to present value all future cash flows. Thus it represents the total compound rate of return that an investor requires during the life of the investment, or the cost of capital. On the other hand, the capitalization rate would be equal to the net cash flow in the next period divided by the present value of the asset, so it is just a divisor used at a specific point in time to estimate a present value, focusing on the return of a single period.

Even though managers use accounting information when doing capital budget analysis, there is really no support in the academic literature for using accounting information such as the return on equity (ROE) or return on assets (ROA) to estimate the cost of capital. However, despite its shortcomings, the E/P ratio is often used by management.

Option-based approach

In 1973, Black and Scholes[2] (B-S) developed a model for pricing options. Their proposal was that we think of the stock, debt or hybrid securities in a firm as analogous to a call option. The equity holders own the option to buy the assets of the company, provided they repay the debt holders. If the firm has outstanding debt that is payable in full on a particular date, the stock in the firm is like an option to buy the firm's assets. This option has an expiration date equal to the maturity date of the debt, and an exercise price equal to the face value of the debt. The debt holders have the risk-free right to receive the return of their loaned monies, minus the value of the default risk. Hence, the value of the debt can be viewed as a risk -free bond minus the value of a put option on the assets.

The B-S option pricing formula expresses the value of a call option in terms of the current price of the stock, the risk-free interest rate, the period until the option expires, the exercise price of the option, and the standard deviation of the rate of return of the stock. A distinguishing feature of the B-S approach is that instead of using beta, this model uses implied volatility calculated from traded options data to describe both systematic and unsystematic risk.

The equity in a firm can be modelled as a call option, where its value would be the price a hypothetical buyer would pay for the possibility that the fair market value of the business enterprise will exceed the face value of the debt at a specified future horizon. The exercise price of the option is the face value of the debt in the firm, and the period until the option expires is the maturity date of the debt. All these variables, with the exception of sigma, the standard deviation of the rate of return on the firm's value, are often known. Then you can simply solve the B-S formula to find an estimate for the standard deviation.

Copeland and Weston (1988)[3] show that the cost of equity for the firm can be expressed as follows:

$$R_E = r_f + N(d_1)(r_c - r_f)\frac{V}{E}$$

Formula 2.40

where r_f is the risk-free rate, r_c the cost of capital for the entire firm, V the current total market value of the firm, and E the current market value of the equity. $N(d_1)$ is the cumulative probability of the standard normal distribution with d_1 as the upper limit, defined as:

$$d_1 \frac{\ln\left(\frac{V}{D}\right) + R_f T}{\sigma\sqrt{T}} + \frac{1}{2}\sigma\sqrt{T}$$

Formula 2.41

where D is the face value of the zero-coupon debt at maturity, T the time until maturity, and sigma σ the standard deviation of the value of the firm's assets.

Although *Formula 2.40* gives helpful insights into the effect that debt and volatility have on the cost of equity, it is difficult to apply. Thus, in 1991 Hsia[4] suggested some modifications to make it easier to use. His idea is that by rolling over the annual interest payments you can think of debt as a perpetuity. This perpetuity can be approximated by a zero-coupon debt with the same duration. Given that the duration of the zero-coupon bond is its maturity, that provides the information for the expiry day of the debt in the formula above. He proves that this is the ratio of the current value of the debt to the annual interest payment.

If the zero-coupon bond appreciates in price at a rate equal to the yield of the actual debt, then the face value of the zero-coupon bond at maturity date is easily defined by multiplying its current value by a growth rate of e (2.71828). After estimating the volatility of the firm (σ) you can substitute the value of the zero-coupon bond into both *Formula 2.40* and *Formula 2.41*.

Hsia suggests estimating sigma using option pricing theory. Given that we know the risk-free rate, the current value of debt, the annual interest payments, and given that the value of equity can be directly observed, it is easy to find the value of sigma that makes the relationship between equity value and the observed variables true.

Hsia manipulates the formula to show that the cost of equity is:

$$R_E = R_f + \left[\frac{A}{B} - R_f\right]\left[\frac{B}{E}\right]\left[\frac{N(d_1)}{N(-d_1)}\right]$$

Formula 2.42

Where R_E is the cost of equity, R_f is the risk free rate, A is the annual interest payment, B is the current value of the debt, E is the current market value of the equity, and d_1 is defined as:

$$d_1 = \frac{\left[l_n\left(1 + \frac{E}{B}\right) + \left(\frac{1}{A}\right)(R_f B - A)\right]}{\sigma\sqrt{\frac{B}{A}}} + \frac{1}{2}\sigma\sqrt{\frac{B}{A}}$$

Formula 2.43

where sigma is the standard deviation of the rate of return or market value of the firm's assets. In this last formula, sigma is the only remaining unknown value. However, it is easily determined by solving the formula to find its estimate.

Even though Hsia does not provide rigorous justification for all his recommendations, his suggestions provide a practical way to use option pricing to find the cost of equity.

Multifactor models
The APT (arbitrage pricing theory)

The two most popular models of risk and return are the Capital Asset Pricing Model (CAPM) and the Arbitrage Pricing Theory (APT). The CAPM, with which we are already familiar, was the first of the pricing models and it is the one most commonly used by practitioners. The APT was presented by Ross in 1976[5] as an alternative asset pricing model. However, it was not until the late eighties that data was commercially available in a form that would permit the application of this theory to regular practice.

Unlike the CAPM, which defined the returns as a function of the systematic risk embedded in the share as represented by the beta, the APT holds that the expected return of a financial asset can be modelled as a linear function of several macroeconomic factors or market indices, where sensitivity to changes of each factor is represented by a factor-specific beta coefficient.

For example, if we think of two companies, one which produces aluminium and another making pharmaceuticals, it is likely that the cash flows of both will be affected by unexpected changes in energy costs. Nevertheless, we might also expect to see that the two companies are not equally sensitive to this factor. This implies that there is an exclusive component to returns, in addition to the common factors. Thus, the APT proposes that the difference between the actual and expected returns on a financial asset is a function of several common factors and an error term that is unique to that security. The returns are assumed to follow the following relationship:

$$E(R_j) = \alpha + \beta_{j1}(F_1) + \beta_{j2}(F_2) + \beta_{j3}(F_3) + \ldots + \beta_{jn}(F_n) + \xi_j \qquad \textit{Formula 2.44}$$

where $E(R_j)$ is the risky asset's expected return, α is the risk-free rate, $\beta_{j1} \ldots \beta_{jn}$ are the sensitivity of the asset to each risk factor, $F_1 \ldots F_n$ are the macroeconomic factors, and ε_j is the unsystematic risk of the asset. If you have a series of historical returns you can use 'factor analysis' to estimate the betas.

Thus, for any individual stock there are two sources of risk: the risk from macroeconomic factors and the risk from possible events that are unique to the company. Since the latter can be diversified, the expected risk premium on a stock is affected exclusively by factor or macroeconomic risk. Given that risks which disappear from portfolio returns ought not to affect the market prices of the assets, the expected risk premium on investment would be the return minus the risk-free rate (the alpha in *Formula 2.44*) which equals the sum of the multiplication of each relevant factor by its beta. Thus, the APT formula makes two statements:

1. If you substitute zero for each of the β's in the formula above, the expected risk premium is zero. A diversified portfolio that is constructed to have zero sensitivity to each macroeconomic factor is essentially risk-free, and therefore must be priced to offer the risk-free rate of interest. If the portfolio offered a higher return, investors could make a risk-free (arbitrage) profit by borrowing to buy the portfolio. If it offered a lower return, you could make an arbitrage profit by running the strategy in reverse: sell the diversified zero-sensitivity portfolio and invest the proceeds in US Treasury Bills.
2. A diversified portfolio that is constructed to have exposure to, for example, factor 1, will offer a risk premium which will vary in direct proportion to the portfolio's sensitivity to that factor. For example, if one has two portfolios A and B which are affected only by factor 1, and A is twice as sensitive to it as B, A must offer twice the risk premium. So if you divide the money equally between US Treasury Bills and A, the combined portfolio would have the same sensitivity to 1 as B, and offer the same risk premium.

This arbitrage applies to well-diversified portfolios, but if the arbitrage pricing relationship holds for all diversified portfolios, it must hold for the individual stocks that make up the portfolios. Each stock must offer an expected return commensurate with its contribution to portfolio risk. In the APT, this contribution depends on the sensitivity of the stock's return to unexpected changes in macroeconomic factors. Thus, the APT has attracted interest because, through its emphasis on multiple sources of systematic risk, it can explain investment results better than the CAPM and help control portfolio risk more effectively. Because a firm's profitability is affected by its sensitivity to underlying macroeconomic factors, the APT is understood to be a 'supply side' model. whereas the CAPM is considered a 'demand side', model given that it results from maximizing the individual investors' utility.

In addition, the APT is less restrictive than the CAPM in its assumptions, it is an explanatory as opposed to a statistical model of asset returns, and it assumes that investors hold unique portfolios with their own specific betas, instead of holding the same 'market portfolio'. In this sense, the CAPM can be considered to be a special case of the APT.

Both the APT and the CAPM stress that expected return depends on undiversifiable risk. In addition, both models find their sensitivities (the betas) through linear regression of historical returns. However, the APT does not identify which are the factors that affect the returns, nor how many factors there are. Furthermore, these factors can change over time.

In this connection, a number of empirical tests have attempted to identify the basic factors underlying security valuation. These include Brown and Weinstein (1983), Chen (1983), Roll and Ross (1980–4), Trzcinka (1986), Reinganum (1981), Conway and Reinganum (1988), Fama and French (1993) and Dhrymes, Friend and Gultekin (1984). In general, these studies point to the existence of at least three or four significant factors of a pervasive macroeconomic nature, such as unanticipated changes in inflation, industrial production, risk premiums and the slope of the yield curve.

In spite of its attractiveness, the APT is not widely applied. The reason lies with the APT's greatest problem: its lack of specificity regarding the multiple factors which systematically affect security returns. On the one hand, the way factors are described is intended to result in high explanatory power, but on the other, computational complications result in factors being defined somewhat arbitrarily. This ends up creating problems when we attempt to link the estimated factors to any macroeconomic variables. Considering the amount of noise in the relationships between macroeconomic factors and individual company returns, finding statistical significance for a practical application of the APT theory has remained a challenge.

A priori models

Given the problems related to the APT's lack of factor specificity, in 1986 Chen, Roll and Ross[6] suggested that one might instead specify the factors a priori. Their hypothesis was that stock returns are a function of changes in industrial production (IP), unexpected inflation (UI), the change in expected inflation (DEI), the risk premium, estimated as the difference between the long-term government bonds and low quality corporate bonds (UPR), and the steepness of the interest term structure (UTS).

Because there is an intuitive understanding of how the proposed macroeconomic variables could affect stock returns, this model was well received. Like the CAPM and APT, the model runs a linear regression using the historical returns of a firm to find its sensitivities to the factors:

$$R_j = a + \beta_{IP} \, IP + \beta_{UI} \, UI + \beta_{DEI} \, DEI + \beta_{UPR} \, UPR + \beta_{UTS} \, UTS + \varepsilon \qquad Formula\ 2.45$$

The expected return on equity is:

$$R_E = r_f + \beta_{IP}\lambda_{IP} + \beta_{UI}\lambda_{UI} + \beta_{DEI}\lambda_{DEI} + \beta_{UPR}\lambda_{UPR} + \beta_{UTS}\lambda_{UTS} \qquad Formula\ 2.46$$

where λ are the risk premiums for the hypothesized factors. To estimate these risk premiums one can conduct a cross-sectional regression for each date in the sample period and then average the estimated risk premiums.

This type of multifactor model can also be run with sensitivities (β_{jn}) specified a priori instead of the factors. For example, in 1992 Fama and French[7] conducted an empirical study during which they found that the firm's size (S) measured by market capitalization, earnings-to-price ratio, debt to equity ratio, and book to market value ratio (b/m) are significantly related to stock returns in addition to the CAPM's market beta which multiplies the equity risk premium (M). As a result, they proposed a three-factor model which is empirically rather than theoretically driven. Since their variables are directly observable, time series regression is not necessary and the cost of equity is defined as:

$$E(R_j) = R_f + \beta \lambda_M + \beta_S \lambda_S + \beta_{b/m} \lambda_{b/m},$$ *Formula 2.47*

As in the previous example, the risk premiums were estimated using cross-sectional regression. Fama and French betas are available from specialized publishers such as Morningstar.

Industry index models

An alternative multifactor model is constructed by including an industry index in addition to the market index. This industry index is obtained by using the returns from a portfolio of stocks from firms belonging to the same sector. The industries are defined by using codes such as a two- or three-digit standard industrial classification code (SIC).

Using this method, we would obtain the return on equity using the following equation:

$$R_E = R_f + b_m \hat{\lambda}_m + b_1 \hat{\lambda}_1$$ *Formula 2.48*

where the lambdas $\hat{\lambda}$ are the average risk premiums estimated, as in the earlier examples, with cross-sectional regressions. The time series regression of the company is:

$$R_j = b_0 + b_m R_m + b_1 R_1 + \varepsilon$$ *Formula 2.49*

where the b's are the estimated regression coefficients and R_1 is the return on the industry index.

Summary

The cost of capital is the expected rate of return the market requires to commit capital to an investment. This rate is used to convert a stream of expected future income into an estimate of its present value. It is market-driven, and is a function of the investment, not the particular investor. At best, past returns provide guidance but the cost of capital is forward-looking, based on expected returns, measured in nominal terms, and at market value rather than book value. The cost of capital is the link that equates expected future returns during the life of the investment with the present value of the investment at a given date.

The weighted average cost of capital (WACC) is the average cost of the permanent financial resources of a firm. The formula of the WACC reaches the average by performing a 'weighted addition' of the capital structure components of the firm multiplied by their costs. The model is concerned with determining the components of the capital structure of the firm, their relative weights, and the cost of each of the sources of funds.

Given that each firm's capital structure is different, a firm's WACC might have any number of terms, each representing the different sources of funds. However, two should be a minimum (debt and common equity). To identify the components of the capital structure of a firm, one can examine the right-hand side of the balance sheet of the non-banking firm under scrutiny. An overall guideline is to consider all components used for the long-term financing of the operations and, in addition, any significant amounts of short-term funds which de facto would be a permanent part of the capital structure of the company.

The return obtained from the investment in a financial asset is correlated to the risk of the cash flows of the financial asset. Each component of an entity's capital structure has its unique cost, depending on its risks. We should double-check our estimates and provide explanations for any findings that deviate from this general statement.

For measuring the cost of equity, various models have been proposed and are in active use by practitioners. However, the capital asset pricing model (CAPM) is probably the best-known and most widely used. The CAPM is the most popular model used to estimate the expected return on a specific share of equity by considering the amount of systematic risk that is embedded in the investment. However, to choose the most appropriate model, we have to determine the reason for our estimate and the data available for the purpose.

3
Problems in Using the Models

Problems in using the models to price risk: An introduction

To value any type of investment including financial assets, projects or complete companies, you need to estimate the cost of the capital components of the proposed undertaking. However, to estimate the cost of capital of any type of project it is first necessary to develop a measure of risk, because the expected return from an investment depends on the risk of its cash flows. Thus, to arrive at the 'desired' return figure, the risk of the investment needs to be determined.

In the previous chapter we reviewed the methods that are most frequently used to capture the relationship between risk and return in financial assets. We introduced several methodologies, not just one, because they take different approaches to measuring market risk. No single model is the most appropriate in all circumstances, because in one way or another each offers an improvement or makes it easier to estimate risk under a particular scenario. For example, if a firm plans to pay no dividends, it is unlikely that the Gordon Method is the most appropriate. If a firm is not publicly traded, deals in several sectors, has little history, pays dividends, and projects constant growth, we might use a model other than the CAPM.

The objective of this chapter is to analyze and discuss in further detail several of the issues with these models that deserve special attention and are usually considered to require some problem-solving on the part of the analyst when she is attempting to approximate the cost of capital. In this chapter we therefore review a number of the difficulties analysts face and the trade-offs they have to make when deciding which methodology to use and how to estimate the variables needed for the selected model.

All the models discussed were expressed by an equation which had the return on the left-hand side of the equation as the variable that needed to be determined. On the right-hand side of the equation, each of these models had a series of variables offered as explaining the asset's return. That is, the dependent variable 'returns' was explained by a series of independent variables which changed with the model in question.

For example, the independent variables in the CAPM were the risk-free rate, the beta and the market risk premium. In the Gordon Model, the return or cost of equity was explained by the current price of the share at the time of the estimate, the cash flows the equity holder would derive from holding the asset, and the growth rate on the cash flows.

Even though these models have different perspectives on forecasting returns, some underlying assumptions are common. For example, they all accept that risk is added to a diversified portfolio as the consequence of accepting an investment project; and risk is understood from the perspective of the marginal, well-diversified investor. Consequently, only systematic risk is compensated; unsystematic or firm-specific risk is diversified.

A second common element in these models is the definition of risk as the difference or variance between some expected return value and the realized return. Consequently, an investment is risk-free or riskless when its actual returns are exactly equal to the expected returns and the variance is zero. A riskless asset is one for which the investor knows the expected returns with one hundred per cent certainty. Hence, for an investment to be risk-free over time, two conditions have to prevail: there can be no default risk, and no uncertainty about reinvestment rates. That is, there can be no cash flows prior to the end of the investment time horizon, since these cash flows would have to be reinvested at rates that are unknown at the time when the asset is purchased.

We illustrate this in Figure 3.1 where we rank a portfolio of investments starting at the bottom, from low to high risk. That is, low volatility-risk, as indicated by the low standard deviation (the square root of the variance) of the returns, and high risk for those investments with high volatility in their returns. The dispersion of the returns around a mean is made clear by the distribution shown on the right-hand side of the graph. The wider the dispersion of returns, the higher the risk. Specifically:

a. Short-term Treasury securities, usually with one year maturities or less, are often used as proxies for the risk-free rate R_f. The low volatility in the graph is indicated by the narrowest dispersion of returns among all the proposed portfolios.

b. Longer-term government bonds with maturities up to 20 or 30 years command higher returns because, for equal changes in interest rates, their prices vary more than those of the shorter-term debt securities. If interest rates rise, then prices of long-term bonds fall, resulting in losses for any investor who has to sell the security prior to maturity. Thus, investors normally require a premium to compensate for this interest rate risk. Consequently, we observe a greater dispersion on the distribution of returns drawn for this basket of securities.

c. Given that the government can always print more money to fulfil their financial obligations, long-term debt securities from a government are usually less risky than those of corporations. Companies with a high default risk must offer high coupon interest rates to sell their debt issues because they are more likely to have difficulty meeting their obligations. For example, the yield in late 1999 on B-rated bonds was over 10.5 per cent, compared to 6.34 per cent for the long-term government bond. The dispersion of returns on corporate bonds is a reflection of both interest rate and default risks.

d. The market price fluctuations of common stocks tend to be wider than those of long-term debt because there is a greater degree of uncertainty associated with dividend payments. The reason is that dividend payments are made from cash remaining after all other corporate obligations are met, and are the first to be cut when the firm encounters difficulties. Furthermore, capital gains (the difference between a higher selling price and a lower purchase price of the share) are also a function of general expectations about the economy and the sector, in addition to the specific conditions of the firm. All these variables cause frequent changes in share prices. Thus, the volatility of returns in common shares tends to be much higher than that of a fixed-income security.

Investments	Average return	Standard deviation	Dispersion of returns
Portfolio stocks	15.2	27.2	
Corporate long-term bonds	6.0	8.7	
Government long-term bonds	5.4	9.2	
Treasury notes	3.8	3.3	−90% 0% +90%

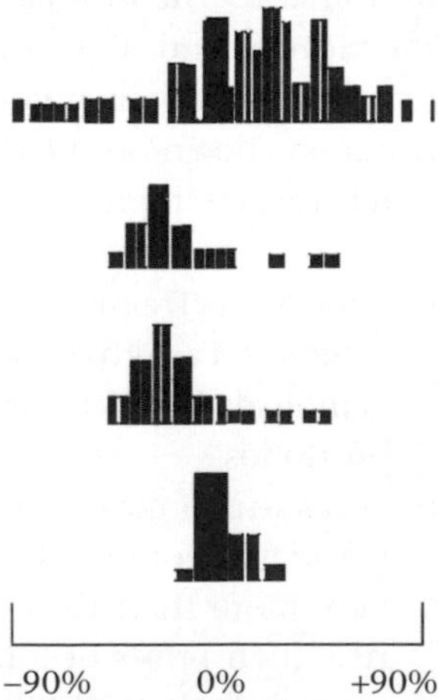

Figure 3.1   Historical returns and standard deviation, US 1926–96

From the explanation and the dispersion of returns shown in the graphs above, it can be derived that if a security has no risk, the difference between the expected and the realized returns would be zero. However, given inflation, interest rate risk, and ultimately the possibility (even if remote) of sovereign defaults, all securities have a variance of returns and no real 'risk-free security' exists.

The CAPM

This discussion of the existence of a risk-free security brings us to the first problem in the application of the CAPM. Recall that the CAPM proposes that the return for any investment is related to the risk added by a specific project to a market portfolio which includes all assets traded. This specific risk is measured with a market beta, leading to an expected return for company J's equity of:

$$E(R_J) = R_f + \beta_J (R_M - R_f) \qquad \qquad Formula\ 2.7$$

In this model, the cost of equity is a function of three inputs: the risk-free rate, the risk premium on the market portfolio, and the beta of the project or firm.[1]

Choosing the risk-free rate (R_f)

The CAPM estimates returns by adding up successive premiums for the risk related to the investment. The first premium added is the 'risk-free rate', the interest rate paid on an investment with zero risk, including default risk.

Given that the probability of default or any other type of risk for a riskless security has to be zero, a risk-free investment does not exist. However, certain proxies are used, because their risk can be regarded as limited and under 'control'. For example, for investments in US dollars, one could say US Treasury bills (T-bills) are risk-free, while for investments in Euros one could use Euribor rates, or German government short-term bills. These securities are considered 'riskless' because the probability of default by, for example, the government, is extremely low at present.

However, in addition to default, a second source of risk in the case of fixed-return investments is interest rate risk. Since these T-bills are short-term funds, the chances interest rates will vary beyond ex-ante expectations over such brief periods is also small. That is, because of the short-term maturity of the instrument, investors are largely protected from the danger that interest rates will increase once the bill is acquired.

Although the concept is quite clear and such instruments do exist, their direct application to the CAPM presents several problems. First, the CAPM assumes each investor has the same investment horizon and the maturity of the project should be matched with that of the risk-free instrument used in the model. However, institutional and private investors usually have horizons of several years, rather than a few months. Thus, to be consistent one must take a risk-free equivalent to be a government bond or note for the relevant date, not the shortest-term security. The implication is that instead of using a short-term maturity risk-free security, one should use a longer-term instrument.

Given these considerations, the preferred instrument used by practitioners is the yield on a 20-year government bond. These long-life investments are thought to provide a closer match to the lifespan of the equivalent investment in the firm. If the yield on the investment and that of a government bond is not equivalent, the analyst can choose the closest maturity available. We can use the return on a 20-year security, for example, by searching for a 30-year obligation with 20 years to maturity. This information can be gathered from the Wall Street Journal, the New York Times or other sources such as the Federal Reserve, which among others also tracks 20-year yields. However, these bonds or obligations are not truly risk-free since, even if free of default risk, they have interest rate risk.

Recall that changes in interest rates present a problem because the current value of these securities is found by dividing their estimated future payments (interest and principal) by the current rate that matches the risk of the security. If one acquires a government bond that pays 5.5 per cent and a few weeks later the same instrument is issued at 6 per cent, given that the interest payments are fixed, the investor is losing half a point return. To avoid this problem, one could use the T-bills, which leave the analyst with a too short implicit horizon. Hence, this is an area where some decision-making on the part of the manager is unavoidable.

A second problem is that the CAPM is a static, single period model. In 1970 Fama offered some explanation for treating the CAPM as if it were to hold inter-temporally, that is, through different periods. Fama showed that if investor's preferences and future investment opportunities are not 'state dependent', then inter-temporal portfolio maximization can be treated as if the investor had a single period utility function. The empirical analysis performed by Black, Jensen and Scholes in 1972 demonstrates that the excess return from holding an asset is not proportional to its beta, given that, for example, on average, low beta assets obtained larger returns than high beta ones.

Among others who have investigated the effects of investment horizon on the estimate of the systematic risk, Levy (1972) proposed that when the holding period assumption is different from the true investment horizon, the performance measure obtained will be biased. Furthermore, Merton proved in a number of examples that portfolio behaviour for an inter-temporal maximizer will be significantly different when she factors in a changing investment opportunity set instead of a constant one. The inter-temporal model proposed by Merton is constructed considering the portfolio selection of investors who can trade continuously and act to maximize their consumption through time. In Merton's inter-temporal CAPM (ICAPM),[2] investors are solving lifetime consumption decisions when faced with more than one uncertainty, such as changes in investment opportunities.

In summary, there is no such thing as a completely riskless asset. In using the CAPM, the analyst will have to decide whether to use a proxy which contains one of two biases: either its holding period is too short to match the investor's true investment horizon, as in the case of T-bills, but will fulfil the CAPM single period assumption; or its investment horizon will be longer, in which case the proxy will contain interest rate risk, in addition to a greater default risk, and will not fulfil the static condition, as would be the case when using a long-term government bond as a proxy.

Given the proposed alternatives, practitioners often opt for the second and choose to match the holding period by using the longer maturity yield on government bonds as of the valuation date. The reason for this choice is that most business projects have long lives through which they are subject to reinvestment risks equivalent to those of long-term bonds. Thus, the better alternative is usually to select the bond that more closely matches the investment horizon and the risks confronting business managers in capital decisions, rather than to compare against short-term T-bills.

When should an analyst use a short-term rather than a long-term government bond rate as a riskless rate? The answer is that it depends upon when the investments cash flows come due. For instance, if the project under analysis has a life expectancy of six years, then it would be appropriate to use a six-year risk-free rate. A three-month Treasury bill is not free of risk for a six-year time horizon. The rationale is that at maturity, the principal will need to be reinvested at an unknown rate. The same is true for any instrument that pays coupons given that these will have to be reinvested at the rates prevailing when the coupons are cashed during the six-year period.

In this example, the only security which fulfils the conditions is a six-year zero-coupon government bond with no default risk and no cash flows paid prior to maturity. However, fulfilling the stated conditions means using a different risk-free rate for cash flows of different durations. This can be quite cumbersome, particularly if we are valuing whole businesses. An alternative approach is to estimate the duration of the cash flows in the project and then use a government bond with equivalent duration to derive a riskless rate.

In finance, duration is a concept most often applied to bonds, and is used to measure the average maturity of a bond's cash flows to serve as a summary statistic of the effective maturity of the bond. In addition, duration is also used to express the sensitivity of the financial asset's price to interest rate movements. The duration of a bond is related to the length of time to its maturity and is estimated as the ratio of the percentage reduction in the bond's price to the percentage increase in the redemption yield of the bond. That is, duration is computed as a weighted average of the times to each coupon or principal payment made by the bond. The weight of each payment is linked to the importance of that payment in relation to the value of the bond. This proportion is the present value of the payment divided by the bond's price. The units of duration are in years, between zero and maturity, and the duration is equal to the time to maturity only if the bond is a zero-coupon bond. The idea is that the longer the time to maturity, the more sensitive the asset is to the interest rate. Hence, duration is useful for estimating the sensitivity of a bond's market price to interest rate (e.g. yield) movements.

Macaulay's[3] duration formula is the weighted average of the times until the receipt of the bond's payments:

$$D = \sum_{t=1}^{T} t * w_t \qquad\qquad\qquad Formula\ 3.1$$

where each of the weights (w_t) is estimated:

$$w_t = \frac{CF_t}{(1+r)^t} \div Bond\ Price \qquad\qquad Formula\ 3.2$$

and w_t is the weight of the cash flow made at time t, r is the bond's yield to maturity, $CF_t/(1+r)t$ is the present value of the cash flow occurring at time t, and the denominator is the aggregation of all cash flows to the bond holder.

For example, the duration of a zero-coupon bond, since it only makes payments at maturity, is exactly equal to its maturity. In other instances, the weight or importance of the payments relative to the total cash flows to be received by the bond holder will shorten the duration.

As far as the cash flows are concerned, Damodaran[4] proposes estimating their duration using the following formula:

$$Duration\ of\ cash\ flows \quad = \frac{\displaystyle\sum_{t-1}^{t=\infty} t * \frac{CF_t}{(1+r)^t}}{\displaystyle\sum_{t=1}^{t=\infty} \frac{CF_t}{(1+r)^t}} \qquad Formula\ 3.3$$

Where CFt is the cash flow in year t and r is the discount rate or cost of capital, when valuing a firm. If the asset's cash flows are received towards the later years they will have a longer duration, whereas if the opposite happens, duration will be short. The estimated duration can be matched with a government security of similar duration to obtain a risk-free rate.

In our discussion, we have simplified the situation by assuming the government whose securities we are using as proxy for the riskless rate is regarded as default-free. However, the governments of most economies in the world do not meet this expectation, and sovereign issues contain some level of risk.

Table 3.1 presents bond ratings and default spreads for several nations. As we see, of the countries in the table, Australia has the maximum rating agencies grant, 'triple a'. The column headings show that this rating, serving as a proxy for the probability of default, commands a risk premium of zero. This is because the consensus on the likelihood of Australia defaulting on sovereign debt is nil at this time. However, as we go down the column, we see that the country ratings worsen, and the risk premium these countries need to offer in order to sell their securities increases.

At the bottom of the table are countries which fall within the category of non-investment grade, with their bonds considered highly speculative to extremely speculative.

A country risk premium must be added to the cost of capital of investments in some markets because the probability that a government will fail to meet its obligations increases as a function of certain macroeconomic and political conditions. Thus, these ratings change as expectations of political and economic conditions within the country evolve.

In the table above, constructed from data posted by Professor Damodaran in his web, Greece is highlighted to show how conditions affect ratings and how these ratings can change dramatically in short periods of time. For example, the A2 rating indicated above for this country was valid as of January 2010

Table 3.1 Sovereign default risk and country risk premium

Country	Long-term Rating	Adj. default Spread	Total risk Premium (%)	Country risk Premium (%)
Australia	Aaa	0	4.50	0.00
Portugal	Aa2	60	5.40	0.90
Botswana	A2	105	6.08	1.58
Greece	**A2**	**105**	**6.08**	**1.58**
Venezuela	B1	450	11.25	6.75
Ukraine	B2	550	12.75	8.25
Argentina	B3	650	14.25	9.75
Ecuador	Caa3	1000	19.50	15.00

Source: Extracted from Damodaran, *Last updated: January 2010* http://pages.stern.nyu.edu/~adamodar/New_Home_Page/datafile/ctryprem.html

when the posting was made. However, by April of the same year, the situation had changed dramatically.

If an investor wants protection from the chance of default she will have to purchase insurance to cover this risk. For example, during the first half of 2010 the cost to insure both Greek and Portuguese debt increased. In the case of Greece, as a result of the budgetary crises, the country's credit default swap (CDS) costs jumped by 435 basis points, which translates into $435,000 per year to insure $10 million of debt for five years. In addition, at the start of May 2010 Greece was further downgraded to BB+, the first level of speculative, or junk, status. In the case of Portugal, CDS costs increased to 183 basis points. Hence, the cost of capital in both economies has increased, providing very different outlooks on expectations compared to only a few months ago.

While it is impossible to measure country risk directly, the ratings assigned to the probability of sovereign default provide strong guidance. A particular advantage is that these ratings help quantify the effect on the equity risk premium given that there is a strong correlation between a country's bond premiums and its equity returns. However, this is just one way of estimating these risks. Another way to estimate country risk for the purpose of determining the right premium is to determine the cost of insuring against it. For this purpose we can use derivative products such as options, futures and forwards. For example, if in the home country the base premium for local investments is 6 per cent and the annual cost of hedging or insuring against the country risk of the economy where the new project is going to take place is 3 per cent a year, then the total premium used for this country will be 9 per cent.

When there is a chance of sovereign debt default, the government is not viewed as default-free. In addition, there are markets where the government does not issue long-term bonds, and the only yields one can get are for short-term Treasury instruments. As mentioned, the long-term government bond rate adjusted for the life of the project is frequently the appropriate risk-free rate. However, when the long-term government bond rate is not available, it may make sense to look at the rate at which large corporations can borrow in the local market. There are different ways to deal with these situations, so in Chapter 5 we cover the subject of country risk in great detail.

Estimating the equity risk premium ($R_M - R_f$)

Often the return on an investment has two components: 1) distributions during the holding period, such as dividends or interest and 2) capital gains/losses in the value of the asset. We already know that the expected return on equities is much less certain than the interest and maturity payments on government obligations. The difference in risk appeared in Figure 3.1 where return distributions of both governmental debt and common stock returns were shown. The greater risk of equity becomes obvious when we see the wider spread of the distribution of equity returns in the graphs. Thus, to accept this risk, investors demand an additional risk premium, sometimes referred to as the 'excess return', 'equity risk premium' (ERP) or 'market risk premium' (MRP).

The equity risk premium measures the weighted average additional return investors demand for moving from a riskless investment into an average (market) equity risk investment. Ergo, this premium is a function of the investors' aggregate risk aversion and the volatility of the market return. The greater the risk aversion, the larger the risk premium required by investors. The weights of the average are related to the savings or the size of the investment the investor brings into the market.

Given economic cycles and innovations, this premium changes over time, as both the variance of the returns in the market and the degree of investor risk aversion change too. However, we cannot foresee the future. Therefore, historical risk premiums are normally used to estimate expectations. That is, we use past information related to the premiums earned by the different investments over time and use these numbers to form expectations about the premiums that should be earned in future.

Even though conceptually this is quite simple, in reality there are several decisions the analyst must make. For example, she will have to determine whether an adjustment for future inflation has to be considered and which historical data (length of the time series, and mean: arithmetic or geometric) better serves the purpose of forming correct expectations at the time the investment is analyzed. The information in Tables 3.2 and 3.3 will help us illustrate these concerns.

The first column in Table 3.2 shows the time period for each of the historical return data collected. The subsequent columns show the arithmetic mean, the geometric mean, and the standard deviation of the arithmetic mean. In the rows there are four blocks containing historical returns calculated for portfolios of short- and long term-government securities, long-term corporate debt, and the market index S&P500.

As in Table 3.2, the first column in Table 3.3 shows the time period for each of the historical data collected. The subsequent columns show the arithmetic mean, the geometric mean, and the standard deviation of the historical equity premium. In the rows there are two blocks containing historical premiums estimated for various periods using the differences between the market proxy S&P500 and either T-bills or long-term government bonds.

At a glance, we can clearly see how the information portrayed in the second and third columns, the arithmetic and geometric means, are different even if both are averages of the same time period's returns. Hence, depending on how we estimate this 'average', we shall come out with quite different expectations about how future returns should look. The table also proves that the choice of the historical period used to estimate the risk premium is a key factor in our results.

Table 3.2   A sample of historical returns

	Arithmetic mean	Geometric mean	Standard deviation
Short-term T-bills			
1928–2009	3.74	3.70	3.03
1926–87	3.54	3.48	0.94
1926–50	1.01	1.00	0.40
1951–75	3.67	3.66	0.56
1976–80	7.80	7.77	0.83
1981–5	10.32	10.30	0.75
1986	6.16	6.16	0.19
1987	5.46	5.46	0.22
2000–9	2.74	2.72	1.88
Long term government bonds			
1928–2009	5.24	4.97	7.78
1926–87	4.58	4.27	7.58
1926–50	4.14	4.04	4.17
1951–75	2.39	2.22	6.45
1976–80	1.95	1.69	11.15
1981–5	17.85	16.82	14.26
1986	24.44	24.44	17.30
1987	−2.69	−2.69	10.28
2000–9	6.62	6.26	9.20
Corporate debt, long term			
1926–87	5.24	4.93	6.97
1926–50	4.82	4.76	3.45
1951–75	3.05	2.86	6.04
1976–80	2.70	2.39	10.87
1981–5	18.96	17.83	14.17
1986	19.85	19.85	8.19
1987	−0.27	−0.27	9.64
S&P 500			
1928–2009	11.27	9.26	20.33
1926–87	12.01	9.90	20.55
1926–50	10.90	7.68	27.18

Continued

Table 3.2 Continued

1951–75	11.87	10.26	13.57
1976–80	14.81	13.95	14.60
1981–5	15.49	14.71	13.92
1986	18.47	18.47	17.94
1987	5.23	5.23	30.5
2000–9	1.15	−0.96	20.86

Source: CRISP.

Table 3.3 Equity risk premiums $(R_M - R_f)$, USA (1926–87) in percentages

	Arithmetic mean	Geometric mean	Standard deviation
T-bills			
1928–2009	7.53	5.56	20.61
1926–87	8.47	6.42	20.60
1926–50	9.89	6.68	27.18
1951–75	8.20	6.60	13.71
1976–80	7.01	6.18	14.60
1981–5	5.17	4.41	14.15
1986	21.31	12.31	17.92
1987	−0.23	−0.23	30.61
2000–9	−1.59	−3.68	21.28
Gov. bonds			
1928–2009	6.03	4.29	21.77
1926–87	7.43	5.63	20.78
1926–50	6.76	3.64	26.94
1951–75	9.48	8.04	14.35
1976–80	12.86	12.26	15.58
1981–5	−2.36	−2.11	13.70
1986	−5.97	−5.97	14.76
1987	7.92	7.92	35.35
2000–9	−5.47	−7.22	29.17

Note: Where RM equals the return on the S&P500, and Rf equals either T. bills or Government bonds for the USA (1926–87).

Source: Crisp, Standard and Poor's.

Historical risk premiums

The most common approach to estimating the risk premium in the CAPM is to base it on average returns on stocks and riskless securities' historical data. Thus, the first question we need to answer is how to select the correct period of data to be used in our estimates.

In Table 3.2 we gave seven examples of means and standard deviations estimated using returns for US data[5] from different time brackets, starting in 1926 and ending in 1987. The purpose of the table is to show that, for instance, if we use a long-term government bond data sample for the period 1926–87, we will be expecting a mean return of 4.58 and 4.27 and a standard deviation of 7.58 per cent. If instead, we focus on the information for 1987, the means are −2.69, and the standard deviation of those returns, 10.28 per cent. So which is true? Which is the better reflection of the future?

In using historical premiums, the implicit assumption is that the risk aversion of investors has not changed across time, and that the relative riskiness of the risky portfolio of stocks has not changed either. Furthermore, included in the premium is an inflation expectation reward that applies to past times, but will be projected to future returns when using the historical estimate.[6]

Since there are economic cycles, including bull and bear markets, a premium estimated using a broad historical period will better capture the behaviour that can be expected from a market in the long run. In consequence, the longest time period possible would be appropriate, provided your investment is also long run, and the market itself has not changed fundamentally.

For example, if our investment has a maturity date of 12 months, it seems the better predictor of the future return would be obtained by using the historical information available closest to the current time, in the hopes it would closely resemble the behaviour of the market over the next year. However, if our investment has a two decade maturity, it makes sense to use data for the broadest time period available, such as that from 1926 to 1987.

This last point will be true except in those instances where the past is no guidance to the future. For instance, if we were looking at a market with a hundred year history but which has fundamentally changed during the past decade (e.g. breath and type of assets traded, liquidity or size), neither past means nor volatilities will help us create reliable expectations of future performance. Extending the time interval of the data used will improve the accuracy of the estimates, but it also strains the reliability of the assumption that the returns are gathered from a stable distribution. In this case, the analyst will have to make an educated guess as to which is the better period to use. The key is to keep an eye on the purpose of the estimate. This will guide the manager in choosing the most appropriate period.

The second question that must be resolved in the process of choosing data for the CAPM equation is whether we should estimate arithmetic or geometric means. For those who are not familiar with this terminology, both means indicate 'the central tendency' or 'representative value' of a set of numbers. In our context these numbers are returns.

The arithmetic mean is what is usually referred to as the 'average'. For instance, we would say that the mean of 1, 2, 3 and 4 is 2.5. We calculate this by adding the set of numbers (1+2+3+4) and then dividing their sum (10) by the number of observations in the sample (4).

The geometric mean is calculated by multiplying the numbers in the sample and then taking the nth root of the result. The geometric mean of (1+2+3+4) is found by taking the 4th square root of their product: $4\sqrt{(1\times2\times3\times4)}$= 2.21. If there were only two observations, one would take the square root, and if there were three, the cube root of their product.

The arithmetic and geometric means produce quite different results. Those who believe the arithmetic mean is the better estimate argue that it is much more consistent with the CAPM framework, and is a better predictor of any future period return. The argument based on consistency relies on the fact that the CAPM is built on the basis that expected returns are averages, with the risk (variance) estimated around this arithmetic mean (not the geometric mean). However, those in the 'geometric camp' argue that the geometric mean takes compounding into account, and thus predicts averages better in the long run. Furthermore, since geometric means yield lower estimates than arithmetic means, it has also been argued that arithmetic mean premiums overstate expected returns.

Suppose, for instance, that a two-period $100 investment has two equally likely outcomes: there is 50 per cent chance that you will obtain a 30 per cent return, and there is a 50 per cent chance that you will obtain a loss of 10 per cent (–10 per cent). The average returns are:

Arithmetic average return = (30% + –10%) / 2 = 10%

Geometric average return = $\sqrt{(1.3)(.9)}$ = 8.1%

Technically both averages are correct. The choice between them depends on the shape of the distributions of the underlying variables used in the estimates. Either way, arithmetic or geometric, in using the average estimated with historical information the underlying assumption is that there are no trends, and investors in current markets expect premiums similar to those of the past.

With regard to the inflation rate, the analyst needs to be concerned with the inflation premium embedded in the historical returns. Thus, if using data gathered from a short historical time period, she would have to consider how similar that inflation premium is to the premium expected in forward projections. In this respect, given the low inflation scenario currently in the markets, some would argue that this return must be decreased (or increased if the contrary is believed to be true) to adjust an expected inflation rate in the future which is higher than that experienced in the past.

Implied equity premiums

A second way of estimating risk premiums is to derive the implied premium in the market. This method has the advantage that it gets around the problems of using historical data. However, it assumes that the market prices stocks correctly.

To estimate the premium using this method we consider the Gordon formula. This is the present value of dividends growing at a constant rate for ever, developed in Chapter 2:

$$P_0 = \frac{D_1}{(R_E - g)}$$ *Formula 2.23*

where

$$D_1 = D_0(1 + g)$$ *Formula 2.24*

and P_0 is the current market price of the common stock, D_1 is the dividend to be paid in the next period, R_E is the return demanded from the company shares, and g is the expected dividend growth rate.

Except for the required return on equity, all inputs in the model can be estimated from current publicly available information. The only unknown is the required return on equity. To find the implied expected return on stocks, we only have to solve for the R_E term in the equation:

$$R_E = \frac{D_1}{P_0} + g$$ *Formula 2.25*

And to get the implied equity risk premium, we just need to subtract the risk-free rate.

For example, assume the current level of the S&P 500 Index is 1000, the dividend yield on the index for the next period is 3 per cent, the expected long-term growth rate in earnings and dividends is 6 per cent, and risk free rate is 5 per cent. Solving for the required return on equity:

$$1000 = (0.03{*}1000) / (R_E - 0.06)$$

Solving for *r*,

$$R_E = \frac{1000(1.03)}{1000} + 0.06 = 9\%$$

If the current riskless rate is 5 per cent, this yields a risk premium of 4 per cent.

The advantage of this approach is that it is market-driven and current, and does not require any historical data. It is, however, limited by whether the valuation model used is the right one, and whether the inputs to the model are available and reliable. For instance, in the above example, both the use of dividends as the expected cash flow to equity investors and the assumption of constant growth might lead to an implied risk premium that is too low.

Having argued the pros and cons of each approach, what should we do? The choice between historical and implied premiums should be based upon the analyst's assessment of the markets. In bull periods more stocks will be overvalued than undervalued, so the implied premiums will yield larger averages than the historical data. The opposite would be true if one were in a bear market. If at the time of the assessment the belief is that the market is pricing stocks correctly, implied premiums can be used in the evaluations. However, if it is believed that these are over or undervalued, and that there is reversion towards historical means, then the historical risk premiums should be used. As stated, each approach carries both advantages and disadvantages that the analyst has to assess.

Calculating the beta (β)

The betas that measure risk in financial models have two basic characteristics that one needs to keep in mind when estimating them. The first is that they measure the risk added to a diversified portfolio, rather than the total risk. Thus, it is entirely possible for an investment to be high risk in terms of individual risk, but low risk in terms of market risk. The second characteristic that all betas share is that they measure the relative risk of an asset, and thus are standardized around one. The market-capitalization weighted average beta across all investments, in the capital asset pricing model, should be equal to one.

To calculate the systematic risk premium in an equity investment we estimate the beta by, for example, running a regression between the historical returns of the market and those of the security under analysis. The dependent variable is the expected company returns including dividends, and the independent variable are those of the market, also including dividends.

Again, making the estimate is simple in itself. However, the validity of the betas obtained is often questioned. The core issues raised refer to the fact that betas are not stable, because both market and company returns (and thus their relationship) change over time, and compromises have to be made in selecting the data to be used for the forecasts. For example, leverage causes betas to rise during recessions, firms with different types of assets will be differently affected by the different parts of the business cycles, and consumers' tastes change.

It has been proven that betas change in time; they show less persistence than variances and covariances (especially those estimated with high frequency, e.g. daily returns); and for single securities, betas are noisy. Nevertheless, in spite of these problems, betas are very helpful in assessing market risk.

In addition to the 'home-made betas' resulting from our regression estimates, 'ready-made betas' can be gathered from sources such as Barra, Value Line, Bloomberg, Yahoo, Merrill Lynch, and the financial press. Either way, given the number of concessions that have to be made to estimate these coefficients, it is important to understand how the estimates can be biased by the choices made in selecting the returns used to obtain them. The main issues that need to be resolved refer to the length and periodicity of the data sample selected, and the choice of market proxy.

Estimation period

To select the period over which historical betas used for forecasting will be estimated, the longest possible data series, with as many observations as possible, will reduce the confidence interval around the estimated coefficient. Extending the estimation period improves statistical reliability. However, increasing the sample size in this manner also raises the chances of adding irrelevant information. While a period that is too short might not provide sufficient information to obtain a representative beta for forecasting risks in the long run, a long series can introduce noise into the estimation.

Data frequency

Likewise, the periodicity of the data selected affects the estimation. The return interval used for the estimate can be daily, weekly or monthly. Using daily data increases the sample size, but it also introduces noise into the sample. On the other hand, running monthly data might not capture important components and introduces greater chances of changes in the betas. When monthly data is used, a minimum of four years' returns would be needed. If we use daily returns, however, two or three years of daily returns would be sufficient.

Market proxy selection

Lastly, the market selected also plays a major role in our results. A number of market indices are used as proxies for the market portfolio. To select the right index one should consider issues such as: how representative is this proxy with reference to the overall market that it is supposed to represent? Or, is it possible that the index (e.g. S&P500) may not completely capture the systematic risk exposure?

For instance, suppose a corporation is very exposed to interest rate risk, but has a fairly low S&P500 beta. If interest rate risk has to be rewarded, one will underestimate it if using only the S&P500 in the calculation of the expected return via a single-factor model, such as the CAPM. Furthermore, to interpret the beta one should understand what the index (given its content and shape) represents.

The reason why the index selection matters is that a series of characteristics differentiate these markers:

A. The sample of data used in the construction of the index varies. Thus, it is important to analyze the composition in terms of the number of shares (size of the index), and how representative of the economy these shares are.
B. The weight given to each share within the various indices also varies. Hence, one should be aware if the index is weighted by price, equally weighted, weighted by value or in any other manner.
C. The computational method used to estimate each index varies.

For example, the Dow Jones Industrial Average (DJIA) includes 30 industrial companies listed on the New York Stock Exchange (NYSE) which are leaders in their industries (blue chips). Compared to the real size of the market this sample is small and not random. Thus, movements in the index are more the reflection of this small subset of shares rather than the overall market average, and the index is prone to be less volatile than the market itself.

The DJIA is estimated by adding the current prices of the 30 shares and dividing by a divisor which has been adjusted for splits and changes that the sample has suffered over time. Because this series is price-weighted, the shares with higher prices will have a greater weight than those with lower prices.

These are the types of concerns we ought to consider in selecting an index. In principle, the right choice should contain the largest possible number of shares, include dividends, and be a weighted average. From the perspective of the CAPM, the S&P500 would be a good choice, given that it includes the 500 largest market-capitalization firms in the United States. However, as mentioned, other indexes can be used as well.

With regard to the sample size needed to estimate the slope in the regression, if there are not sufficient observations, the estimate will have a high standard error, which will make the estimation unreliable and not fit for use. In the extreme case, when few or no observations are available (e.g. the firm is of recent creation or not publicly traded) we can use comparable betas from other firms in the sector to supply the data needed. This is reasonable, given that the systematic risk exposures for companies within the same industry have to be quite similar. Several examples of how this method is used will be provided in later chapters. Another concern when using same-sector betas is to choose a set of firms that could be considered competitors, rather than companies within the same industry, but with fundamental key differences such as size. In addition, when estimating betas, one should control for differences in leverage among the firms used in the comparison.

The compromises underlying the beta estimates result in different coefficients. For example, consider the case of Microsoft. Bloomberg's estimate of Microsoft's beta is calculated with 103 weekly returns, relative to the NASDAQ (where the shares are traded), and gives a coefficient of 0.791. The same estimate run against the S&P500, the index used most often by specialized services estimating betas, produces 0.750. However, if instead of weekly, we use 99 monthly returns against the NASDAQ, we get a 0.773 beta coefficient.

In the case of Microsoft there is not much variation. Nevertheless, carrying out the same experiment with JPMorgan Chase & Co. produces values for beta from 1.334, using 430 weekly observations against the NASDAQ, to 1.743 if run against the S&P500 for the same period and type of observations. Even worse, in the case of Citigroup, beta ranges from 3.310 if we run returns against the S&P500 for 103 weekly observations, to 2.495 if we extend the period to 430 observations, to 1.786 if we run the last regression against the NASDAQ rather than the S&P500. Given these wide ranges in beta estimates, justifying the choices and choosing the one that makes sense in each case is important.

Figure 3.2 shows the regressions produced by Bloomberg for JPMorgan and Citigroup. Interestingly, Bloomberg's screens show the fit of the regression and the dispersion of the observations, including important outliers scattered around the quadrants. Furthermore, we can see that each beta estimate comes with a standard error. For example, in the dramatic case of Citigroup where the beta has risen to 3.310, the standard error is 0.349. Assuming the beta is normally

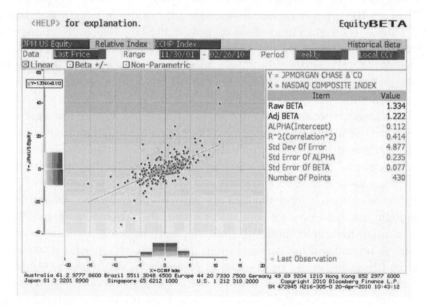

Figure 3.2   Beta for J. P. Morgan U.S. equity relative CCMP index

distributed, with a probability of 67 per cent we can say that the 'true' beta for Citigroup is somewhere between 2.961 and 3.659. This is the result of adding the mean of 3.310 to plus or minus one standard error of 0.349 (Figures 3.3–3.6).

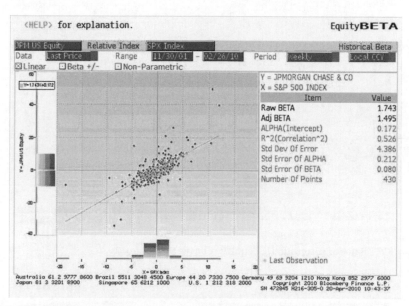

Figure 3.3 Beta for J. P. Morgan U.S. equity relative SPX index

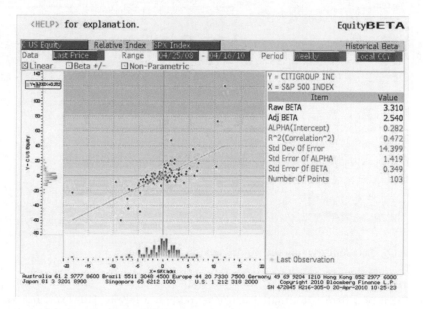

Figure 3.4 Beta for Citigroup U.S. equity relative SPX index 1

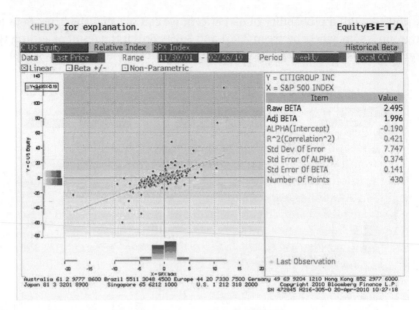

Figure 3.5   Beta for Citigroup U.S. equity relative SPX index 2

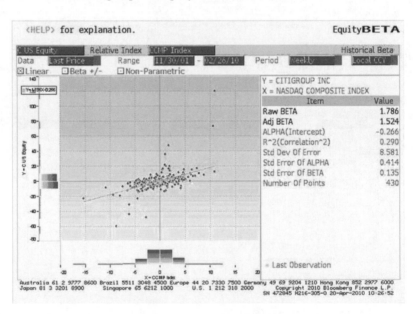

Figure 3.6   Beta for Citigroup U.S. equity relative CCMP index

Determinants of betas

The beta of a firm is estimated using regression analysis. However, notwith-standing the calculation problems, the beta is just the result of the nature of the business and the decisions made by its managers. When, where and how to invest, and what capital structure supports the corporation are what determine its beta. With an understanding of these questions analysts can get an overall idea of the type of beta a firm should have. This concept not only applies to CAPM betas, but to any betas, including those derived using the APM or multifactor approach.

Type of business

Since betas measure a relationship between two variables, higher betas will be obtained from businesses that are more sensitive to market conditions, and lower betas from those that remain unaffected by cycles or other macro idiosyncrasies. For example, the demand for certain types of minerals is inelastic, so we would expect to see very low betas for such products, given that they do not react to changes in the business environment. Furthermore, it is possible (at least in theory) that such a business could be sensitive to cycles in other markets. For example, a mining business in South Africa might be dependent upon the business cycle of metal manufacturing in China, rather than the South African market itself.

Other things being equal, cyclical firms can be expected to have higher betas than non-cyclical firms, that is, of course, unless the market itself is equally cyclical.

Degree of leverage

A company with high operating leverage (for example, one with high fixed costs relative to total costs), will also have more volatility in earnings before interest and taxes (EBIT) than an otherwise equal company with low operating leverage. This volatility in EBIT will result in higher betas than for other firms with less operating leverage.

The same is true for firms carrying more financial leverage. In comparison, companies that are identical except for the amount of debt in their capital structures will also be more affected by higher earnings variability. Debt obligations increase the riskiness of the cash flows and reduce corporate flexibility. If all of the firm's risks are borne by the stockholders, the beta of debt is zero, and debt has a tax benefit, then:

$$\beta^L = \beta^U \left[1 + (1 - t)\left(\frac{D}{E}\right) \right]$$
Formula 3.4

where

β^L = Leveraged beta for equity in the firm
β^U = Unleveraged beta of the firm (the beta of the firm without any debt)
t = Corporate tax rate
D/E = Debt/equity ratio

In many instances practitioners do not use the $(1-t)$ term, reducing and simplifying the formula accordingly.

In addition, if the debt of the beta is not zero, and the debt has market risk, this formula can be modified to take this factor into consideration:

$$\beta^L = \beta^U \left[1 + (1-t)\left(\frac{D}{E}\right) \right] - \beta_D \left(\frac{D}{E}\right) \qquad \qquad \textit{Formula 3.5}$$

where β_D is the beta of debt.

Thus, the equity beta of a company is determined by the risk of the assets or operations as well as by the amount of financial leverage the firm has taken on.

The Gordon or constant growth model

The CAPM is the model most frequently used to estimate desired rates of return and the cost of capital of investment projects. Nevertheless, in the preceding chapter we offered some alternatives to this methodology. For example, under the alternative Gordon Model:

$$P_0 = \frac{D_1}{R_E - g} \qquad \qquad \textit{Formula 2.23}$$

$$R_E = \frac{D_1}{P_0} + g \qquad , \qquad \qquad \textit{Formula 2.25}$$

where

$$D_1 = D_0(1+g) \qquad \qquad \textit{Formula 2.24}$$

In the formula, P_0 is the current market price of the common stock, D_1 is the dividend to be paid in the next period, R_E is the return demanded from the company's shares, and g is the expected dividend growth rate.

The Gordon Model offers some advantages over the CAPM in those instances when its application is advisable. For the most part, the data needed to feed the model is readily available, since both current share prices and annual dividends paid can be easily obtained from the financial press and specialized sources. However, the anticipated rate of constant growth, g, is not observable. This is crucial, given that most of the value of holding the share will come from the dividend payment. Hence, the key to obtaining a realistic estimate is to assess the dividend growth rate accurately.

To estimate a credible g one can, for example, review analysts' forecasts or look at the historical dividend growth. Either way, some decisions will have to be made in order to establish how to use these data. For example, if one is collecting forecasts one has to determine how many to use and how to weight the various opinions. Similarly, if historical information is used, the length of the historical series will need to be determined, as well as the methodology used to estimate an average. Furthermore, in the process it is very likely that a number of technical problems will also need to be resolved.

The effort that goes into solving a problem has to be related to the relevance of the issue we are attempting to tackle. Assuming getting the most accurate cost of equity is important, a good idea is to get an estimate, contrast this result with the opinions of experts, and assess whether the outcome is 'reasonable'. In finance, things have to make sense. The following will provide some guidance, but is no substitute for the analyst's specific knowledge of the company, sector and economy.

1. Dividend payments come out of earnings. They cannot grow permanently at a rate greater than the growth in net income.
2. Dividend payments are often smoothed. Companies tend to be cautions in changing dividend policy, since this affects the valuation of their shares and their clientele in the market.
3. Dividend payments are made out of the cash flows that are available once all other current expenses are taken care of. Therefore, changes in efficiencies, additional investments and losses on sale, for example, will affect the ability of the firm to increase and/or support dividend payments.
4. Dividend policy is a function of the sector, the amount of leverage and the life cycle of the business, but it also depends upon management's beliefs and their assessment of their investors' wants.
5. A company's retention ratio (the portion of net income that is reinvested in the company rather than distributed in the form of dividends) can change. Furthermore, some companies pay a given amount (e.g. $40 per share) and not a proportion of net income.

Given these comments, a good way to start is to assess the historical behaviour of the firm with regard to the payment of dividends, because if management has followed a given policy in the past, provided no major changes have occurred or are forecasted in the company or sector, it is likely that the same policies will be followed in the foreseeable future. In addition, it is worth bearing in mind that any company in the market will have to reward the investors equally for the risks they take. Thus, if the company's competitors are paying, for example, 11.5 per cent, other things being equal, our company cannot be far from that figure and any deviations will have to be justified.

More specifically, if our only source of information is analysts' forecasts, we can do one of three things: choose the estimate provided by the analyst we believe is more correct, calculate an average, or calculate an average with different weightings of the various opinions. The best alternative will depend on the circumstances.

If we decide to use historical data, the first step is to select the time horizon. When the company fundamentals or dividend policy have not changed, we can use up to seven or ten years of information. However, when major changes have occurred, this series will be truncated to start after those changes, because the older data will not be relevant for future development. If there is an outlier within the chosen series, one should consider 'normalizing' the distribution by removing the outlying observation from the data set, and investigate the reasons for the different behaviour of one period.

Once the time horizon has been selected the next decision will be to determine if equal weight is going to be given to all of the observations. Sometimes, more weight is given to more recent years, since these are thought to be more relevant. To get an average both the geometric mean and the arithmetic mean can be used.

In addition, a decision will have to be made as to whether future growth is likely to be constant, or whether dividends will change at a non-constant rate for a number of years before a constant growth rate can be applied.

Once a g is calculated, we need to assess whether our estimation is 'reasonable'. Assume we estimated a g of 20 per cent for the equity of a firm within an economy that has an annual inflation rate of 3 per cent. This large g applied to the cash flows in perpetuity implies the firm is growing constantly at a rate greater than that of the economy overall. Although this could be true for a number of years, it is extremely unlikely in perpetuity. The growth rate cannot be equal to the cost of equity capital; indeed, in the long run it should be much lower. As the growth rate approaches the return, the price of the share increases dramatically. However, if the growth rate is less than the return or cost of capital and diminishes, the price converges to the value of a perpetuity with no growth. These statements can be tested by plugging different numbers into the Gordon formula.

The subjective or risk premium model

According to this methodology, the cost of equity capital is:

$$k_E = k_D + \rho \qquad\qquad\qquad\qquad \textit{Formula 2.28}$$

where K_D is the cost of debt before taxes and ρ is the subjective premium component.

The subjective component is the compensation granted to the company's investors for giving up their option to purchase a fixed-income investment in the company's debt and getting a return equal to K_D and, instead, becoming shareholders. The main challenge of the model is how to evaluate what this rate should be.

We can use some guidelines to help us find a value for ρ. For example, we could examine the premiums paid by companies similar to the one in question. In addition, we could consider anchors for the lower and upper bounds of this premium such as those imposed on regulated utilities or suffered by high volatility firms. Several adjustments might need to be considered. If the company is publicly traded, one such adjustment could be related to company size. If the firm is privately held, 'key person' premiums, among others, might be advisable. In this way we arrive at a range of values in the setting of K_E.

From cost of equity to cost of capital

In working out the specific issues related to each source of financing, it is important to understand the general principles that affect all these sources of funds. In this connection, a key concern much debated in estimating the weights of the debt and equity components is whether the weighted average cost of capital should be based on market value or book value.

The simple answer to this question is that all components of the cost of capital, the value of debt, equity and any hybrids the firm might be using to finance their operations should be estimated at market value. This is because securities are issued at market values, and all other value measures such as prices, forecasts or securities are also set at market value. Furthermore, if one wishes to change the capital structure of the company, this will also have to be done at market value.

The defenders of book value use several arguments:

a. Book value is more reliable than market value because it does not change as often.

   Actually, for financial purposes this is more of a weakness., because the value of a firm changes in time, so market information, which picks up such volatility and reflects it in market prices will provide a better reflection of the true state of the value of the assets than accounting values.

b. Estimating debt ratios with book values is a more conservative approach.

   This statement assumes that being conservative is an objective, and that market debt ratios are lower than accounting debt ratios. The truth is that given the volatility of prices in the market the latter assumption is not valid. However, even if it were valid, it would also turn into a disadvantage, because the cost of capital resulting from using lower ratios will be a less conservative estimate, given that it will underestimate the value of both the debt and the equity. In addition, being conservative is not an objective in itself. The purpose is to be as 'correct' as humanly possible, given the nature of the data. That is, given that we do business in the real world it makes no sense to use out dated information in the hope that we shall err on the conservative side. Likely deviations from means ought to be reflected using scenario analysis and statistics, not by using methods that incorporate a bias in a particular direction.

c. Lenders look at book values.

This might be true in some instances, given that market price volatility will bound the value of the asset in question. However, this is not a universal truth. Furthermore, assets have to be sold at market value, regardless of what their accounting values show.

The impact of price changes in the markets will not affect all firms in the same manner. Some sectors carry little debt, and thus will be somewhat better sheltered from the full impact of changes in the value of their equity.

Finally, it is worth remembering that the weights of the components of the capital will change over time, especially in the case of start-ups. It is therefore advisable to assess how the structure will develop over time until the firm reaches a level of maturity.

Summary

To estimate the cost of capital, a series of methodologies have been proposed, because no one model is the most appropriate under all circumstances. Furthermore, in practice, each of these methods requires some problem-solving on the part of the analyst.

The common predicament is that expected (ex-ante) returns are determined by risk, but expected returns are not observable. Therefore, historical data is fed into our models instead, to provide a figure for the expected or desired return.

A jump is therefore made in going from ex-ante theories to ex-post data. This situation presents a number of challenges, as the analyst or manager will have to select data periods, frequencies and mean estimation methods, just to name a few, to represent a likely set of occurrences from which to project the future.

If the multivariate probability distribution of returns has remained stationary over time, historical returns can be used to estimate expected returns, variances and covariances. However, non-stationarity in this distribution can cause complications in forming these estimates.

In simple words, insofar as the past resembles the future, expectations created with historical data will approximate the true outcomes. However, if the data has trends, the means and variances of the information set (data) change over time. If this is the case, using historical information such as the beta to assess a future outcome will lead to wrong predictions. Making informed decisions when selecting these data is therefore vital.

Appendix: A more detailed analysis of the CAPM

This Appendix tries to clarify some of the technical jargon to help readers understand the trade-offs the analyst has to make when selecting data for the inputs, and understanding the economic and econometric meaning of the results he obtains. The discussion below is concerned with technical issues and includes some statistical and econometric vocabulary that is needed to achieve a deeper appreciation of the CAPM. Thus, it is only recommended for those readers who are specifically interested in the more technical aspects of the CAPM.

Following Markowitz's (1952) mean-variance optimization theory, the CAPM explains how investors form efficient portfolios. In this context, rational investors will choose to invest in portfolios which fall on the efficient frontier. These are characterized as providing the maximum return for each unit of risk. The CAPM sets up a structure to explain how these assets are chosen.

A key differentiating element of the CAPM is that it assumes that the only source of risk that matters is systematic risk. Unsystematic risk is diversifiable, while the market risk cannot be diversified and has to be hedged. Accepting market risk is compensated by a risk premium proportional to the risk that investors acquire:

$$R_{j,t} - R_f = \alpha_j + \beta_j \left(R_{m,t} - r_f\right) + \varepsilon_{j,t} \qquad \text{\textit{Formula 3.6}}$$

with j $=1,...,N$ and t $=1,...,T$

where

$R_{j,t}$ = return on asset j at time t
R_f = return of riskless asset at time t
$R_{m,t}$ = return on the market portfolio at time t
α_j and β_j are the coefficients to be estimated.

$$\mathrm{Cov}\left(\left(R_{m,t}, \varepsilon_{j,t}\right)\right) = 0$$

If $\alpha_j = 0$, then

$$E[R_{j,t} - r_f] = \beta_j \, E[(R_{m,t} - r_f)] \qquad \text{\textit{Formula 2.6}}$$

where,

$E[R_{j,t} - R_f]$ is the market risk premium that compensates shareholders for acquiring risk beyond that contained in a risk-free security. The expected return on asset j over the risk-free rate is proportional to the market risk premium, and the beta β_j is the measure of sensitivity to market risk and plays the role of the proportionality factor.

A key element of the CAPM is that the market portfolio R_M represents all the wealth in the economy. That should consist of not only the shares trading in the markets, but all private and public wealth, including human capital.

The CAPM is used by more than 80 per cent of financial managers and advisors.[7] Several features explain the popularity of the model. For example, it is simple to understand and use, and it provides a good benchmark for performance evaluation. However, the model has also been subject to criticism. Below we list a series of conceptual and econometric difficulties that plague the practical use of the CAPM.

Conceptual problems using CAPM

1) The CAPM states that the expected (ex-ante) returns are determined by risk. However expected returns are not observable. Therefore, tests of the CAPM must be conducted with historical (ex-post) returns. A jump is made in going from ex-ante theory to ex-post data. If the multivariate probability distribution of returns has remained stationary over time, historical returns can be used to estimate expected returns, variances and covariances. However, non-stationarity in this distribution can cause complications in forming these estimates.

   In other words, a stationary process is a stochastic process (think of a time series of data in which observations are random or non-predictable, such as returns) whose joint probability distribution does not change over time. As a result, parameters such as the mean and the variance remain stable. On the other hand, if the process is non-stationary, for example, if the data has trends, the means and variances of the information set (data) change over time. If this is the case, using historical information such as the beta to assess a future outcome will lead to wrong predictions.

   A stochastic process is one whose path is non-deterministic. For example, if we are thinking of share prices, the next state (price P_1) is determined both by the process's predictable actions (the last share price on the prior date P_0) and by a random element (e_1, error term). That is, we cannot determine precisely the share price even if it has a known component.

2) Even if the probability distribution of returns has been stationary, some variables such as betas cannot be observed. Although these variables can be estimated, this introduces measurement error into the econometric tests.

3) The market portfolio, central to the CAPM, has never been precisely defined. Stock market indices are just proxies: many CAPM assets cannot be quantified although the portfolio should contain all the assets.

4) There is also a related difficulty specifying the risk-free rate.

In 1977, Roll published an article where he argued that although the CAPM is testable in principle 'no correct and unambiguous test of the theory had appeared' and that it is practically impossible that such a test could ever be carried out. His reasoning was that the only testable hypothesis of the CAPM is that the true market portfolio lies on the efficient set: that is, the market portfolio is mean-variance efficient. All other hypotheses, such as the linear relationship between beta and expected return, can be shown to be redundant, given the main hypothesis. However, the main hypothesis cannot be tested, since the true market portfolio cannot be observed, given that it must include all assets.

Roll also argued that the practice of using proxies for the market portfolio is beset with problems because, for example, they might be efficient when the true market portfolio is inefficient or vice versa. Roll's critique does not reject the CAPM per se, only its testability.

Some of the consequences of not knowing the market portfolio's true value are explained by Roll. For example, in his 1977 and 1978 works, the author points out that the ambiguity of the market portfolio leaves the CAPM untestable (does the market portfolio actually lie on the efficient set?), and that using proxies has problems. Even if the returns are highly correlated, different proxies would lead to different beta estimates for the same securities.

In spite of Roll's critique, several tests of the CAPM have been conducted. For example, some researchers suggest that there are other ways to test the model since it proposes that the market portfolio is efficient, and efficient portfolios offer the highest expected return for their risk.

The work of Black, Jensen and Scholes (1972) shows that while the CAPM predicts the expected excess return from holding an asset is proportional to the covariance of its return with the market portfolio, in reality this is not the case. In particular, the authors found that low beta assets earn higher returns on average, and high beta assets earn a lower return on average, than forecasted by the model. These studies suggest that the slope of the CAPM model is lower and the intercept higher than predicted by the traditional theory.

In their 1973 classic paper, Fama and MacBeth went about testing the model in a slightly different way. The authors grouped all NYSE stocks into 20 portfolios, and plotted the estimated beta of each portfolio in a five-year period against the portfolio's average return over a subsequent five-year period. If the CAPM is correct, investors would not have expected any of these portfolios to perform better or worse than a comparable package of T-bills and the market portfolio. However, the actual returns did not exactly fall on the market line and alphas were found to be significantly greater than the mean of the risk-free interest rate. Once more, it is difficult to draw a definite conclusion from the findings given that the results could be due to the fact that (1) the CAPM is a rough approximation to real markets, (2) the authors did not include all the risky assets in the index, or (3) the tests were not appropriately performed since they use actual rather than expected returns.

The CAPM predicts that beta is the only reason expected returns differ among assets. Nevertheless, there is evidence that the average return on small firm stock has been substantially larger than predicted by the CAPM (the size effect), that firms with high book to market ratios outperform those with low book to market ratios (the value premium), and that stocks with high price–earnings ratios earn lower returns over long periods than those the model would predict. Thus, there seems to be more than one source of risk.

Other 'anomalies' found include:

a. The Monday Effect and the January Effect: the Monday effect (French, 1980) and the January effect (Reinganum, 1983; Roll, 1983). Research has shown that some of the biggest price deviations from random walks result from seasonal and temporal patterns. The Monday and January effects are two examples. On Mondays stock prices go down more than on any other day, while in January, returns significantly exceed those in other months.

b. Long-term reversals: DeBondt and Thaler (1985) grouped companies in two sets as extreme losers and extreme winners. For each year, starting in 1933, they formed portfolios of the best and the worst performing stocks over the three preceding years. They then tracked the returns on these portfolios for the subsequent five years. Their findings showed that over three- to five-year holding periods, stocks that performed poorly over the previous three to five years achieved larger returns than those which performed well during the same period. The authors used overreaction to justify the differences in returns. The extreme losers become inexpensive, whereas extreme winners become too expensive. Thus, prices reversed themselves.

c. Momentum: Jegadeesh and Titman (1993) showed that movements in individual stock prices over the period of six to twelve months tend to predict future movements in the same direction. Thus the observed tendency is for rising asset prices to rise even further in the short run. Unlike the long-term trends spotted by De Bondt and Thaler (1985) which tend to revert to the mean, the short-term trends continue, leading to short-run momentum for equity returns.

d. *D/E* leverage effect: In 1988 Bhandari published results showing a positive relationship between leverage and returns, controlling for the beta, firm size and the January effect. The relationship proved insensitive to variations in the market proxy and the estimation technique.

To date, it appears that the post-Roll tests have not determined whether the CAPM is an empirically feasible model given that all the studies have been the subject of some degree of criticism. However, Markovitz (1983) pointed out that sensible practical use of portfolio analysis and the CAPM does not depend on the success of this empirical research, but on its ability to predict and that this is therefore the critical issue.

Over time, researchers have tried to get around the difficulties described above. For example, two approaches have evolved to solve the non-stationarity problem:

1) Form portfolios that have stationary betas, and
2) Interpret the tests in terms of the distributions of asset returns conditional on aggregate wealth.

The expected returns and betas can be measured by the distributions of asset returns conditional on aggregate wealth. If these distributions are stationary over time, then a time-series of returns on assets may be used to test the unconditional CAPM. Conditional aggregate wealth implies that prior knowledge or information affects judgement and thus affects the probabilities. The fact that the market portfolio is on the frontier of the portfolio based on the unconditional distributions does not imply the validity of the conditional CAPM; it is a strong prediction of the unconditional form of the CAPM.

Three approaches have evolved to remedy the unobservability problem:

1) Ignore the problem, assume the disturbance terms are uncorrelated with the true market portfolio, and that the proxy portfolio has a unit beta. This is equivalent to assuming the market proxy is the minimum variance portfolio.
2) Interpret the test as a test of whether the market proxy is on the portfolio frontier, and
3) View the test as a test of a single-factor APT.

We can explicitly demonstrate the implicit assumption made when the unobservability of the true market portfolio is ignored:

1) Given that the market proxy has a unit beta, it is shown that the beta with respect to the proxy is equal to the beta with respect to the actual market portfolio. Therefore, true betas can be estimated if the market proxy has a unit beta and the disturbance terms are uncorrelated with the true market portfolio.
2) It is also demonstrated that the betas of all assets in this proper subset of assets with respect to the minimum variance unit beta portfolio are identical to their betas with respect to the true market portfolio.

The CAPM suggests three empirical models for testing monthly rates of return on common stocks:

1) A cross-sectional regression of average monthly excess returns.
2) A series of monthly cross-sectional regressions of the realized rates of return on the betas.
3) A series of time-series regressions for each asset or portfolio in the sample.

Econometric problems using CAPM

Regression analysis is a technique for analyzing the relationship between a dependent and one or more independent variables, and is used for prediction and forecasting. The regression parameters provide information as to how the typical value of the dependent variable (e.g. returns) varies when any of the independent variables (e.g. beta) changes while the others remain fixed. Hence, the regression estimates show the average value of the dependent variable when the independent variables are held fixed, or the conditional expectation of the dependent variable given the independent variables when these are held fixed. The regression results include the variation of the dependent variable around the regression function.

The better known methods for carrying out regression analysis are linear regression and ordinary least squares regression. In order to obtain meaningful results some assumptions are made by the methods, although regression analysis can still be used when the assumptions do not fully hold. Classical assumptions include:

- The sample must be representative of the population in quality and size.
- The error is a random variable with a mean of zero, conditional on the explanatory variables.
- The predictors must be linearly independent. That is, independent variables cannot be the combination of other independent variables and these cannot be highly correlated among themselves.
- Errors have to be uncorrelated.
- The variance of the error is constant across observations (homoscedasticity). If this assumption is violated, other methods might be used to assess the relationships. An example of homoscedastic distribution is provided in Figure 3.7.

Fulfilling these assumptions implies that estimates will be unbiased, consistent and efficient. These are sufficient conditions, but not all are necessary and several of these assumptions can be relaxed by using more advanced treatments. Nevertheless, when treating returns, a real problem is finding trends and spatial autocorrelation.

The most relevant econometric problems associated with the CAPM are:

1. The disturbance terms are heteroscedastic (random dispersion) and correlated across assets, because the variances of the rates of return differ across assets and the asset returns are correlated. Therefore, the ordinary least square (OLS) coefficients (those obtained by regressing the returns) are inefficient estimators.

    The distributions in the graphs in Figure 3.7 can be compared to observe the differences between sequences of data with finite variance or infinite variance.

    Additionally, the coefficients are biased because the estimates of the variances are biased. Possible solutions to this are to use generalized least square (GLS) estimators or to use OLS estimators and calculate the correct variance of the coefficients.

    The estimator is unbiased and consistent if the errors have finite variance and are uncorrelated with the regressors. The bias of an estimator is the difference between its expected value and the true value of the parameter being estimated. A series of estimators for a parameter is consistent if the series converges in probability to the parameter.

2) We do not observe true betas but their estimates, and these contain measurement errors. Possible solutions to this problem are:
    a) Use grouped data to reduce the variances of the measurement errors in betas.
    b) Use an instrumental variables approach.
    c) Use an adjusted GLS approach that takes account of the variances of the measurement errors in betas.

Focus on the heteroscedasticity and correlation of the disturbance terms:

1) Assume that the betas are fixed independent variables without error.
2) Also assume that the test sample consists of linearly independent monthly rates of return.
3) Therefore, the variance–covariance matrix is non-singular and strictly positive.

Three remedies for the measurement errors in the betas:

1) Group assets into portfolios – the variance of the measurement errors for the portfolio betas would approach zero as the number of assets in each portfolio increases.

2) Use the instrumental variables approach. A variable that is highly correlated with the true beta but uncorrelated with the measurement errors is used to obtain the estimators (i.e. previous betas).
3) Subtract the average variance of the measurement error from the cross-sectional sample variation of the estimated betas.

Grouping assets into portfolios – If the criterion used to group the assets is uncorrelated with the measurement errors, the variance of the errors approaches zero as the number of assets in the portfolios increases. If measurement errors are correlated, the variance is only reduced by grouping and not eliminated.

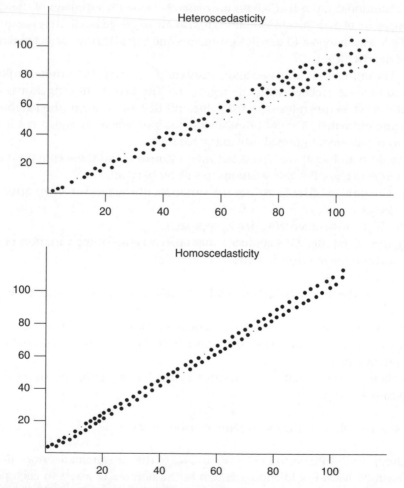

Figure 3.7   Heteroscedasticity and homoscedasticity

Although grouping reduces or eliminates the inconsistency resulting from measurement errors, it also diminishes the efficiency of the estimators. The efficiency of the OLS estimators is equal to the ratio of the between-group variation in estimated betas to the total variation in estimated betas. This ratio is less than unity and therefore indicates a loss of efficiency.

This loss of efficiency can be minimized by placing the assets into groups in such a way that the within-group variation is minimized and the between-group variation maximized. Forming the groups according to the true beta would be ideal. However, the true beta is unobservable and estimates of betas contain measurement errors. Therefore, the next best method is to use a variable highly correlated with the true betas but that does not contain the measurement errors (previous betas). In other words, when we use the portfolio grouping procedure in order to get consistent estimates, we will lose some estimating precision because we will incorrectly estimate the sample variance.

The failure to reject a strong prediction is usually due to a weak statistical test. Use of a stronger test should reject because these predictions are only true in an idealized world. A weak prediction is a prediction whose validity is broadly implied by, but does not imply, the underlying theory. An example of a weak prediction of the CAPM is that ex-post betas are positively related to ex-post returns. Since these imply weaker relationships, it is easier to find statistical support.

The CAPM is a static (single period) model. Fama (1970) proposed that it could be treated as if it holds inter-temporally if preferences and future investment opportunity sets are not state-dependent. Nevertheless, Merton (1971) has shown in a number of examples that portfolio behaviour for an inter-temporal maximizer will be significantly different when a changing investment opportunity set instead of a constant one is factored in. There have been several attempts to construct a multi-period capital asset pricing model on the basis of a multiple horizon for investors. The only way in which these models are inter-temporal is in their specification of a multi-period horizon for the investor, who is then assumed to solve a stochastic dynamic programming problem. The resulting demand functions are still used to solve for prices in a static framework.

The effects of investment horizon on the estimation of systematic risk were investigated by Jensen (1969). Basing his argument on the instantaneous systematic risk concept, he concluded that the logarithmic linear form of the CAPM can be used to eliminate the effects of the time horizon and the estimated systematic risk. Levy (1972) has shown that the assumption of a holding period that is different from the true investment horizon will indeed lead to systematic bias of the performance measure. Cheng and Deets (1973) show that the logarithmic linear form of the CAPM not only implies a linear relationship but produces an instantaneous risk, dependent upon the length of the observed horizon. In addition, they proposed a new instantaneous systematic risk entitled the 'Cheng–Deets instantaneous systematic risk' as a replacement for the Jensen instantaneous risk. Neither Jensen nor Cheng–Deets has ever investigated the effects of a finite investment horizon when market equilibrium is not instantaneous.

Regardless of the various problems in applying the CAPM, the model provides a rationale for passive portfolio strategy. Investors should

a) diversify holdings of risky assets in the proportions of the market portfolio, and
b) mix this portfolio with risk-free assets to achieve the desired risk–return combination.

This passive strategy can serve as a risk-adjusted benchmark for measuring the performance of active portfolio selection strategies and is attractive for two reasons:

1. Historically, it has outperformed most actively managed portfolios, and
2. It is comparatively less expensive since the costs of transactions and research are lower.

In portfolio management the CAPM is mainly used in two ways:

1) To establish a logical and convenient starting point in asset allocation and security selection, and
2) To establish a benchmark for evaluating portfolio management ability on a risk-adjusted basis.

4
Caveats

WACC, average risk and the divisional cost of capital

A firm's weighted average cost of capital (WACC) is simply the return investors expect to earn on the average market risk of their firm's investments. Thus, when using the CAPM in assessing whether a new projects is viable, we need to find out if the project is of 'average' risk.

The 'hurdle rate' is the minimum acceptable rate of return from an investment project. For projects of average risk, it is usually equal to the firm's cost of capital. Practitioners use the hurdle rate to describe any risk-adjusted discount rate.

Suppose we have a new investment project of average risk named X. If all the projects of our company also had average risk, the hurdle rate of this project X would be the same as the WACC, for example 12 per cent. In addition, the hurdle rate of any individual project carried out by the company would be the same, that is, the WACC, because all its projects have average risk, and therefore, they require average return.

Suppose we are analyzing an additional new project Z. We calculate its IRR and this turns out to be 11 per cent, so according to our minimum acceptable return requirements we would not undertake project Z, because it is below our 'hurdle': the minimum acceptable return. Nevertheless, if we do realize that this project Z, has less or more risk than average we should adjust our required return accordingly.

For example, the company ACMA is analyzing a project with the following characteristics:

The required net investment is $50,000, the estimated life of the project ten years, the positive cash flows generated during those ten years $10,000 per year and the company's WACC is 12 per cent. With this information, if we calculate the NPV for the project, we obtain a positive figure, so it is an acceptable project. Nevertheless, let us say that we know the project has greater than average

131

risk and the appropriate discount rate should be 16 per cent. Then, as the estimations in Table 4.1 show, we should not undertake the project.

Figure 4.1 illustrates the difference between the use of a single discount rate (WACC) to accept or reject any project, and the use of a discount rate based on the security market line (SML) for each project.

The figure shows four different projects (A, B, C and D), a constant horizontal line representing a WACC of 12 per cent, and a discount rate based on the SML for each project. Using the WACC, projects C and D are acceptable. Nevertheless, if we do consider the risk differential among projects, and therefore adjust the required return for each of them, the only acceptable projects are A and C.

The risk-adjusted discount rate approach is considered preferable to the WACC approach when the projects under consideration differ significantly in their risk characteristics.

Table 4.1 ACMA project

Year (t)	Net cash flow	Weighted average cost of capital (k_a = .12)		Risk-adjusted discount rate (k_a = .16)	
		Interest factor	Present value	Interest factor	Present value
0	$-50,000	1.000	$-50,000	1.000	$-50,000
1–10	$10,000	5.650	56,500	4.833	48,330
NPV			$6,500		$-1,670

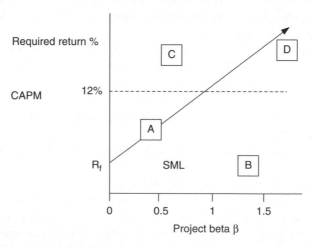

Figure 4.1 Security market line and project risk

We introduced this topic in earlier chapters; but in the context of evaluating different investment alternatives, ensuring we that scrutinized the projects on the basis of both the return and the risk.'

In this section we want to call readers' attention to aspects of the risk of the projects themselves, as the different investment alternatives available to the firms can be grouped according to their level of risk. For example, a firm's Manual of Accounting and Finance might identify different categories for investment proposals such as: 1) safety, 2) convenience, 3) quality, 4) revenue-increasing and 5) others. The procedures for the proposals and the criteria for the acceptance of the projects will vary according to where the projects fit within these categories.

Cost-reduction opportunities and new undertakings initiated to either increase production capacity or manufacture a new product would fall within the fourth group above. In this sense, the key to using the WACC as a hurdle rate for discounting the estimated cash flows is whether the new projects under analysis are in the same risk category as the firm's average.

Does it fit within the industry or industries where the company has done business in the past? If so, have these industries themselves evolved? For example, 30 years ago, IT companies were concerned mainly with providing telephone services in a monopolistic environment. Both the scope of the business and the regulatory situation has significantly evolved since those times. The average risk of the sector has therefore changed, and consequently that of any company within it. It is also true that not all firms within a sector are like the sector's average. The market risk of both the project and the firm will depend on the sensitivity of the firm to the industry and to the overall economy. If the new project shares the average firm's profile, the project's cost of capital will be the same as the firm's average cost of capital. However, if the project falls within a new industry with a greater or lower market risk than the firm's overall assets, then adjustments to the discount rate are necessary.

Consider a manufacturer of children's household products which distributes cradles, tables, chairs and goods of that nature. Given their target market expertise, in time the firm decides to extend its product line and start producing diapers. A few years later they further broaden their focus to manufacture baby formula and other baby foods. Even though our firm still specializes in the children's market, it is clear its operational risks have shifted. Furthermore, each new product brings with itself uncertainties not present when manufacturing new designs of tables and the like. The reason is that with a new product the firm is testing many hypothesis or assumptions, whereas with an improvement or change in an existing one (i.e. the same table but now offered in a new colour) that is not the case.

In our example, the WACC of the firm and after the dipper/baby formula products were launched will change. It will be an average of the returns demanded by investors for the different risks the company acquires: those of selling children's tables and those of distributing dippers and baby food in addition to those of the projects mentioned not to be within category four.

When a project does not have the average company risk, the financial managers will need to determine the appropriate return. There are several reasons for this. First, if you discount by a lower cost of capital, you will be overestimating the value the specific project adds to the company. That is, the project will look more attractive than it really is. The other side of this is that its returns will not be rewarding the investor appropriately for the risk it adds to the portfolio of investments. On the other hand, if you are using a higher rate than needed, first, you might reject perfectly good projects, and second, given the greater return by which you discount, riskier projects will always look more attractive than those which are not as risky. Thus in a situation of limited capital availability there will be a tendency to accept riskier projects instead of others within the firm that might have great profit potential but which look less glamorous. An extreme example would be a company within a regulated industry with a line of products which offers constant low returns but has low risk, and a second line of business within the IT industry which offers high returns but with huge volatility.

In summary, if we are evaluating investments with risks which substantially differ from those of the firm overall, using the WACC to discount the cash flows will lead to poor decisions. Using the WACC is only appropriate when the risk of the proposed investment is similar to that of the firm's existing activities. If different divisions or products within the company compete for funds, those with higher risk will offer higher returns and they will tend to be the winners in the allocation of the firm's scarce resources. Consequently, one must not forget that the adequate discount rate has to be selected in accordance to the use that is going to be made of the funds.

In cases when the right discount rate is not equal to the company's WACC, we can use different approaches to assess the adequate return given the risk of the project under evaluation. One such approach is to examine other investments outside the firm that are in the same risk class. Because for each unit of risk the market demands a specific return (as indicated by the security market line), it is easy to get guidance on what these rates ought to be. We just need to identify other companies involved in equivalent businesses and observe their returns. Thus, for example, if we produce and distribute dippers we shall discount the cash flows of those projects by rates close to those offered by other dipper manufacturers. There are many sources that publish this type of information, such as Ibbotson Associates.

A second approach to adjusting the WACC to reflect risk differentials among projects within a single firm would be to add or deduct a premium depending upon the category in which the investment is classified. For example, the cost of funds destined to develop a new product in a new industry could be considered within category four and very high risk. The firm might therefore want to adjust the WACC by adding a high premium, such as six per cent. This premium would be common to all projects within that category.

On the other hand, if the project were to be the replacement of some existing equipment to improve quality, then we could use a discount as an adjustment factor to the WACC, for example by deducting four per cent from the weighted average. A graphic illustration of this approach is presented in figure 4.2.

Firms with different product lines might also be structured by divisions and reporting units. The divisional cost of capital is relevant given that the firm's WACC will be a weighted average of the costs of capital of the different reporting units. As explained earlier for the case of new product lines, divisions with risks different from the firm's average risk have to determine their own appropriate discount rates.

The process is analogous to the one described for the products: one can use the discount rate offered by 'pure plays' – companies in a single line of business, with assets and activities equivalent to those of the division we are analyzing. When using the CAPM to estimate the cost of equity, the betas of the pure plays have to be adjusted for the differences in the capital structure of each firm. This is done by unleveraging and leveraging the betas. In implementing this approach, the main difficulty is in finding companies comparable to the division for which costs of equity need to be estimated.

Suppose we have a company (ACMA) with several lines of business, including one in the residential construction sector. In order to determine whether a specific investment opportunity has a positive net present value, we need to

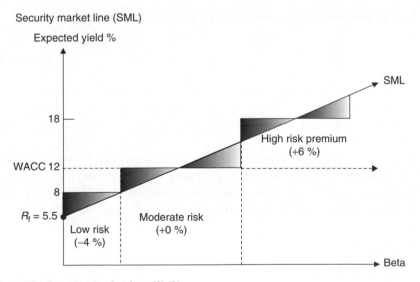

Figure 4.2   Security market line (SML)

estimate its equity cost of capital. We do not have a beta for the portion of the firm that deals with this line of business, but we know the current and target debt to equity ratio of this division.

Following the strategy explained earlier, we select several publicly traded companies with observable betas which are pure plays within the construction business. The firms selected must resemble our division as closely as possible. A good way of choosing among the various alternatives is to consider those we think of as competitors, with similar asset composition and size.

Given that the capital structure information of traded companies is in the public domain, it is easy to determine the debt to equity ratio of each of these firms. With several sector betas, and information regarding the leverage structure of these corporations, we can get an unleveraged beta for the construction sector and a leveraged beta for our division.

We start with the leveraged beta formula reviewed in Chapter 3:

$$\beta^L = \beta^U \left[1 + (1-t)\left(\frac{D}{E}\right) \right]$$

Formula 3.3

where

β^L is the leveraged beta
β^U is the unleveraged beta
t is the effective tax rate
D is the market value of the debt
E is the market value of the equity

We can substitute the values in the above formula or simplify into:]

$$B^L = \beta^U * \left(1 + \frac{D}{E} \right)$$

Formula 4.1

which is the version most often used by practitioners, where, again, β^U is the unleveraged beta, β^L is the leveraged beta and D and E are the market values of the debt and equity in the capital structure of the company under observation.

Given that companies carry debt in their capital structures, what we observe are leveraged betas. Thus, in order to find a representative beta for the assets of the sector irrespective of the leverage of each individual firm, we need to turn the formula around to remove the impact of the debt from the beta:

$$\beta^U = \frac{\beta^L}{\left(1 + \frac{D}{E} \right)}$$

Formula 4.2

In the first column of Table 4.2 we name the firms chosen as competitors of ACMA. In the second column we list their betas. Notice that we put a question mark in ACMA's place since this is the one we are attempting to estimate. In the third column we provide the debt to equity ratio of each of the firms. In the last column we use these data to estimate the unleveraged beta of each firm. In the Total row we add all of these unleveraged betas and divide by the number of companies in the sample to get an industry average. Then, we use this sector's average and ACMA's debt to equity ratio to estimate the firm's leveraged beta for the residential construction division:

$$\beta^L = \beta^U * (1 + D / E) = 0.972 * 1.5 = 1.458$$

This approach to estimating a beta is based on the idea that the systematic risk for a particular line of business is common to all firms which compete in that market. This is a reasonable assumption which has been proven to work. However, often it is quite difficult to apply it properly since there are many lines of business for which pure plays are hard to find.

Finally, looking at a slightly different scenario, it could be the case that we are working with a company made up of different divisions. If we know the overall cost of capital of the firm and we have all the data necessary for estimating the cost of capital of all divisions except one, we could determine this unknown by solving a simple equation.

Assume we have a company Smith's Goods and Services (SGS), with three divisions. This company is publicly traded and we know the market value of their debt and equity. Given that we find pure plays for two of its divisions and that we know their target debt to equity ratios, we are able

Table 4.2 Beta for ACMA division

Company name	Observed equity beta	Ratio D/E	$\beta U = \beta L / (1 + D/E)$
ACMA division whose cost of equity we wish to determine	?	0.50	?
Haube	1.747	0.73	1.010
Gadaros	1.434	0.24	1.156
Cebartes	1.829	0.20	1.524
Groman	1.781	1.65	0.672
Acosi	1.406	1.82	0.499
Total	–	–	4.861 / 5 =
Average	–	–	0.972

to determine the cost of equity capital for these by repeating the process described above.

We therefore, use the CAPM to compute the WACC for the company and each of its divisions, and in all the instances when we find pure plays we calculate the cost of equity using betas of comparable corporations, adjusting for the different capital structures.

In the process of making these estimations we might overlook two facts. First, we should make sure we do not unleverage and leverage the overall company beta by the same debt to equity ratio. The correct procedure is to unleverage by the current debt to equity ratio, and to leverage by the 'target' debt to equity ratio.

Second, when choosing the right risk-free rate for the CAPM of each division, we should ensure we take into account the life of the projects in their respective line of business and match this to the time to maturity of the bond which proxies the risk-free rate. For example, if we are in the real estate sector, given that the lives of assets in this sector are very long, we should use a long-term risk-free asset, that is, 20 years.

At this point in our example we have all the data needed to estimate the cost of capital for two of the divisions and the overall company. We now need to obtain the information for the third division. In this example we use the CAPM to compute the WACC for the company and each of its divisions, and we calculate the cost of equity for each division using betas of similar corporations adjusting for the different capital structures.

To help the reader through the process we copy here those formulas we already analyzed in Chapter 2, while recalling that to determine the WACC we multiply the percentage of each type of funding within the capital structure by its own cost and then add up all the different costs from the different sources of funds.

Since we do not have industry betas we could use to estimate the equity capital of the third division, this cost has to be estimated in a different way. The key to this procedure is to realize that the beta of the company's assets is only a weighted average of the betas of the different divisions, where the weights are a fraction of the value of the equity of each division. In this example, as a proxy for those weights, we have used the identifiable assets of each unit. However, if more relevant, we could utilize other variables such as sales.

ß Assets (the unleveraged beta) of SGS =

$$\beta\,A = \left(\frac{V_{RE}}{V_{SGS}}\right)\beta_{RE} + \left(\frac{V_{R}}{V_{SGS}}\right)\beta\,A_{R} + \left(\frac{V_{SGS}}{V_{SGS}}\right)\beta\,A_{TS}$$

Formula 4.3

where:

βA = is the beta of the assets (unleveraged beta) of SGS = 0.65
βA_{RE} = is the beta of the assets of the real estate division = 0.407
βA_R = is the beta of the assets of the restaurant division = 1.44
βA_{TS} = is the beta of the assets of the travel agency services division = ?

and V_{SGS}, V_{RE}, V_R, V_{TS} are the values of the company and each of its units. Using the identifiable fraction of the assets of each division as a proxy of the relative value (60%, 10% and 30%), and the previously estimated betas (listed above):

0.65 = 60% * 0.407 + 10% * 1.44 + 30% * β_{TS}

β_{TS}, the beta of the travel agency division, is the only unknown. Thus we clear the equation to determine its value:

(0.65–0.3882) / 0.30

$\beta T_S = 0.87$

Considering the goal of 40 per cent debt, the beta of the equity is:

β_{TS} = 0.87 *(1 +0.4/0.6) = 1.45

Now, we use the CAPM to estimate the cost of equity:

$K_E = R_f + \beta\ [R_M – R_f]$ *Formula 2.22*

where the equity risk premium is the difference between the expected return on the market portfolio R_M and the risk-free rate (R_f).

$K_E = R_f + \beta$ [Risk premium] = 5.5 + 1.45 * 7.43 = 16.30%

Considering the debt to equity target of 40% to 60%, and the marginal tax rate of 44 per cent, and a cost of debt 1.5% above the risk-free rate, the WACC of the travel agency division is:

60% * 16.30 + 40% * (5.5+1.5) (1–0.44) =

= 9.78 + 1.568 = 11.348%

Mergers and acquisitions

We can continue to study the same topics – project risk and average company risk – for a different business context: mergers and acquisitions. It is clear that, just as in the case of project analysis, a realistic cost of capital estimate is needed to properly evaluate a prospective merger. However, failed acquisitions are often the result of mistakes in understanding what this rate should be. Not surprisingly, the guiding light in this context is the same we have used before: the rate of return on the acquisition earned by the purchasing firm ought to be equal to that of the competitors of the purchased enterprise. We have already stated the reason for this: equal risk commands equal return. Firms within the same industry carry out operations using similar assets and thus share the same operational risks.

A typical mistake in company valuation is to use the weighted average cost of capital of the purchasing firm as the rate to discount the cash flows of the target company. The WACC used to discount the cash flows of an enterprise should match the risks of that enterprise's cash flows. It is clear that the risks of the operations of the target company will not change just because someone else coming from a different line of business has purchased them. For example, if a multinational bakery were to purchase a chain of nuclear reactors, that would not change the operational risks of the nuclear reactors. Furthermore, even if the acquiring firm can by its mere size and reputation acquire cheaper debt, it does not mean a transfer of wealth should be done between both companies. The costs of debt of the target firm should still reflect its own debt capacity.

The capital structure of a firm encompasses all the elements that help finance the long-term assets of the firm. Accordingly, the focus of the capital structure analysis for a merger should be the target capital structure of the combined company. That is, the long-term WACC of the overall merged structure should reflect the debt capacity of the target company plus that of the acquiring company, and the cost of equity of the acquiring company plus those of the target, all in the appropriate proportions.

Flotation costs

If a firm finds acquires external capital, then it incurs flotation costs. Flotation costs are the costs of floating or issuing new securities. If the issue is sold through underwriters, the flotation expenses include administrative costs such as filing, legal and printing fees as well as costs which result from using the services of investment bankers who assist the firm in selling their securities to the market. These costs can be quite significant, in the magnitude of ten per cent of the proceeds,[1] although they vary widely, for example, between 0.5 per cent and 15 per cent depending on the size of the issue and the type and quality of the security. These costs are usually larger for equity issues than for preferred, which in turn are larger than for those of debt. The reason is that underwriters incur greater risks when issuing variable return securities than with fixed-income securities. Low quality issues are also more expensive than high quality, and smaller size issues more expensive than larger.

Sometimes the WACC is increased to reflect flotation costs. However, through these pages it has been reiterated that the cost of capital must reflect its use, not its origin. Thus, a group of academics and practitioners have proposed that these expenses should be included in the cash flows and not in the WACC. However, those who claim they should be included in the cost of capital argue that, typically, flotation costs are not applied to operational cash flows.

Suppose the firm ACMA wants to issue equity to finance a project with a cost of $100 million. If the issuing or floating costs are 10 per cent of the proceeds, the firm will only receive 90 per cent of the issued amount. Given that the firm needs $100 million, it will be necessary to issue additional capital to recover those expenses. The gross issue will therefore be the project costs divided by one, minus the cost of the issue, which in this case means $100 million divided by 0.90, which equals $111.11 million. The total expenses of the flotation are $11.11 million, making the true cost of the expansion $111.11 million.

If instead ACMA's capital structure includes 40 per cent debt, the flotation expenses related to the equity issue are 10 per cent and those associated with debt are 5 per cent, we need to estimate the total costs in a slightly different manner. To calculate the weighted average total flotation cost (F_A) we simply multiply the flotation expenses of equity (F_E) and of debt (F_D) by their respective proportions within the total capital structure, and add them up:]

$$(F_A) = \left(\frac{E}{V}\right) * (F_E) + \left(\frac{D}{V}\right) * (F_D)$$

Formula 4.4

$$= 60\% * 0.10 + 40\% * 0.05 = 8\%$$

This result tells us that we will now need to adjust the weighted average cost of the capital by an additional 8 per cent to account for the flotation costs. For each dollar of external financing, the firm needs to raise $1 / (1 - 0.08) = $1.087. In our example, this will translate to: $ [100 million / (1 - F_A)] = $100 million / 0.92 = $108.7 million.

Rather, if we are attempting to estimate the external cost of capital (including flotation costs) of a specific source of funds, let us say preferred stock, we shall use the formula from Chapter 2:

$$K_P = \frac{D}{P_0}$$

Formula 2.21

and make a substitution:

$$K_P = \frac{D}{P_{net}}$$

where K_P is the cost of the preferred stock, D is the annual preferred dividend, and P_{net} is the net proceeds to the company from the sale of the stock after subtracting the flotation costs, instead of the current price as in the earlier formula. For example, assume a dividend of $2.5, a price per share of $20, and flotation costs of $0.50 per share, then K_P= 2.5/ (20 − 0.5) = 12.8 per cent.

Similarly, if we are estimating the cost of external common equity, then instead of using:

$$R_E = \frac{D_1}{P_0} + g$$

where

$$D_1 = D_0 (1 + g)$$

we make a small transformation to:

$$K_{E'} = \frac{D_1}{P_{net}} + g$$

where $K_{E'}$ is the cost of external common equity, D_1 is the next period's dividend, P_{net} are the proceeds per share to the company after deducting flotation costs and g is the perpetual growth rate on the dividend payments.

An alternative approach to accounting for flotation costs is to adjust the project's cash flows instead of the WACC. The APV method of dealing with flotation costs by adjusting the initial investment is feasible for a general capital budgeting/financing case, because circularity can be avoided by using an algorithm that matches each project's NPV with the incremental flotation cost of the security potentially issued to finance the project. This approach is widely used in project financing, where large-scale projects such as oil refinery or power plant projects are financed with debt and other securities, backed by specific claims on the project's cash flows. This cash flow-based borrowing is different from the usual asset-based borrowing that most firms use. Since project financing is funded via securities with claims tied to a particular project, the flotation costs can be included with the project's other cash flows when evaluating the value of the project.

Cost of capital and inflation

Inflation is the widespread and sustained rising of prices for goods and services in a given market. Not all price increases can be regarded as inflation.

Specifically, we do not use the term to refer to a price increase of a good, service, industry or sector in particular, but to the increase in the general price level of goods and services offered within an economy. After the Second World War, inflation rates in economically developed countries generally stayed below 20 per cent annually. However, in developing countries there have been instances when general price increases of more than one thousand per cent annually have been recorded. When this occurs, another currency such as the US dollar or a series of goods (such as cigarettes, beverages, diamonds or oil) end up re-placing the official mint as a means for exchanging goods and services.

Country inflation can be the consequence of a number of problems, such as:

1. A surplus in the amount of money in circulation within a country. This surplus results in demand growing faster than the supply of goods and serv-ices.
2. Expectations of future price increases, which result in the raising of wages and other payments to match the projected price increases.
3. Cost increases in the factors of production (raw materials, labour, etc.)
4. Increase in the speed at which money circulates in the course of current transactions.
5. The allocation of large amounts of resources to a sector.

Inflation is measured with the consumer price index (CPI), a statistical device that reflects the changing prices of a set of goods and services. To estimate this figure the prices of hundreds of articles are obtained from different locations in the economy. The CPI is often used both to measure inflation and to compensate for the loss of purchasing power suffered by economic agents. For example:

(1) Leasing real estate. Contracts often specify that the annual cost of a lease contract will be updated on the basis of changes in the CPI.
(2) Wage bargaining and pensions. The inter-professional minimum wages, pensions or the salaries of civil servants, are usually updated by the gov-ernment on the basis of its inflation forecasts. Furthermore, annual wage increases are also negotiated on the basis of the expected inflation rate.
(3) Income taxes. In most developed countries, the authority which deals with income tax collections takes inflation into account when adjusting personal exemptions and standard deductions on an annual basis. The purpose is to ensure contributors preserve their capacity to save and contribute to their retirement plans.
(4) Finance. When inflation rises, interest rates increase. Mortgage owners or borrowers with variable-interest loans will be forced to increase their con-tributions. Consequently, most lenders will have to purchase fixed-income securities, affecting the stock exchange.

An inflationary process results in a continuous decline in the value of money. In this scenario, price-fixing agents will attempt to pass the costs resulting from the loss of purchasing power of the currency to consumers by raising prices. Consumers, with the same salary level, will have to pay more for goods and services. The result of this process is fewer purchases of goods and services and a decrease in economic activity.

In general, inflation hurts individuals receiving income in nominal terms and those who receive income that grows less than the inflation rate itself. However, inflation can benefit debtors, because the loss in value of the currency allows them to provide lower returns in real terms than the amounts of the debt that were initially contracted, with the consequent loss to creditors and lenders.

Rising prices in a market creates a comparative advantage for imported goods, while it worsens the situation of the exports which are now more expensive. Consequently, inflation benefits those whose economic activities are related to imports, while it negatively affects those involved in exports. If the rate at which prices increase is much higher than that in the countries with which the nation competes in international markets, the inflationary nation will see its competitiveness reduced. Furthermore, inflation generates other costs, such as those arising from uncertainty about future prices. This lack of ability to forecast prices will affect decisions about spending, saving and investments, causing an inadequate allocation of resources and therefore hampering economic growth.

Inflation and accounting information

The main objective of accounting reports is to provide information on the financial situation of a firm to all those who have some form of economic association with it, such as managers, suppliers, banks, the tax revenue service, and potential investors. However, to a large extent, trust in the reliability of such information has been eroded in recent years. This is partly the result of accounting regulations which in some instances permits the recording of facts and economic operations on the basis of 'creative accounting', with no regard to the ideal of a true picture of the economic reality of operations. In addition, financial scandals such as those of Enron and WorldCom, the loss of credibility in their auditing companies, the burst of the real estate bubble and the ensuing financial crises, have resulted in this negative perception becoming widespread.

Although great efforts are being made to unify legislations and avoid significant biases in the comparison of accounting information across countries, with the globalization of the world economy, interpreting financial statements has become more complex. One reason has to do with the assessment of the elements disclosed in the itemized accounts of a company. For example, an important aspect of this assessment is to determine whether the disclosed amounts are expressed in terms of the current currency value or on historical terms. This issue is not relevant in very low inflation countries. However, for those where the loss of purchasing power of their currency is constant and growing, not using an appropriate way of adjusting to reflect this situation can lead to a very significant distortion of the values contained in the accounting information.

As a general rule, accounting valuation criteria based on historical values does not consider changes in the purchasing power of the currency, because the assumption is that the currency is stable. For example, most countries which converted their local currencies to the euro suffered inflation for several years. The situation with the euro is just one example which can help us understand the differences in purchasing power before and after a specific event. In countries with high inflation, this loss of purchasing power multiplies several times yearly, and the value of the currency falls on a monthly basis.

To ignore the loss of purchasing power of a currency would seriously affect the homogeneity of the posted accounts, damaging our ability to compare corporate data at different times in the firm's history or that of different companies. Furthermore, neglecting to take this into account would also distort the figures which by their nature arise from the addition or subtraction of items which are not homogenous.

In a firm's income statement, such distortions would arise because between the sale process or the creation of income, and the generation of the necessary expenses associated with those revenues, time elapses. In an inflationary environment, the currency can suffer considerable loss in value during such period. That is why adjustments for inflation are necessary, the main purpose being the smoothing of defects in the information recorded.

In the balance sheet, some assets and liabilities, by their intrinsic nature, are expressed in current monetary values. These are the so-called monetary assets, such as cash the company holds in its current account. For example, a 10 euro bill is always 'ten euro', and it cannot be recorded at a different value. However, in contrast, non-monetary assets are expressed in the currency of the time when the incorporation of the asset into the balance sheet took place, so these are not homogeneous values. A clear example is the value at which fixed assets are originally recorded. Adjustments in values ought therefore to be performed for these non-monetary assets and liabilities, as well as for items within the income statement.

If the accounting practice lacks a standardized process for such important issue as providing information on homogeneous units, one can wonder about the soundness of the accounting information. If there is not a generally accepted and standardized fashion of dealing with the loss of purchasing power between the time sales are produced and costs paid, one can easily imagine the problems that could be generated in reference to dividend payments and taxes. For example, the firm could face liquidity problems. Furthermore, this situation could result in the erroneous estimation of profitability and solvency, as these would result from the aggregation of figures in different units of measure.

In business management, distortions in accounting information result in large inefficiencies, because management cannot use these data to make decisions. A clear example is the methodology utilized for the estimation of prices. In the scenarios we are considering, pricing decisions cannot be made using the cost information derived from the accounting records, because these items are expressed in currency which has different values. Thus, management is forced to spend time and resources gathering additional information needed for decision-making.

Some remedies have been devised to handle this situation, at least in part. For example, one could use the accelerated imputation of the costs to the results, or in the balance sheet the revaluation of fixed assets and depreciation costs. However, these are just partial solutions and do not resolve the problem that is created by not applying a homogeneous unit of value in a comprehensive manner. Consequently, the adjustment mechanism that should be made is the conversion of the different values obtained through time to current value equivalents. This requires defining the index that will be used to perform such conversion.

Since the aim of this operation is to reflect the loss of purchasing power of the currency in an economy, and not a specific asset revaluation, the index that should be used for this correction will be one which marks the general evolution of prices. The indices will depend on each country and not on the specific industry in which the firm develops its economic activities. The selection of the best index will depend on theoretical and practical aspects such as its availability, so that it can be accessed frequently and in a timely manner.

The adjustment to the accounting figures that results from changes in the general level of prices or inflation is not in any way intended to reflect the value of those assets or liabilities at current prices; these adjustments only seek to make accounting data comparable and consistent through time. This type of adjustment is necessary for the correct assessment of investment projects, for the realization of economic budgets, for assessing the cost of different funding options and for other economic operations which could be of interest in countries where the loss, or even the risk of loss, of the purchasing power of the currency is sufficiently significant.

Real versus nominal returns

The nominal cost of capital that derives from market interest rates and the expected returns of equity is a function of anticipated inflation. During periods when high inflation is expected, investors and creditors will demand higher returns to compensate for their reduced spending power. Investors will lend their savings, but by the time they get their principal back, its value will be diminished, in the sense that the investors will be able to purchase fewer goods with it because of the general increase in prices.

We therefore need to consider the impact of inflation when dealing with projects that generate cash flows over long periods. If inflation is higher than anticipated, those cash flows might not be worth as much as expected when the investment was first analyzed. The nominal return on an investment has not been adjusted for inflationary effects, whereas the real return has already been adjusted for the effects of inflation. In the absence of inflation, the real rate would be equal (or very close) to the nominal rate, and the real cash flows equal to the nominal cash flows.

If that we expect inflation to grow at the rate i, all of our project's cash flows (revenues and expenses) will rise at that rate. For example, we are considering a $100 investment that we can sell in one year's time for $112. The nominal return on such investment will be 12 per cent. However, if we assume an inflation rate of 2.5 per cent, our return is worth 2.5 per cent less, that is: 112/1.025 = 109.26. We are giving up the opportunity of consuming $100 today in exchange for getting $112 back in a year. However, by that time we shall be able to purchase fewer goods with that $112: the equivalent of today's $109.26.

The relationship between nominal and real returns and inflation is called the 'Fisher Effect'. To understand this relationship let us examine the following equivalencies.

Nominal cash flow = Real cash flow * (1 + inflation)

Using Fisher's theorem,[2] the real cost of capital is estimated:

(1 + nominal rate) = (1 + real rate) (1 + i)

Then, returning to our example above, we could directly estimate our real return by applying the formula:

(1 + 0.12) = (1 + real rate) (1+ 0.025),

Rearranging terms to clear for the real rate:

1 + real rate = (1 + nominal rate) / (1+i),

1 + real rate = 1.12 / 1.025 = 1.0926,

real rate = 1.0926 − 1 = 9.26%

In general, there are two ways of estimating cash flows that allow for inflation. The first is to express all future cash flows on a real basis and then discount them by the real cost of capital. The second is to repeat the same operation but using nominal figures. Both approaches are theoretically sound, but using nominal numbers might be easier to implement, because most real numbers are derived from their nominal counterparts (given that it is in nominal terms that prices are usually specified). Furthermore, there are complications when one tries to estimate depreciation, working capital, insurance or tax charges in real terms, because these are estimated in nominal terms. For example, depreciation is a percentage of the nominal book value of the asset. Therefore, unless there are specific reasons not to do so, the nominal method is the preferred method.

The principle of consistency requires that we use values determined on the same basis in the numerator and denominator. Nominal cash flows must be discounted at nominal discount rates; real cash flows must be discounted at real discount rates.

Inflation affects the cost of capital. Recall how the rates of return are estimated for different financial securities: in Chapter 1 we explained these were the results of a risk-free component plus a compensation for the time value of money.

In an environment of low inflation, postponing consumption is not as 'expensive' as in a high inflation scenario. Furthermore, as we move from fixed-income securities such as Treasury notes to the equity cost of capital, we see how inflationary effects compound around the estimation. For example, a treasury note would just require adjustment in the one component that compensates for the time value of money, which is directly related to inflation. However, if we think of the cost of equity capital and its estimation using the CAPM, several adjustments would be required to adjust the risk-free rate, the beta and the equity risk premium, because each of these components separately reflects expected inflation, as they all value systematic risk.

In normal inflationary environments, when the nominal default-free spot rates is thought to capture inflation expectations, the models can function without major distortions. However, in hyperinflationary environments or when working on projects with very long life spans, one could estimate variables such as changes in working capital, depreciation, insurance and taxes in nominal terms and then deflate them by the forecasted inflation.

Uncertainty about inflation compounds over time: long-term projects will be penalized more than short-term projects, and firms will be much less willing to make commitments for extended periods of time.

The following example illustrates the effect of inflation on discount rates and cash flow valuation.

MACMA has cash flows of $100 million which are expected to grow in real terms at 7 per cent annually for the next two years, and at 4 per cent thereafter. The firm's beta is 1.2, the equity risk premium is 5.42, and the risk–free rate 5.5 per cent. The expected inflation rate is 2.5 per cent.

First, we shall estimate the growth rates and then the discount rate in both real and nominal terms, and then the present value of the cash flows. Growth rate in first two years at 7 per cent:

$(1.07)(1.025)-1 = 9.675\%$

4 per cent perpetual growth rate after initial two years:

$(1.04)(1.025)-1 = 6.6\%$

Discount rate:

$E(R_M) = 5.5\% + 1.2(5.42\%) = 12\%$ $1.12/1.025 - 1 = 9.26$ per cent

The terminal values are estimated for both real and nominal cash flows as follows (Table 4.3):

Terminal value (nominal cash flows) $= \$120.28*1.066/(0.12-0.066) = \$2,374.53$

Terminal value (real cash flows) $= \$114.49*1.04/(0.0926-0.04) = \$2,263.68$

These estimates assume that growth rates after the second year are perpetual. The present value of the cash flows can then be calculated using the appropriate discount rate:

PV nominal cash flows $= \$109.67/1.12 + \$120.28/1.12^2 + \$2374.53/1.12^2 = \$2086.7$

PV using real cash flows $= \$107/1.09 + \$114.49/1.09^2 + \$2263.68/1.09^2 = \$2099.81$

Table 4.3 Real versus nominal cash flows

Year	Real cash flows		Nominal cash flows	
	CF to equity	Terminal value	Nominal cash flows	Terminal value
1	$107	–	$109.675	–
2	$114.49	2,263.68	$120.286	2,374.53

Risk premiums for non-traded stocks

We have so far focused our discussions on publicly traded firms. When we estimated the rate of return required by public stockholders, we used stock prices
to determine the market value of equity and stock returns to estimate beta as
an input for the CAPM approach. But how should we measure the cost of equity
for a firm that is not traded? Are there any additional adjustments we should
make when considering our participation in publicly traded corporations?

In addition to considering the risk of a project when this is the case under
analysis, there are several other adjustments related to risk that must be used to
increase or reduce the fair market value of the equity of a company. Adjustments
such as liquidity risk discounts, control premium, and key person discount are
applied as necessary when valuing businesses.

We know that WACC should be determined using market value debt and
equity ratios. However, in the cases of privately owned companies we might
not be able to observe those values. To get around this, some analysts choose
to use the target debt/equity ratio of the firm or the average debt/equity ratios
of publicly traded comparable firms.

We can begin by identifying publicly traded firms that are in the same industry and approximately the same size and similar capital structure as the privately owned firm. We then calculate the betas for these publicly traded firms
and use the average betas as an estimate for the beta of the privately owned
firm. This is the same procedure we followed to estimate the divisional cost of
capital.

While the above approach might appear straightforward, there are a few
issues we need to bear in mind when determining the cost of equity in privately owned firms:

Liquidity Risk Discount: a company that is not traded publicly is an illiquid
investment, because whoever buys the firm might have difficulty in selling it
within a reasonably short period of time. The risk of the investment increases
if, when an investor tries to sell, she cannot find a buyer. In principle this could
happen with any sort of investment, but when the company in question is
small and not publicly traded, this risk is particularly high. The liquidity discount that is applied to the cost of equity ranges between 4 per cent and 87 per
cent, although usually, when there are no additional special circumstances, it
lies somewhere between 35 per cent and 50 per cent.

The liquidity premium is not used solely in the cases of privately owned
firms but is also sometimes applied to the cost of equity for small publicly
traded firms. Many analysts make an ad hoc adjustment of 1 to 3 percentage
points to reflect the liquidity premium.[3]

· In the case of privately held firms, the owner is often the sole investor and all
her wealth is invested in her private business. Because the owner does not have

the opportunity to diversify, she is exposed to all of the firm's risk, not just the systematic risk measured by the beta. In such a case, it might be advisable to adjust the industry beta to account for the undiversifiable risk. To arrive at the total beta of the firm, we divide the market beta of the industry by the correlation coefficient of the industry and the market proxy.

$$\text{Total Beta} = \frac{\text{Market beta of industry}}{\text{Correlation coefficient of industry and inde}}$$

$$\text{Total Beta} = \frac{\text{Market Beta}}{\sqrt{R \text{ Squared}}}$$

Formula 4.5

For example, if a firm in a given sector has a beta of 1.2, and the average proportion of the risk that is market risk (R^2 of the regression) is 32 per cent, then the total market beta is 2.121 (1.20 / $\sqrt{0.32}$).

Minority Interest Discount: If a shareholder owns a minority of the outstanding shares of a company, she can only participate in the management or decision-making if allowed to do so by the controlling shareholder. This risk is reflected in the rate used to discount the Free Cash Flows (FCF), because the risk premium of the equity of a large publicly traded company is based in the small shareholder who participates in this type of company. Consequently, we do not usually apply a discount for minority interest to adjust the fair market value of a company, whether it is traded or not, unless the FCF have already been calculated to reflect a controlling interest.

Control Premium: If the participation we are valuing grants control over the company, and this was not already reflected when estimating the FCF, it is usually necessary to add a controlling premium to the estimated fair market value of the equity. For example, if a company has 100 shares selling at $37, and we are planning to purchase 51 per cent of those (that is, 51 shares), then we should pay $37 per share for 51 shares, that is $1,887, plus a premium. Most control premiums range between 15 per cent and 50 per cent. In this example, if we were to pay a premium of 25 per cent, our final payment for the controlling portion of this company would be $37 * 51 * (1.25) = $2,358.75. The difference between 2,358.75 and 1,887 (471.75) would be the premium.

Sometimes it is appropriate to apply other discounts to the fair market value of equity. A typical example is the 'key person discount'. This is often used when there is an individual who is key to the development of the business (particularly when the business is small). In these instances, reaching the estimated FCF depends on this one person (or a few people) whose disappearance (voluntary or otherwise) would seriously damage the ability of the company to generate earnings. In large companies, managers are often more 'generic' or have fewer competences. It is therefore easier to replace them, and this discount does not apply. However, in instances when an owner sells her small company, or when a key account manager has a special type of control, this discount could be required.

Another example is 'diversification discount'. This discount is considered if, for example, we are trying to purchase a company and its products are diversified. It is commonly thought that a diversified company (one that operates in two or more industries) reduces its operating risks. Nevertheless, it is often difficult to find buyers who are interested in exactly those specific lines of business or product mixes. In practice, it is usually easier to find buyers interested in one specific product or line, the additional products acting as a deterrent for the purchaser. This type of discount is therefore often considered.

Suppose a financial entity is purchasing a minority interest in a company that is not publicly traded. Through DCF techniques, they reach the conclusion that the total value of the equity of the company (total value of the DCF of the company minus the value of the debt) is $20,000 million. To simplify, let us assume this company has no debt, so the value of the company equals the value of the equity. Since this company is not publicly traded and we are not purchasing all of the equity, but just a minority interest, to determine its value to us, we would need to subtract two discounts from the total value of $20,000 million: 1) for minority interest, and 2) for lack of liquidity.

We would therefore carry out the following adjustments:

Value of the company

− value of the debt

= Value of the equity for a shareholder with controlling interest
in a publicly traded corporation

− discount for minority interest

= value of the shares for a minority shareholder, as if it were a
liquid investment

− liquidity discount

= value of the shares of a minority interest of a non-liquid
investment (not traded in the market)

Note: This is a good time to reflect on the difference between the free cash flows to all investors (FCF or FCFF, or free cash flow to the firm), whether debtors or shareholders, and the free cash flows to the equity holder (FCFE, or free cash flow to equity). When we are trying to determine the value of the company to all investors, we use FCF (as defined below) and discount the cash flows at the WACC. We can then use this estimate to calculate the value of the company as is, or subtract the debt to reach the value of the equity of the company:

FCFF (Free Cash Flow to Firm), calculated as:

Earnings before interest and taxes (EBIT)

− taxes

+ Depreciation, amortization and depletion

+/− changes in working capital

+/− capital expenditures

Alternatively, we can also use FCFE, as defined below. The only additional consideration is that, in this case, we discount them by K_E and not by the WACC.

FCFE (Free Cash Flow to Equity holders), calculated as:

Net Income

+ Depreciation, amortization, and depletion

+/− changes in working capital

+/− additional capital expenditures

− Principal repayments

+ New debt issues
− Preferred dividend payments

Specific concerns for regulated industries

In the preceding sections we assumed that the companies in our examples were free to choose the products and services they provide, and how much they charge. This is not always the case. For example, electricity and water utilities are constrained from setting their own prices. Also, they do not compete in a normal open market, as most of the services they offer are ruled by oligopolistic or even monopolistic environments. Thus, when estimating the cost of capital for companies in regulated sectors, we need to take into consideration some of these special circumstances.

Public utilities cannot set or change prices without the approval of their regulatory bodies. Establishing these prices is a balancing act between considerations related to consumer needs and ensuring these companies stay in business. Prices cannot be so high that consumers at large cannot afford the use of these services, nor can they be so low that costs of production, taxes, interest payments and equity capital put these enterprises at risk.

To determine the cost of capital in this environment, a typical process is to establish a base rate: often the sum of the accounting values of all the funding sources, such as debt and equity. The cost of debt is determined by estimating a weighted average of the coupons of the existing debt of the firm. The cost of equity is most often estimated with the dividend growth model. The reason for this is that models, such as the CAPM, incorporate assumptions which will not apply in a regulated environment. For example, one of the CAPM's assumptions is that expected returns follow a normal distribution. However, in a regulated environment where prices are not set freely by the firms in response to the market forces of supply and demand, there is an upper limit to the earnings potential that can be generated by the companies. Thus, this condition of normality is not fulfilled and the price distribution is likely to be skewed.

In the first chapter, when commenting on Jane's trials and tribulations, we described what a normal distribution of returns looks like. Specifically, we said that the normal curve describes a probability distribution where the majority of the observations cluster around a central value (the mean), and the higher and lower values taper off smoothly according to their probabilities of occurring. As a visual aid, we provided the figure again as Figure 4.3. Given that the area below the curve describes the probability of each event, and given that the figure is symmetrical, we can begin to understand how if prices are not set freely, the probability distribution of returns will not have the shape of the drawing below. Instead, the hump or 'belly' of the curve will be to the right or the left and the distributions will be skewed.

Compare the normal distribution in Figure 4.3 with those in Figure 4.4. The tails on both sides of the curve's 'belly' will help us assess which type of skewness affects each distribution. For example, if we have a negatively skewed distribution, then the left tail is longer and the bulk of the observations are on the right of the figure. The side to which the curve is skewed shows where the observations are clustered. In this case, if most observations are really large,

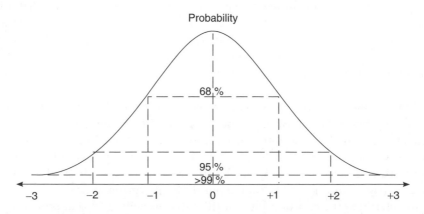

Figure 4.3   Normal curve

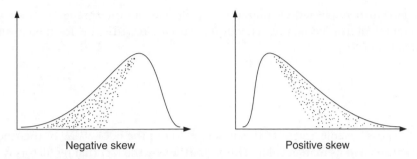

Negative skew   Positive skew

Figure 4.4 Skewness

this type of distribution is said to be left-skewed. On the other hand, if a curve is positively skewed, then the opposite happens: the right tail is longer and the bulk of the distribution is to the left of the figure. This means that most values are small. This type of distribution is said to be right-skewed.

In financial modelling, skewness risk means that observations are not distributed symmetrically around an average value. That is, the average or mean and the median[4] value of the distribution are different. Skewness is a problem because, unless recognized, it can lead to an underestimate of the risk of variables.

The pricing constraints in regulated industries are said to result in the skewness of returns. Therefore, to estimate the cost of equity, models other than the CAPM are recommended. In this environment, the Dividend Growth Model (also called the Gordon Model) is a good choice because most utility companies pay large and stable dividends.

As we saw in Chapter 2, the Dividend Growth Model was represented as:

$$P_0 = \frac{D_1}{(R_E - g)}$$

where

$$D_1 = D_0 (1 + g)$$

In the formula, P_0 is the current market price of the common stock, D_1 is the dividend to be paid in the next period, R_E is the return demanded from the company shares, and is g the expected dividend growth rate. To find the return required, we only solve for the R_E term in the equation:

$$R_E = \frac{D_1}{P_0} + g$$

The return requested by shareholders, R_E, can be interpreted as the cost of capital of the company. Therefore, we can rewrite the formula using K instead of R:

$$K_E = \frac{D_0(1+g)}{P_0} + g$$

One possible adjustment to this model is to use the book value of the stock price instead of its market value. This is justified by the fact that regulators will apply the rate of the accounting equity value.

The suggestion is that we replace P_0, the current market price of the common stock, by its book value. This replacement of market values by book values should not result in a large change in the estimate of the cost of equity because for utilities, the market and book values are close to each other.

In addition to the Gordon Model, the 'three moment model' by Kraus and Litzenberger (1976)[5] can also be used because it allows for skewness:

$$K_J = R_f + b_1\beta + b_2\gamma \qquad \qquad \textit{Formula 4.6}$$

Where the equity return or cost of capital of security j (K_j) is a function of the risk-free rate (R_f), the beta (β) and the gamma (γ), which are the measures of risk, and b_1 and b_1 their risk premiums. In this equation, the beta coefficient which measures the systematic risk of j with respect to the market is defined as in the CAPM, the covariance between the returns of the firm and the market divided by the variance of the returns of the market:

$$\beta_J = \frac{\rho_{JM}\sigma_J\sigma_M}{\sigma_M^2} \qquad \qquad \textit{Formula 2.3}$$

where ρ_{JM} is the correlation coefficient between the rents of share J and those of the market portfolio M, σ is the standard deviation of each of the variables, and σ_M^2 is the variance of the returns of the market portfolio. Thus, to get the beta of a share J we just divide the covariance between the historical returns of the share J and those of a market proxy (such as the S&P 500) 'M', by the variance (the standard deviation squared) of the market.

The gamma (γ) is the measure of risk due to skewness defined as the coskewness between the returns of the firm and those of the market divided by the skewness of the market:

$$\gamma = \frac{\sum(x-u_x)(y-u_y)^2}{\sum(y-u_y)^3} \qquad \qquad \textit{Formula 4.7}$$

where x and y are the specific observations for the J share (*x*) and the market (*y*), and $(\mu_x)(\mu_y)$ the means of all X and Ys respectively.

In statistical terms, the skewness of a random variable (such as realized returns) is the 'third standardized moment' with the first and the second moments referring to the mean and the variance, hence the name given to this model.

A third model that can be used in this context is the APT method reviewed in Chapter 2. As a reminder, let us recall that the APT holds that the expected return of a financial asset can be modelled as a linear function of several macroeconomic factors or market indices, where sensitivity to changes in each factor is represented by a factor-specific beta coefficient. The returns are assumed to obey the following relationship:

$$E(R_j) = \alpha + \beta_{j1}(F_1) + \beta_{j2}(F_2) + \beta_{j3}(F_3) + ... + \beta_{jn}(F_n) + \xi_j$$ *Formula 2.43*

Applied research with this model indicates that it has more explanatory power than the CAPM and is superior in estimating returns for companies in the utility industries.

Stock options

In Chapter 2, we covered some of the basics of options jargon when reviewing the equity cost of capital according to the option-based approach developed by Black and Scholes (B-S) in 1973.[6] In this chapter we consider option pricing in the context of executive compensation and corporate governance. We therefore start with a brief review of the concepts essential for understanding these derivative products and the factors affecting their value and pricing.

In finance, an option is a contract between a buyer and a seller, by which the buyer acquires the right to purchase or sell an underlying asset (e.g. raw materials, property, financial securities or derivative instruments) on or before the date of expiration of the option, at an agreed price (the strike or exercise price). For this right, the buyer pays the seller a premium, which is the price of owning the option.

There are two main categories of options. An option to buy is a *call* option. If, in contrast, the acquired right gives the option to sell, it is a *put* option. A trader who thinks a stock's price is bound to increase will buy a call option. The benefit to her will equal the difference between the lower purchase price and the future higher market price, minus the cost of the premium. Thus, if the market stock price at expiry is above the exercise price by more than the premium paid, she will profit. Although under any other circumstance the buyer will lose, the important characteristic of this derivative instrument is that it limits or bounds the losses. This is because if the stock price in the

market at expiration is below the exercise price (the price at which she purchased the right to buy), she will simply let the call contract expire, and only
lose the amount of the premium. On the other hand, the potential for gains
is infinite.

If the trader thinks the stock's price will decline in the future, she will buy
a put option. In this case she will benefit if the market stock price at expiration has moved in the direction she bet on and is below the exercise price
(the price at which she purchased the right to sell) by more than the premium
paid. Again, if this is not the case she will let the option expire and just lose
the price paid for the right. Thus, the buyer might choose not to exercise her
right by allowing the options to expire. However, if the purchaser decides
to exercise her right, the seller is forced to sell or buy the asset at the agreed
price.

A call option is valuable when the price of the underlying security is high
relative to the exercise price (the contrary is true for a put option). When the
option is 'in-the-money', exercising its will return a positive payoff to the
holder, whereas if it is 'out-of-the-money', its value will be near zero. The payoff
to the call buyer at expiration will be equal to:

$$S_T - X \qquad \text{if } S_T > X, \text{ or}$$

$$0 \qquad \text{if } S_T \leq X$$

where S_T is the value of the stock at the expiration date and X is the exercise
price.

Independently of the model used for its valuation, the value of an option is
related to the price of the underlying security, the exercise price of the option,
the time to expiration, the future volatility of the underlying security's price
over the life of the option, and the cost of holding a position in the underlying
stock (i.e. interest and dividend).

Stock options have been widely discussed in recent times as a form of compensation to employees and managers of companies. Stock options create
heated discussions for two main reasons. First, it is feared that granting such
rights to managers may introduce incentives *not* to act in the best interests of
existing and long-term shareholders, and second, because of disagreements
about how to account and value these stock option costs.

A stock option plan is a remuneration strategy by which a company pays a portion of an employee's salary by giving her stock options. As in the general case
described at the beginning of the section, options that grant the right to purchase shares of a company's stock are called 'call options'. Thus call options give
the employee the right to purchase shares at a future point in time (the exercise
time), at a price per share which is established in advance (the exercise price).

Once the holder of the asset (the employee) is allowed by the option agreement to exercise her rights, she will do so or not, depending on whether the exercise price is higher or lower than the market value of the shares at the exercise time. Again, the gains to the option holder derive from the price differential between the cost to market participants and the price at which the employee can buy the shares. The option will be more valuable the larger the difference between the price at which the option holder can buy the shares by exercising her rights and the cost of obtaining those same shares in the market.

Given that the option's value is a function of the value of the underlying stock, it is claimed that granting these rights to employees aligns the interests of the executives with those of the stockholders. Because the executives themselves will make more profit the higher the value of the equity, it is assumed they become more likely to make decisions that will benefit the stockholders. However, it is also recognized that granting such options does not result in a perfect alignment of interests. One reason is that options increase in value when there is volatility in the underlying stock. Thus, executives might take on unwarranted risks to drive up stock prices. In addition, holding options also encourages management to send 'signals' to the market or to push accounting procedures in order to affect the value of the shares in the short run. For example, some executives might smooth earnings, or make false statements in order to drive up stock prices just before exercising their stock options.[7]

It is known that a motivation for management to engage in fraudulent financial reporting is more likely when a significant portion of management's compensation is represented by bonuses, stock options or other incentives, that are contingent upon the entity reaching aggressive targets for financial results. Thus, much of the focus of forensic analysis is on detecting misleading and inaccurate accounting practices that can lead to such problems.

Granting stock options to employees can be done in a variety of ways. For example, the firm might purchase the options in the market by paying the premium, or it might issue new shares for this purpose and take them from their treasury stock account. Whichever way is used, the immediate effect is a dilution of earnings per share for existing shareholders. The reason for this is that when the first method is used, the cost of the premium will reduce the earnings available for distributions, whereas when the second method is used, the firm will increase the number of shares while its earnings remain constant.

Employee stock options are part of the equity capital of the company and should be clearly recognized in the balance sheet. In addition, issuing stock options has a cost which must be expensed in the income statement. Thus in making assessments about the book and market value of companies, adjustments might have to be made to reflect option market values fairly. If a firm has outstanding stock options, adjustments to the equity value of the firm might be necessary. Fair market values are usually estimated using the Black-Scholes model.

Convertible stock

Adding more sophistication to the share structure of a corporation can be the best way to deal with delicate situations. For example, this might assist a firm to achieve its goals in takeovers, position itself more effectively in the security markets or align its stock better to fit the needs of their various investors.

For example, in a corporate takeover a firm might find itself competing for the targeted firm, completing the deal and attempting to please its own shareholders, those of the targeted corporation, and the investors of both companies. The solution might be to create a range of instruments that encompass cash, equity and hybrid options. A firm might create a series of common stock with no voting rights, or which can be converted into other types of common stock at a given ratio. Alternatively, it might create convertible redeemable preferred shares, or different classes of share such as targeted stock, which might represent an interest in the financial performance of a specific project share and which could also be exchanged at a later date.

In more normal situations, firms often issue different classes of common stock, distinguishing each class by voting rights, dividends rights or new issue subscription rights. Two typical instruments that provide funding flexibility are preferred equity and convertible debt. There are many reasons why these types of solutions might be warranted. For example, the firm might wish to minimize share dilution, or avoid taking on additional debt to pay for the deal.

Convertible debt and convertible preferred equity are hybrid instruments which combine the characteristics of two securities in one: a regular debt or preferred equity instrument plus a warrant. The warrant entitles its holder to buy stock of the company at a given price. These instruments are usually attached to bonds or preferred stock and, given that they provide an option to the holder, they reduce the interest rates or dividends that the company has to offer., These warrants are frequently also 'detachable', that is, they can be sold in the market independently of the bond or stock.

If an instrument is callable, this feature benefits the issuing company, because the investor can be forced to convert the instrument whether she wants to or not. The cost of capital for the convertible instrument is the sum of its elements: the warrant (equivalent to a long-term call option) and the straight debt or preferred element.

In theory, the market price of a convertible debenture should never drop below its intrinsic value, which is derived from the value of a security contained in the security itself. The intrinsic value is also called the fundamental value and is usually calculated by summing the future income generated by the asset and discounting it to its present value. For example, the intrinsic value of a share is simply the number of shares being converted at par value, times the current market price of common shares.

A convertible bond is described as being 'in-the-money' when the conversion price is lower than the equity price; 'at-the-money' when the conversion price is equal to the equity price, or 'out-of-the-money', when the conversion price is greater than the equity price.

A simple method for determining the value of a convertible involves estimating the present value of the future interest and principal payments at the cost of debt and adding the present value of the warrant. However, this method does not take into account certain aspects of the security, such as stochastic interest rates and credit spreads, or regular features including the issuer's call rights.

There are several attributes of convertible bonds that make them attractive to certain investors. For example, they are usually issued at a higher yield than the shares into which the bonds convert, and they are less volatile and risky than preferred or common shares. Convertibles are often used as part of a hedging strategy, for example by simultaneously purchasing the convertible instrument and shorting the same common stock.

For issuers, convertibles are attractive in that they result in lower fixed-rate borrowing costs which allow locking into low-cost fixed long-term borrowing. Convertibles are also useful, for example, in deferring voting dilution, increasing the amount of debt a company has in issue, or as currency in takeovers.

Taxation

The tax rate a firm needs to pay can be expressed as 'the marginal rate', which is the rate on each additional dollar earned or spent, and the 'effective rate', an average rate calculated by dividing the total value of taxes paid by the taxable income. If the tax legislation is 'progressive', meaning that the tax rate increases as the taxable base grows from low to high, then the average effective tax rate is less than the marginal tax. As the amount subject to taxation rises, both the marginal and effective rates will increase usually up to a maximum, and there might be ranges where the marginal rate will stay flat.

Tax laws in most countries allow firms to deduct the interest payments paid on debt from the taxable income they report. This tax subsidy from the government lowers the effective cost of debt financing for companies. In contrast, payments made to equity holders, such as dividends and retained earnings, are non tax-deductible expenses as they are distributed after taxes are paid.

In addition to the debt allowance, the corporation's tax liability will be affected by any type of deductability schemes the government might offer. For business, tax-deductible expenses usually include the cost of goods sold, sales and administration expenses, depreciation allowances and the interest expenses already mentioned. The basis for the recognition of an 'optimal capital structure' is the fact that taxes affect the WACC. However, this effect goes beyond the consideration of the items listed above. One reason for this is that code provisions, including those of the US, offer net operating loss carry backs and carry forwards. That is, corporations that sustain net operating losses during one period are allowed to set those losses off against any taxable income in another year, lowering its taxes. The fact that business may carry back losses for two years and forward for 20 will affect the assumed marginal tax rate.

Corporate income taxes have implications for financial managers. In the text we analyze the tax effect where appropriate. For example, in Chapter 2 we estimated the after-tax cost of debt, and in Chapters 6 and 7 we shall analyze its impact on the optimal capital structure. However, below we list some of the critical areas of concern.

The tax advantages associated with debt financing are an important reason behind debt financing, financial restructurings and leveraged buyouts. Dividend policy is also affected by taxes. The rationale behind this is that when dividends are paid to stockholders, they are immediately taxed as income. Dividends are therefore affected by double taxation, as these monies, which come out of the corporation and into shareholders' pockets, are already on an 'after-tax' basis. However, if the corporation retains the earnings rather than paying them out, taxes on stock price appreciation are deferred. Thus, the ability to defer taxes influences decision-making towards retention.

Capital expenditure choices are also affected by corporate taxes. There are two reasons for this: first, because capital expenditures are made on an 'after-tax' basis, and second, because of the ability to depreciate the assets and other expenditures associated with capital expenditures. The choice of depreciation method will affect the corporation's cash flows.

To determine which projects add value to the company, in the capital budgeting process marginal costs associated with the proposed venture are related to its marginal benefits. Thus, the costs of funding (debt, equity, etc) must also be stated in marginal terms. This mirrors the fact that when computing the project's net present value, firms will try to estimate expected cash flows rather than historical figures. It is self-evident that if the costs of capital change significantly during the coming year, those are the costs we need to consider, rather than any historical estimates. Lastly, note that pre-tax cash flows should be discounted at pre-tax discount rates; and after-tax cash flows should be discounted at after-tax discount rates. The nominator and denominator of the present value ratios should be consistent.

Summary

This section summarizes our review of the factors that affect our cost of capital estimates.

A firm's weighted average cost of capital (WACC) is simply the return investors expect to earn on the average market risk of their firm's investments. Thus, when using the CAPM to assess whether a new project is viable, we must find out whether the project is of average risk.

Different investment alternatives available to a firm can be grouped according to their level of risk. The procedures for project proposals and the criteria for their acceptance will vary according to where the projects fit within these categories. In cases where the right discount rate is not equal to the WACC of the company we can use different approaches to help us assess an adequate return, given the risk of the project.

One such approach is to examine other investments outside the firm that are in the same risk class. For each unit of risk the market demands a specific return, so it is easy to get guidance on what these rates ought to be. A second approach is to add or deduct a premium depending upon the category in which the investment has been classified. This premium would be common to all projects within that category.

If a firm obtains external capital, then it incurs flotation costs, which are the costs of floating or issuing new securities. If the issue is sold through underwriters, these costs can be quite significant. To reflect flotation costs the WACC is sometimes increased. However, it has been proposed that these expenses should be taken into account in a different way, given that the cost of capital must reflect the use of the capital, not its origin.

Inflation is the widespread and sustained rising of the prices for goods and services in a given market. It affects our assessment of the elements disclosed in the itemized financial statements of a company. In countries where the loss of purchasing power is constant and growing, an appropriate adjustment to prevent significant distortion in the values contained in the accounting information is necessary. Some partial remedies could be the use of accelerated assigning of the costs to the results, or the revaluation of fixed assets and depreciation costs in the balance sheet. However, these are just partial solutions and do not resolve the problem that is created by not applying a homogeneous unit of value in a comprehensive manner. Thus a recommendation would be to convert the different values obtained through time to current value equivalents. This requires defining the index that would be used to perform such a conversion.

A second consideration is that the nominal cost of capital that is derived from market interest rates and the expected returns of equity is a function of anticipated inflation. Thus, during periods when high inflation is expected, investors and creditors will demand higher returns to compensate for their reduced spending power. We therefore need to consider the impact of inflation when dealing with projects that generate cash flows over multiple periods. The relationship between nominal and real returns and inflation is called the 'Fisher Effect'.

When a firm is not publicly traded, there are a few issues we need to bear in mind: (1) the liquidity of an ownership stake is less than the liquidity of publicly held stock, (2) we are unable to observe a privately held firm's equity market value and (3) the owner is often the only investor and tends to have his wealth invested in the private business and does not have the opportunity to diversify. Other typical adjustments related to risk are the liquidity risk discount, the control premium and the key person discount.

In the preceding sections we assumed that the companies in our examples were free to choose the products and services they provide, and how much they charge. However, this is not always the case. Thus, when estimating the cost of capital for companies in regulated sectors, we need to take into consideration some of these special circumstances.

Employee stock options are part of the equity capital of the company and should be clearly recognized in the balance sheet. In addition, issuing stock options has a cost which must be expensed in the income statement. Thus in making assessments about the book and market value of companies, adjustments might have to be made to reflect option market values fairly. If a firm has outstanding stock options, adjustments to the equity value of the firm might be necessary. Fair market values are usually estimated using the Black-Scholes model.

A firm might create a range of flexible or adaptable instruments that encompass cash, equity, and hybrid options. Some examples would be a series of common stock with no voting rights, or which can be converted into other types of common stock at a given ratio, convertible redeemable preferred shares, or different classes of share such as targeted stock which might represent an interest in the financial performance of a specific project share and which could also be exchanged at a later date. Appropriate methods can be devised for determining the value of these instruments.

Taxes affect the cost of capital. Tax laws in most countries allow firms to deduct the interest payments paid on debt from the taxable income they report. In addition, the corporation's tax liability will be affected by any type of deductability schemes the government might offer, such as tax-deductible expenses, net operating loss carry backs and carry forwards. Tax advantages are an important consideration in debt financing, financial restructurings and leveraged buyouts. Dividend policy is also affected by taxes, as the ability to defer taxes influences decision-making towards retention.

5
Country Risk

Country risk premiums

Suppose you are interested in expanding overseas to an emerging country. With this goal in mind, one of the options you are analyzing is the purchase of a company in that country. To find out whether this opportunity is acceptable, as with any other investment project, you need to estimate the value of this business to you and compare it to its cost.

In previous chapters, we showed how to do this valuation: calculate the operative and financial cash flows generated by the hypothetical acceptance of the project. That is, estimate the net cash inflows the project would generate in each period, and discount them by the appropriate cost of capital.

Nevertheless, in contrast to our earlier examples, the fact that this company is located in foreign territory presents an additional challenge. While the demographic and market characteristics of this emerging economy may present very attractive business opportunities, starting operations in this territory could also bring additional exposure to risk. When this is the case, a supplementary risk premium should be added to the cost of capital in order to reflect the emerging market status of the country of interest. That is, our discount rate for the cash flows derived from this project should include compensation for all the risks of the cash flows of the project, including those of being in a developing economy. If those risks are not reflected in the operative cash flows, they should be reflected in the financial cash flows.

Therefore, the first question that comes to mind is whether the company we are planning to acquire is exposed to country risk. If the answer to this question is affirmative, we would need to figure out by how much, how to quantify this country risk, and how to incorporate this cost into the cash flow analysis of our expansionary project.

It is worth mentioning that not all firms operating in countries other than the one where they happened to be first established are subject to country risk. In addition, it is also advisable to consider that one might be exposed to this kind of risk even if trading in developed markets, because a significant percentage of our revenues and or costs are generated in emerging markets. Furthermore, not all companies within a market (even an emerging market) are equally exposed to that country's risk. The question we need to answer refers to our own situation, given the project and the circumstances under consideration.

Going back to our original line of thought, if in fact we are exposed to country risk, it becomes obvious that different countries, at different times, should demand different premiums. For example, the risk of investing in a nation with a stable government and growing economy could not be compared to that of moving into a war-torn area where the government changes every few months. Therefore, you would need to derive a measure for the risk associate with *this* country at *this* point in time.

To help you do this, companies such as Standard and Poor's, Moody's, and Fitch IBCA, the world's main rating agencies, professionally dedicate themselves to assessing sovereign risks. You should be aware that, as with so many other issues in finance, producing these ratings is not a scientific exercise, but includes qualitative and quantitative aspects, as well as judgemental criteria. As a result, different rating agencies may not agree completely on their assessments of the same country. It is also important to understand that rating a country is no trivial matter, since the yield demanded from the issues of public debt from different states depends to a large extent on the credit ratings granted by the agencies to those states. Consequently, the rating process is carefully scrutinized by the international financial community and all the parties involved.

Sovereign credit ratings

A credit rating can apply to any types of issuer of debt, including sovereign countries, supranational institutions, autonomous regions, local authorities, international institutions and corporate businesses. Just as with corporate debt, sovereign credit rating is the publication of an educated judgement, based on multiple variables, on the probability that a specific borrower may default on its commitments with respect to the service of its debt. One thing to keep in mind is that the rating of sovereign debt is the upper limit to any other debt issued within the country, such as those sold by local entities and companies. Also, in the case of sovereign credit ratings, the rating granted not only determines the yield to be generated by the state, but also facilitates the sale of the issue into the market. In addition, it is important to remember that just as in the corporate case, these ratings measure default risk. However, equity risk and default risk are not the same, even if they are driven by many common factors.

Understanding country ratings is key to adjusting the cost of capital when necessary. We also need to remember that although the agencies focus on default risk, this might not be the only risk affecting the market.

In analyzing the steps and specific considerations by which sovereign credit ratings are assigned, one should be aware that, understandably, the information disclosed by the agencies about this procedure is limited. This lack of transparency may prevent observers from understanding the relative weight that is assigned to each of the relevant variables, or specific considerations that apply in every instance. Thus it may seem that a few of these variables, such as the GDP per capita, the growth of GDP and CPI, the gross external debt relative to earnings and the classification of a country as industrialized or not can explain the average rating given to issuers of long-term foreign currency debt. Therefore, the discussion that follows does not claim to be a complete and detailed explanation of the process followed by each of the agencies. For that purpose, one should consult the agencies directly.[1] This text just tries to provide an overall idea of the general steps followed in granting sovereign credit rating, so that the concept of country risk premium, and how it is derived, becomes understandable and manageable.

When assigning sovereign debt ratings, the main agencies follow a similar process: they determine the original rating for the issue of debt to be sold in the primary market, and then follow up the country's development through time to assess whether changes on the original ratings are warranted. We can summarize the process as follows:

1. A sovereign state and a rating agency reach an agreement to classify the state as an 'issuer'.
2. The agency sends the issuer a questionnaire requesting information about its level of indebtedness and capacity to service debt.
3. To clarify any issues that arise, the country's economic authorities and agency representatives may hold personal meetings.
4. The agency analysts draft a report which includes aspects related to the country itself as well as a comparison to others in the region, or countries similar in other ways. This report is sent to the sovereign country authorities for their review.
5. Once objections have been reported or the issuer indicates conformity, the report is passed to the Sovereign Risk Committee of the agency, and a definitive rating is assigned.
6. After the rating is granted, the agency will keep monitoring the country to reassess the rating granted. When a review process is started, it is made public. This process can result in changes (upgrades or downgrades) that will affect the yields demanded in the secondary market for debt issued by those nations, as well as future issues to be sold in the primary market.

With regard to the last step, point 6, when the agency starts the process the information released to the public includes whether the outlook for the rating is positive, negative or stable and includes the kind of indebtedness the country is facing. This could be long-term or short-term, in foreign or local currency. However, in most cases, the credit rating of the country refers to long-term foreign currency debt, unless specified otherwise. Sometimes we can observe that the debt issued in local currency is rated slightly better than that in foreign currency. This is because repayments in foreign currency require having sufficient reserves, whereas local currency can be issued more or less at need (but, of course, not without some collateral effects that for brevity, and because they are not related directly to the issue at hand, are not going to be discussed here).

Points 2) through 4) above indicate that the rating agencies analyze both quantitative and qualitative data about the country in question. This data would typically include information about economic policy and sectors, stress factors and political risk.

This information would include (within economic policy) the efficiency of the public administration, the ability of the Treasury to manage the external debt, their understanding of international financial markets, the fiscal balance, the surplus or deficit in the public accounts, the ratio of public sector debt to GDP and the capacity to grow despite any deficit. In addition, the agencies would also examine indicators such as growth of GDP, inflation, balance of payments and the unemployment situation. Additional factors to take into account would include population growth, age distribution, the productivity of the agricultural and industrial sectors, the degree of urbanization and the effectiveness of the education system.

In the process of country analysis the sectors that might have the greatest effect on the balance of payments would be granted more attention. The agencies would therefore be interested in determining the country's ability to generate foreign exchange earnings, so issues such as sector market shares, the diversity of the markets, and the composition of exports would be of interest. Consequently, the openness of the economy, its attitude towards foreign investment (including issues such as repatriation of profits), and the level of protectionism would also be relevant.

The ratings granted are forward-looking, in the sense that they reflect an assessment of the probability that the debt will be repaid under the conditions stated. Thus, the stress variables incorporate possible reactions to international events such as world recessions, changes in interest rates, or the prices of raw materials on the international markets. In this category the labour force is a particularly relevant variable.

Lastly, political factors are also analyzed. Within this category matters such as the stability of the government or whether it belongs to international organizations such as the IMC or EU would be considered.

Although this process is broadly followed by the three agencies, there are significant differences between them. For example, Moody's analyzes 39 variables in four categories: monetary, liquidity and vulnerability indicators; external payments and debt; fiscal indicators; and performance and economic structure. Fitch, in contrast, analyzes 139 variables in 14 categories: balance of supply and demand in the economy; balance of payments; banking and finance; constraints on medium term growth; demographic, educational and structural factors; dynamism of the private sector; external assets; external liabilities; international position; labour market analysis; macroeconomic policy; politics and the state; structure of output and trade; and trade and foreign investment policy. In practice, though, the overall effect of these differences is less than you might expect: most countries get equivalent ratings from the different agencies.

As mentioned in point 5, the information derived from the analysis of these variables is incorporated into a risk model that helps each agency determine a score (see the fifth column in Table 5.1). This score is translated into a specific rating for each country, expressed in a combination of letters similar to those already introduced in Chapter 2 in the case of corporate debt. These ratings can be grouped in two general categories: investment grade, and speculative debt. Table 5.1 shows the assigned value, its corresponding rating by the three major agencies, and an average risk premium for each rating, whereas Table 5.2 shows the information for a sample of rated countries.

Table 5.2 presents a 15-country sample of the ratings granted by the three agencies to the long-term debt in foreign currency issued by these countries as of May 2010. The updated information can be extracted from the web sites of the three agencies.

Some examples of the correspondences between the bond ratings and average risk premiums are given in Table 5.1.

Modelling country risk

In the example at the beginning of this section our concern was to determine a risk premium to add to the discount rate used to bring to present value the future cash flows generated by our investment opportunity. So far, we have said that this premium is linked to a country's debt default risk. We already know what this means and how specialized agencies evaluate this sovereign debt default-free risk to come up with different ratings. Nevertheless, several questions remain unanswered. For example, we would need to know how to incorporate a Ba2 rating into our cost of capital, if this is all the risk we need to consider, and whether there are other methods we could also use to value this premium. Our discussion of the first question will lead us through these pages to the second and third.

Table 5.1   Comparative ratings by three agencies Risk premiums in basis points according to rating

S&P	Moody's	Fitch	Probability of default[2]	Assigned value	Average premiums country risk government bonds	Average premiums country risk corporate bonds
AAA	Aaa	AAA	Obligations rated Aaa are judged to be of the highest quality, with minimal credit risk.	8	0	0
AA+	Aa1	AA+	Obligations rated Aa are judged to be of high quality and are subject to very low credit risk.	7.33	60	75
AA	Aa2	AA	Obligations rated Aa are judged to be of high quality and are subject to very low credit risk.	7	65	85
AA–	Aa3	AA–	Obligations rated Aa are judged to be of high quality and are subject to very low credit risk.	6.66	70	90
A+	A1	A+	Obligations rated A are considered upper–medium grade and are subject to low credit risk	6.33	80	100
A	A2	A	Obligations rated A are considered upper–medium grade and are subject to low credit risk	6	90	125
A–	A3	A–	Obligations rated A are considered upper–medium grade and are subject to low credit risk	5.66	100	135
BBB+	Baa1	BBB+	Obligations rated Baa are subject to moderate credit risk. They are considered medium grade and as such may possess certain speculative characteristics	5.33	120	150

Continued

Table 5.1 Continued

S&P	Moody's	Fitch	Probability of default[2]	Assigned value	Average premiums country risk government bonds	Average premiums country risk corporate bonds
BBB	Baa2	BBB	Obligations rated Baa are subject to moderate credit risk. They are considered medium grade and as such may possess certain speculative characteristics	5	130	175
BBB–	Baa3	BBB–	Obligations rated Baa are subject to moderate credit risk. They are considered medium grade and as such may possess certain speculative characteristics	4.66	145	200
BB+	Ba1	BB+	Obligations rated Ba are judged to have speculative elements and are subject to substantial credit risk.	4.33	250	325
BB	Ba2	BB	Obligations rated Ba are judged to have speculative elements and are subject to substantial credit risk.	4	300	400
BB–	Ba3	BB–	Obligations rated Ba are judged to have speculative elements and are subject to substantial credit risk.	3.66	400	525
B+	B1	B+	Obligations rated B are considered speculative and are subject to high credit risk.	3.33	450	600

Continued

Table 5.1 Continued

S&P	Moody's	Fitch	Probability of default[2]	Assigned value	Average premiums country risk government bonds	Average premiums country risk corporate bonds
B	B2	B	Obligations rated B are considered speculative and are subject to high credit risk	3	550	750
B–	B3	B–	Obligations rated B are considered speculative and are subject to high credit risk.	2.66	650	850
CCC+	Caa1[3]	CCC+	Obligations rated Caa are judged to be of poor standing and are subject to very high credit risk.	2.33	750	900

Note: Investment grade ratings are in bold.
Source: www.Moody's.com, www.fitchratings.com, www.standardandpoors.com, and www. bondsonline.com. For complete and fully updated information communicate directly with the agencies.

Table 5.2 Country equivalency ratings from the three agencies as of October 2010

	Fitch	S&P	Moody's
Argentina	B	B–	B3
Austria	AAA	AAA	Aaa
Bermuda	AA+	AA	Aa2
Brazil	BBB–	BBB–	Baa3
Bulgaria	BBB–	BBB	Baa3
Colombia	BB+	BB+	Ba1
Ecuador	CCC	B–	Caa3
Egypt	BB+	BB+	Ba1
Indonesia	BB+	BB	Ba2
Korea	A+	A	A1
Malaysia	A–	A–	A3
Malta	A+	A	A1
Papua New Guinea	Rating withdrawn	BB	B1
Ukraine	B	B+	B2
Uruguay	BB	BB–	Ba3

Source: www.standardandpoors.com; www.fitchratings.com; www.moodys.com

Once more it is useful to remember that the country risk premium refers to the higher interest rates that would have to be paid for loans and investment projects in a country compared to some standard (such as our home country). In our example, the cash flows of the project under consideration are more risky than those coming from our regular projects. Obviously, a company's exposure to country risk comes from where it does its business not from where it was founded or where it trades its financial assets. The idea can be illustrated with the following example.

Before we undertake our new international project, 100 per cent of our operating cash flows have similar risk and demand a return of 15 per cent. Therefore, our average cost of capital is 15 per cent. If we take on a new project with a higher risk, the return demanded will also be higher, let us say 20 per cent. If 25 per cent of all expected future cash flows for our company are expected to come from this riskier project, our overall cost of capital should be 20*25 per cent + 15*75 per cent = 5 + 11.25 = 16.25 per cent. The overall return for our investors would have to increase from 15 per cent to 16.25 per cent in order to acknowledge the additional risk, because, overall, the operating cash flows to the company will be riskier after the new project is running.

Once we have determined that our project is indeed exposed to additional risk, there are different ways in which we can include the likely premium during the project analysis. Some managers choose to adjust the cost of capital, while others prefer to work with the cash flows. The norm is that systematic risks ought to be accounted for in the denominator (cost of capital) whereas the firm-specific or unsystematic risks ought to be considered in the numerator (the cash flows of the investment project). In this section, we will look at different approaches. Our list is by no means exhaustive as numerous authors and practitioners have contributed to this subject in an attempt to find refinements that work better in different scenarios. However, in our review we discuss the approaches used more frequently and the most common problems analysts encounter in using these methods. As we shall see, each of these models provides an angle on how to treat this type of risk. However, it is also true that each of the proposals is subject to a series of criticisms. If this were not so, there would be just one universally accepted approach to treating country risk.

Analyzing why a range of models are used will help us understand the complications and tradeoffs a financial manager has to face when determining the country risk premium, and more generally, when assessing the cost of capital in multinational contexts.

The models below are presented concisely, to make them easier to compare. We use a common framework for the different proposals, including a description of the model, its adequateness, and criticisms made of it.

The challenge of determining the right premium for international investments – when this is indeed a problem – is that we typically have an equation with four variables, of which two are unknowns. That is, we often have a project (investment) in a home country and an equivalent project in a foreign market. Usually we either know, or can establish relatively inexpensively, the risk and required return for the home country investment. We need to calculate the values of these two variables for the equivalent venture in the foreign market.

The difficulties arise from the fact that the proxies we use in both the estimation of risk and return are correlated in a way that cannot be translated into the new market at face value. That is, the relationship between the bond and equity markets in the US is not necessarily the same as that, for example, in Argentina. Furthermore, the US bond market is quite different from that of Argentina in terms of the instruments traded, volume, liquidity, and so on. The same applies to the equity markets of both countries which have, for example, different volatilities, liquidity, volume and size.

For example, when thinking of a local market, we assume certain characteristics and behaviour on the part of that market and the securities traded on it that help us assess the correct premiums. However, when we try to apply an equivalent approach by arithmetically measuring the proportions of the returns of the instruments in the different markets, we cannot make a direct comparison. We might say, for instance, that the market risk premium, measured as the difference between the return on the equity market in the US (e.g. S&500) and the risk-free rate, is 7.45 per cent on average. This 7.45 per cent is not equivalent to the same percentage applied to a market with different characteristics. An additional problem is that a specific type of model might not work across all countries independently of their stage of development of their market.

CAPM + country risk premium (CRP)

The first method we are going to review uses the CAPM, with which we are already familiar, and adjusts the cost of equity by adding a country risk premium (CRP). This premium can be estimated in a number of ways, as described below. The model will be:

$$E\left(R_{i,x}\right) = R_f + \text{Beta}_i[E\left(R_M\right) - R_f] + \text{CRP}_x$$

Formula 5.1

where

$E(R_{ix})$ = is the expected return from project i in country x (our developing country);

R_f = is the risk-free rate (for example, the immediate return or yield on a ten-year maturity US Treasury bond);

Beta_i = the beta of an equivalent project in developed country (e.g. USA);

$E(R_M)$ = the expected rate of return on the developed market (e.g. S&P500) or a global index (e.g. MSCI);

CRP_x = country risk premium of the developing country, which can be estimated in a number of ways. For example:

- Method 1: CRP_x = using an agency-assigned rating translated into the number of basis points that need to be added to a specific risk category. For example, 900 points would equal 9 per cent.
- Method 2: CRP_x = by taking the range of default risk calculated as the differential between the yields of both countries (developed and undeveloped) of a fixed-income risk-free asset, issued in the same currency, and with equal maturity. For example, suppose the yield on a ten-year maturity Treasury bond issued in US dollars in the developed country is six per cent, and the yield on a ten-year maturity US Treasury bond in US dollars in the developing country is 13 per cent. The CRP would equal: 13–6 = 7 per cent.
- Method 3: CRP_x = using the historical risk premium of the equity over fixed-income instruments in the developing country. For example, if the return on the equity market R_{MX} is 17 per cent on average, and the historical average return on the bond market of the developing country is nine per cent, the CRP would equal: 17–9 = 8 per cent.

Criticisms of these methods

Country risk is not the same for all projects. For example, within different countries, for whatever reasons, some sectors of the economy will be more reputable than others and would carry less than the average risk of doing business in the country, while others which are more protected or are common nationalization targets of certain governments will be riskier.

Some parts of the project may not be exposed to the risk.

Country risk is not totally systematic but part of it is diversifiable. To determine whether risk is systematic you can look at the correlation between the market proxies of both countries using, for example, the market indices. If there is little correlation, that means risk can be diversified and only the systematic part should be included in the discount rate. It is worth remembering that the diversifiable risks go into the cash flows of the project to be discounted, whereas the non-diversifiable risks are those reflected in the cost of capital used as a divisor.

Country risk is not exactly the same as the default risk of a debt issue in a foreign currency. There will be a relationship between both variables, given that both are affected by issues such as political risk and inflation, which is why it is used as a proxy, but that is all. For example, the default risk could depend on the foreign currency reserves a country holds, which is totally unrelated to country risk as such.

The ratings provided by the agencies often do not completely reflect expectations about the future, but they have an important historical component.

The default spreads of the debt reflect the future better than do the ratings. However, this proxy still has the disadvantage that both countries must issue debt with the same maturity and in the same currency.

Typical adjustments

- Try to isolate country risk from other types of risk;
- Adjust the risk of that business in that country (the relationship between the market and the business in one country might not be the same as in another);
- Make sure that the country risks have not been taken into account both in the cash flows and in the discount rate at the same time.

Example

Method 1: CRP_x = agency rating translated into the number of basis points we need to add for each specific rating.

If we are considering an investment in Bulgaria, a country with ratings of BB, BB+ and B1 and that rating demands an additional premium of 4.5 per cent, we would add 4.5 per cent to our cost of equity and 4.5 per cent to our cost of debt.

While these ratings provide an adequate measure of country risk, as we have mentioned, there are problems associated with them. First, rating agencies are often late updating their ratings to reflect the underlying risks. Second, the goal of the rating agency is to qualify default risk, which might obscure other risks that affect the stock markets. What are the alternatives? One is to make a historical estimation which provides an average default risk, not adjusted for the different companies which are neither equally exposed nor fully updated.

Method 2: CRP_x = the default risk range estimated as the differential between the yields of a risk-free asset of both countries, issued in the same currency and with equal maturity.

One way of solving one of the above mentioned problems is to calculate the CRP as the spread of default between fixed financial assets of equal rating, maturity and issued in the same currency by both countries. If both countries issue risk-free debt with equal risk and currency, a first step to this adjustment is to compare the returns of both financial instruments. Both assets must be issued in the same currency, because otherwise the calculated premium might reflect inflation differentials instead of risk differentials perceived by the market. The index would be measuring two effects: currency exchange rate risk and default risk.

Assume the US government issues a ten-year maturity bond with a 5.5 per cent return. The Colombian government has an instrument of similar characteristics except that the return offered is 8.5 per cent, a three per cent difference. If the Colombian bond is liquid, and the yield reflects investors' views of the Colombian market, the country risk premium (ρ) for Colombia should be three per cent or 300 basis points, which is the difference between the returns (8.5 per cent – 5.5 per cent).

Working on this problem one has to remember that the only relevant index is the current return or yield, which may or may not be equal to that on the coupon when the instrument was issued. That is why we need to highlight that the 3 per cent would be the correct value if the return at maturity is expressed as the yield. Otherwise, for example, if it were expressed as an annual effective rate, we would need an additional adjustment, and we would calculate the risk as follows:

$$\left[\frac{1 + \text{Colombia's rate}}{1 + \text{US rate}} \right] - 1$$

Formula 5.2

That is: $1 + \rho = [1.085\% / 1.055\%] - 1 = 0.0284\%$

The evidence that spreads change over time has led some analysts to suggest that instead of taking the current yields to estimate the spread, it would be more reasonable to consider the average spread calculated over a period of time. Figures 5.1a and 5.1b illustrate this idea and the argument made by such analysts.

Figures 5.1a and b show the different pattern of the yields of the US and Colombian bonds. Furthermore, medium- and long-term Colombian bonds might

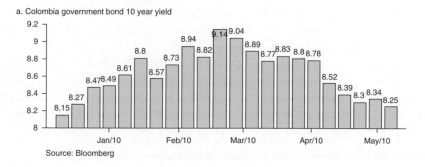

a. Colombia government bond 10 year yield

Source: Bloomberg

Figure 5.1a   Colombia government bond 10 year yield

Source: www.tradingeconomics.com/Economics/Government-Bond-Yield.aspx?Symbol=USD#ixzz0nhLCK42s

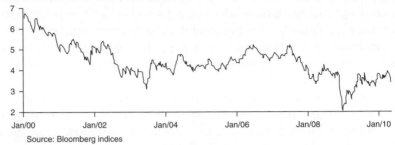

Figure 5.1b   United States government bond 10 year yield

Source: www.tradingeconomics.com/Economics/Government-Bond-Yield.
aspx?Symbol=USD#ixzz0nhMFWMkU

not be available at all times and thus show that the default spread is not constant over time. Therefore, if we are convinced by this argument and follow the suggestion, we would take the yields of the bonds of both markets for a period of at least three years, average them out, and find the difference, as in the example above.

Analysts who use default spread as a measure of country risk typically add them to both the cost of equity and debt of every company traded in that country. For instance, the cost of equity for a Colombian company estimated in US dollars will be three per cent higher than the cost of equity of an otherwise similar US company using our measure of the default spread.

To address the issue that not all companies are equally affected by country risk, some practitioners add the default spread to the US risks premium and multiply it by the beta. This increases the cost of equity for high beta, and lowers them for low beta companies.

Other analysts go a step further and make an additional adjustment by multiplying the default spread to the US risk premium and multiplying it by the company beta. That way, the cost of equity for higher risk companies compared to that for low beta or low risk firms would be increased further. Whichever way we do the calculation, once the difference in spreads has been determined, we would add that to our original cost of capital as a risk premium. For example, the cost of equity for a Colombian company estimated in US dollars would be three per cent higher than the cost of equity of a similar US company.

Method 3: CRP_x = historical risk premium of fixed versus variable return
If the excess return from an equity portfolio over a bond portfolio has averaged six per cent over a period of time, it might seem reasonable to assume this return differential will prevail in the future. However, although this expectation might seem logical, the problem with the historical premiums

is that they are not very precise. Furthermore, to estimate them one needs quality information, including historical data. These requirements are often a problem in developing markets with a short history, liquidity issues and huge volatility. After all, the premiums are extracted from the returns of shares and bonds that are themselves volatile. Hence, a historical premium of six per cent may be subject to a very large standard error, which renders the estimate useless.

How can we estimate that standard error? In general, the standard error in the risk premium is a function of the standard deviation of the returns of the equity and the number of years of data we use as observations:

$$\text{Standard error in the risk premium} = \frac{\sigma_{US} \text{ of the annualized equity returns}}{\sqrt{number\ of\ years\ of\ data\ in\ the\ sample}}$$

where

σ is the standard deviation

To show the standard error in the historical risk premium in the US using 84 years of data:

Standard deviation in the risk premium of USA = 20% / $\sqrt{84}$ = 2.18%

With an annualized standard deviation of the returns of the values of 20 per cent, the standard error, even with 84 years of data, is approximately 2.18 per cent.

The problem worsens when dealing with emerging markets, as accessing data for these economies is often a problem: the collection of such data began quite recently and for many countries it is difficult to obtain time series longer than ten years. Furthermore, even if we can obtain the prices they are usually plagued with problems such as excessive volatility, so our estimates of the historical risk premium for these markets might be useless, because of the large standard errors.

Modified historical risk premium

Given that we still need to come out with a method to assess a risk premium in developing countries, one proposal is to use a 'modified historical risk premium'. This works as follows:

$$(K_{Mx} - R_f) = K_{Mx} + CRP_{EX}$$

Formula 5.3

We can read the above formula by saying that the equity risk premium for the developing country equals the market risk premium for the equity market plus an equity country risk premium. The idea is that the country factor might contain risk elements additional to those experienced by the equity market, reflecting the fact that it is not a mature securities market.

To estimate the equity risk premium for a mature market we just look at average historical returns, which are readily available and widely published. For example, we can use the Stocks, Bonds, Bills and Inflation by Ibbotson Associates and find out that on average, stocks returned approximately 7.54 per cent above the risk-free rate for the period 1928 and 2005.

To estimate the equity risk premium of a country we would need to measure the risk of country and turn the country risk into a 'premium'. Regardless of how we make this adjustment, once the difference in the spread has been determined, we would add it to our original cost of capital as a country risk premium. For example, the cost of the equity of a Colombian company, estimated in US dollars, would be three per cent higher than the cost of equity of a comparable American company.

We need to draw attention to the fact that an underlying assumption of the above methodology is that the foreign country's equity and bond markets have the same volatility as that of our home country. Since this is rarely the case, it is suggested that an adjustment be made to allow for this. The usual measure of equity risk is the standard deviation in stock prices. Therefore, we can apply the ratio of the standard deviation of the equity markets of both countries to obtain a measure of relative equity risk, as calculated by the volatilities of these markets.

Relative equity risk

$$\sigma_x = \frac{\sigma_x}{\sigma_{US}}$$

Formula 5.4

where
  σ is the standard deviation
  x is the developing country
To get a measure of the total risk premium for any country we could multiply the relative standard deviation derived from the above formula by the premium used for US stocks:

ERP_x = risk premium $_{US}$ * relative σ_x

Assume we are using 7.54 per cent as the equity risk premium (ERP) for the US. The annualized standard deviation in the S&P 500 between 2000 and

2009, using weekly returns, was 20.86 per cent, and the standard deviation in our developing equity index over the same period was 35 per cent. Using these values, we would calculate of a total risk premium for our developing country x as follows:

$$ERP_x = 7.54\ \%* (35\% / 20.86\ \%) = 12.65\%$$

The country risk premium (CRP) can be isolated as follows:

$$CRP_x = 12.65\% - 7.54\ \% = 5.11\%$$

A problem with this approach is that it compares markets that may have very different structures and liquidity. If share are infrequently traded, standard deviations can be small. The explanation is not low risk but lack of liquidity, which in fact means that the risk is greater. This is particularly true of developing markets. When such issues affect a market, this technique is not going to pick up on all the equity risk and the premiums will turn out to be too low. In addition, since prices are quoted in the country's currency, each standard deviation is expressed in a different currency. Nonetheless, this could be fixed by converting everything into US dollars. We must therefore stress again that although tools do help us analyze the information, they are no substitute for the analyst's scrutiny of the specific factors of the case under consideration. That is, if we find a low standard deviation, the analyst should be able to explain why and act accordingly.

Country default spreads only measure the premium for default risk and equity markets are riskier than bonds, so we would expect the country equity risk premium to be larger than the country default risk spread. To confirm this, we can compare the volatility of the equity and bonds markets within the country. Under this method the country's risk premium would equal its default spread (the risk premium for default spread) multiplied by the difference between the risk in the equity and bond markets:

$$CRP_x = \text{Default spread for country} * \left(\frac{\sigma_{x\ Equity}}{\sigma_{x\ Bond\ Market}} \right)$$

Formula 5.5

Let us use the same market to provide an example. Suppose the default spread on developing country X's 10-year bond issued in US dollars is 8.51 per cent and the annualized standard deviation in the equity market proxy 35 per cent. Using monthly returns for a three-year period, the annualized

Table 5.3　Country and total equity risk premium: Developing country March 2010

Method	Developed country equity premium (%)	Developing CRP (%)	Total equity risk premium (%)
Country Bond Default Spread	7.54	5.51	13.05
Relative Equity Standard Deviation	7.54	5.11	12.65
Mixture	7.54	10.39	17.93

standard deviation in the bond is calculated at 28.65 per cent. The resulting equity risk premium for country X is as follows:

Additional $CEP_X =$

Default spread $_X$* $(\sigma_{X\,Equity}\,/\,\sigma_{X\,Bond\,Market}) = 8.51 * (35\%\,/\,28.65\%) = 10.39\%$

As you might have noticed, this premium is added to the mature market equity premium because investors who can obtain from the developing country bond market a dollar-denominated return of, for example, 13 per cent, will not find a 12 per cent return in the equity market acceptable.

In our summary of results in Table 5.3, we can see that each approach gives a different answer. The question that comes to mind is: which is the better approach?

Local CAPM

When considering that markets are segmented (not integrated) and investors are diversified, one can use the local CAPM. We can test whether the market is segmented by doing a correlation of the R_M of the developed country and that of the developing country. Segmented markets present barriers to the movements of the international cash flows. If there were no arbitrage, these barriers would result in differences between the prices paid for the same good traded in the different countries. However, in an integrated market, such differences would be instantaneously eliminated by arbitrage, and adjustments to risk and returns would occur simultaneously in all integrated markets. The model to use when the markets are not integrated is:

$$E(R_{ix}) = R_{fx} + Beta_{ix}\left[E(R_{Mx}) - R_{fx}\right]$$

Formula 5.6

where
$E(R_{ix})$ = expected return of project i in country x (developing country);
R_{fx} = risk-free rate in country x;

$Beta_{ix}$ = project i beta with respect to market x;

$E(R_{Mx})$ = expected return of the market in country x;

Criticisms

- All the parameters refer to country x;
- Even if we run a correlation, the results might not be reliable because of the characteristics of small markets, which usually have few stocks, and:
  - High volatility of these markets make it very difficult to estimate average returns with a high degree of confidence in that sense that the mean will be a good representative of expectations.
  - Emerging markets are usually illiquid and most of the shares do not trade continuously. Pricing information is therefore irregular and infrequent.
  - It is difficult to find comparable businesses, as there are probably only a few companies in the market, so the returns of the index do not necessarily reflect the market but just a few stocks.
  - It could also be the case that an exchange whose overall index shows lack of correlation with that of the developed country is integrated in one sector or industry.

International CAPM

The International CAPM is used when we consider the markets to be integrated and the institutional investors well diversified. A distinctive assumption of the model is that investors consume in 'hard currency' (e.g. dollars), so the model must account for losses in purchasing power. The International CAPM picks up on the risks that arise from deviations in Purchasing Power Parity (PPP) by adding a term to the CAPM, which measures the risk of exchange rate movements between the local and the developed country currency (e.g. the US). The model is as follows:

$$E\left(R_{i,x}\right) = R_f + \text{Beta}_i\left[E\left(R_M\right) - R_f\right] + \gamma_{i,x} * E\left(s_x + r_x - R_f\right)$$

Formula 5.7

where

$E(R_{i,x})$ = expected return from project i in country x (developing country);

R_f = the risk-free rate;

Beta_i = the beta of investment i, determined with reference to a proxy for the global portfolio (e.g. MSCI);

$E(R_M)$ = the expected return from the developed market (e.g. S&P500) or global index (e.g. MSCI);

$\gamma_{i,x}$ = the beta of the risk-free rate of the developed country with reference to the exchange rate with the local currency;

s_x = the percentage change in the exchange rate between the developed country's currency and that of the local currency;

r_x = the risk-free rate of the local country;

The model is simplified by assuming that PPP prevails in the long run for major capital investments and the currency term which accounts for exchange rate risk disappears, leaving:

$$E(R_{ix}) = R_f + \text{Beta}_i \left[E(R_M) - R_f \right]$$

Formula 5.8

that is, the developed country CAPM, except for the beta term, estimated as indicated above.

Criticisms

- The estimated beta is not reliable since the local stock may be illiquid and have a short history.
- The model is simplified because of the assumption that PPP prevails in the long run. However, in some instances the 'long run' might be far into the future.
- Furthermore, there are other ways of taking care of exchange rate risk.

The Modified International CAPM (MICAPM)

The Modified International CAPM (MICAPM) is used when markets are thought to be integrated and the institutional investors well diversified. It assumes that PPP prevails for long-term capital investors and basically just modifies the beta of the International CAPM.

The model is:

$$E(R_i) = R_f + \text{Beta}_p \left[E(R_M) - R_f \right]$$

Formula 5.9

where

$E(R_i)$ = the expected return of project i;

R_f = the risk-free rate;

$E(R_M)$ = the expected rate of return of the developed market (e.g. S&P500) or global index (e.g. MSCI);

Beta_p = the weighted beta, estimated as in the following example:

Assume we are interested in a sector such as apparel manufacturing (AM) which trades in one developed – the US – and two developing countries, C1 and C2. We then take these steps:

- obtain the industry betas of the US ($\beta_{t, US}$);

- estimate the betas of C1 and C2 with reference to the developed country by regressing the market proxy of each of C1 and C2 against that of the US ($\beta_{t\,C1,\,US}$ and $\beta_{t\,C2,\,US}$);
- calculate the beta of the project in each market with respect to the US, where

$$\beta_{t\,C1,\,US} = \beta_{t,\,US}\,\beta_{t\,C1,\,US}$$

$$\beta_{t\,C2,\,US} = \beta_{t,\,US}\,\beta_{t\,C2,\,US}$$

and

$\beta_{t,\,US}$ = is the beta of the project in the US

$\beta_{t\,C1,\,US}$ = is the beta of C1, with respect to the US market

$\beta_{t\,C2,\,US}$ = is the beta of C2, with respect to the US market

- find the weighted average beta using:

$$\text{Beta}_p = \alpha_{US}\,\beta_{t\,US} + \alpha_{C1}\,\beta_{tC1,US} + \alpha_{C2}\beta_{tC2,US}$$
Formula 5.10

$\alpha_{US} + \alpha_{C1} + \alpha_{C2} = 1$, alphas or percentages representing the income originated in each market which add up to 1.

Godfrey and Espinosa

The model of Godfrey and Espinosa[4] is concerned with adjusting returns for three types of risks that they believe affect all investments in developing countries. The authors account for these political, business and currency risks by using an adapted version of the CAPM, which modifies the CAPM beta to account for business risk and adds a country risk premium term to correct for political risk. Currency risk is resolved by using a hard currency (e.g. $US).

The model is:

$$E(R_{ix}) = R_f + \text{Beta}_{adj}[E(R_M) - R_f] + CRP_x$$
Formula 5.11

where

$E(R_{ix})$ = the return expected from project i in country x (developing country);

R_f = the risk–free rate, for example a US $ bond with 10 years maturity, expressed as instant return or yield;

$E(R_M)$ = the expected rate of return of the developed market (e.g. S&P500);

CRP_x = the country risk premium, estimated as the ratio between the long-term risk-free rate in the developing nation (as represented, for example, by a Treasury Bond issued in US dollars) and the long-term risk-free rate in the developed nation (as represented for example by a Treasury Bond in the same currency);

Beta $_{adj}$ = the adjusted beta, estimated as the ratio between the standard deviation of the returns in the developing market, which in turn is estimated by using a market proxy (local R_{MX}) and the standard deviation of the USA markets returns (R_M, e.g. S&P500),

$$\text{Beta}_{adj} = \frac{\sigma_X}{\sigma_M}$$

Formula 5.12

Criticism

Since the relevant economic and political facts affect both the quality of the debt returns and the volatility of the local market, the adjusted beta and country risk premium are related. Adjustments are therefore necessary to account for this. Erb, Harvey and Viskanta[5] report that 40% of the volatility of the equity is a function of changes in debt quality. Consequently, the beta in the model is adjusted by the percentage:

$$E\left(R_{ix}\right) = R_f + \left(0.60 * \text{Beta}_{adj}\right)\left[E\left(R_M\right) - R_f\right] + CRP_x$$

Criticism

- the model uses the debt risk premium to assess country risk;
- the adjusted beta depends on historical information about the local market returns;
- the adjusted beta represents local equity market risk and it is not clear how this is related to the specific project;
- the relationship between credit quality and equity volatility is estimated with historical data, and this relationship might not be constant.

Erb, Harvey and Viskanta[6]

In 1995, Erb, Harvey and Viskanta published the first of a series of articles in which they argued that in segmented developing countries, country credit risk is a proxy for the 'ex-ante' risk exposure. The authors used country credit risk ratings from the Institutional Investor to test the relationship between expected returns and volatility in 135 countries. Their tests showed that the use of beta with a world market portfolio in segmented countries can result in underestimation of the cost of capital. Instead they proposed the following model estimated, using regression with semi-annual data:

$$E(R_{ix}) = \gamma_0 + \gamma_1 * CRP_x$$

Formula 5.13

where

$E(R_{ix})$ = the return expected from project i in country x (developing country) in $US;

$\gamma_0 + \gamma_1$ = the estimated regression parameters;

CRP_x = the country risk premium, which in their model is the credit rating of country x.

Criticism

The main criticism of this method is that it only explains how to calculate an expected rate of return for the 'average' project, and does not explain how to adjust for the specific risk of the project.

Estrada[7]

Estrada (2000, 2001) succinctly framed the issue of estimating the cost of capital in the international context by pointing out that the problems related to its calculation in developed and emerging markets are substantially different. The author recognizes that practitioners in the real world use a CAPM-based model, which can be modified to account for variables such as size and book-to-market ratios and will work relatively well. His proposal for emerging markets, however, rests on the recognition that the international CAPM implicitly assumes integrated markets, which is at odds with reality in many instances. Estrada suggests estimating the costs of equity in emerging markets using the semideviation with respect to the mean, as he assumes that returns are a function of the downside section instead of the total variance of the local returns. The model is as follows:

$$E(R_{i,x}) = R_f + CRP_M * R_{Mix}$$

Formula 5.14

where

$E(R_{ix})$ = the expected return for project i in country x (developing country)

R_f = the developed country's risk-free rate

CRP_{MW} = a world market risk premium

R_{Mix} = the risk measure of negative volatility, estimated as the ratio of the semi-standard deviation of returns with respect to the mean in market x and the semi-standard deviation of returns with respect to the mean in the world market. The semi-standard deviation of returns is given by:

$$R_{Mix} = \frac{\sqrt{\left(\frac{1}{N}\right) \boxtimes \text{EMBED Equation. 3 } \boxtimes\boxtimes\boxtimes (R_{ix} - R_{ix})}}{\sqrt{\left(\frac{1}{N}\right) \boxtimes \text{EMBED Equation. 3 } \boxtimes\boxtimes\boxtimes (R_{ix} - R_{iw})}}$$

Formula 5.15

For $R_{ix} < R_{ix}$ and $R_{ix} < R_{iW}$
where
   N is the number of observations
   R_{ix} is the return of asset i in market x
   R_{ix} is the mean return of asset i in market x, and
   R_{iW} is the mean return of asset i in the global market

APT

Finally, the last model we propose here is Ross's (1976) APT reviewed in Chapter 2. Recall that this method proposes that an asset's returns are sensitive to several factors rather than just systematic risk, and assumes arbitrage that eliminates all profit opportunities. According to the model, the returns can be derived as follows:

$$E(R_i) = R_f + \beta_{i1} * f_1 + \beta_{i2} * f_2 + \beta_{i3} * f_3 + \ldots + \beta_{in} * f_n$$

Formula 5.16

where
   $E(R_i)$ = the expected return of project i
   R_f = the risk-free rate, say, for example, 10 years' maturity in dollars for a US Bond, expressed as instant return or yield
   f = a factor affecting the return
   β_i = the sensitivity of project i to each factor

Criticism

The APT applied in the international context is subject to the same criticisms as when it is applied to the home country, that is, that factors are difficult to identify and tend to be correlated with each other. Variables that affect a particular result are said to be orthogonal if they are uncorrelated, so this problem can be solved by 'orthogonalization': a way of removing the correlation among the factors by regressing them against each other.

Cash flows

At the beginning of this discussion we mentioned that country risk could be allowed for by adjusting the cost of capital or the cash flows to be derived from the project. Some of the advantages of the method presented now are that historical data are not needed and we do not have to make corrections for country risk. Nevertheless, it does make a couple of assumptions, such as that the market is correctly priced and that the growth in the cash flows is known. To use this method we go back to the Gordon or constant growth model presented earlier. According to this model, the formula for the present value of a dividend stream to be received, starting next period, that would have a perpetual growth rate of g was the following:

$$P_0 = \frac{D_1}{(K_E - g)}$$
Formula 2.23

where $D_1 = D_0 (1 + g)$
Formula 2.24

In the formula, P_0 is the current market price of the common stock, D_1 is the dividend to be received in the next period, K_E is the return demanded from the company shares, and g is the expected dividend growth rate. To find the return demanded, we only have to solve for the K_E term in the equation:

$$K_E = \frac{D_0(1+g)}{P_0} + g$$
Formula 2.25

$$K_E = \frac{D_1}{P_0} + g$$

For the purpose of the current discussion, we introduce a small modification in the formula, changing the denomination of the numerator and, instead of dividends, using the more general indication of 'cash flows' and the required return on equity K_E by required return K:

$$PV_0 = \frac{\text{Expected Cash Flows}}{(K - g)}$$
Formula 5.17

where
Expected Cash Flows$_1$ = CF$_0$ (1+g)
PV_0 = the present value of a series of cash flows growing at rate g to be received in the future
K = the required return
g = the perpetual growth rate of the cash flow
Given that the price is obtained from the market and that growth and projected cash flows are part of the estimations done by a firm in analyzing a

new investment venture, much of the data is already available. Thus, we just need to solve for K to get an implied number for the expected return on stocks. From this figure, we deduct the risk-free rate and obtain the implied equity risk premium.

For example, assume the S&P500 Index is at 1088, the expected dividend yield on the index is 3.2 per cent, and the expected long-term growth rate in earnings and dividends is five per cent. We can solve the equation for the required return (K) using Formula 5.17:

$1088 = (0.032*1088) / (K - 0.05)$

$(K - 0.05)1088 = 0.032*1088$

$1088K - 54.4 = 34.816$

$1088K = 34.816 + 54.4$

$K = (34.816 + 54.4) / 1088$

$K = 89.216 / 1088$

$K = 8.2\%$

If the current risk-free rate is 3.44 per cent, this will yield an equity premium of 4.76 per cent.

We discussed earlier how we can generalize this model for more than one growth rate. For example, if the risk-free rate is 3.44 per cent, the S&P500 1088, the dividends' yield and stock returns in the index during the previous year was approximately 3.2 per cent; and the consensus estimate of the expected growth of the companies in the index is five per cent for the next five years.

A constant five per cent growth rate in the cash flows might be too high a rate to be sustainable in perpetuity. However, because this rate affects periods closer to the time when the valuation is done and therefore has a lot of weight in the estimation, 'averaging across' might distort the result significantly. In this instance, it might be better to use the two-stage option, by splitting the growth rate in two: five per cent for the next five periods and then a sustainable perpetual growth closer to an average inflation or growth rate of the Treasury bond of 3.44 per cent. Given that the return on a risk-free instrument is the sum of expected inflation and a real rate, if we think the real rate will approach real growth, then the perpetual growth rate should that of the bond.

Following the two-stage method we: 1) estimate the individual cash flows of the first five periods, 2) calculate the perpetuity portion of the cash flows that will be received after the fifth period, and 3) discount all the cash flows. Since we are attempting to determine K, the discount rate, we have to solve all the terms at the same time. This can easily be done using a spreadsheet;

for example in Excel we can use the IRR (internal rate of return) function. Otherwise we can use trial and error.

The cash flows in year one are found by multiplying the index by the dividend yield and the growth rate. The second period's cash flow is obtained by multiplying the first cash flow by its growth rate, and so on for successive periods:

Period 1: Dividend yield*index*growth rate = 0.032*1088*1.05 = 36.55

Period 2: Cash flow on index for period one * 1.05 = 38.38

Table 5.4 shows the expected cash flows for the next five years of high growth, and the first year of stable perpetual growth thereafter.

Assuming our assumptions and estimates for the cash flows and growth are correct, and the index is a good estimate of value, we just have to solve for K:

$36.55/ (1+ K) + 38.38/ (1+ K)^2 + 40.30/ (1+ K)^3 + 42.31/ (1+ K)^4 +$

$(44.43*1.0344)/(K - .0344)) / (1+ K)^5 = 1088$

then $K = 7\%$

and

$K_E = K - R_f$

$K_E = 7 - 3.44 = 3.56\%$

Thus, the implied equity premium is 3.56 per cent for the US in such date and the same method can be used for any country.

While implied premiums are market-driven, current, and forward-looking this method does not entirely avoid the need to use historical data, because we have to assess growth estimates and dividend payments, which are also a function of the firm's income statement structure and governance policy.

Table 5.4 Cash flow estimation

Year	Formula	Cash flow on index
1	$CF_0 * (1+g)^1$	36.55
2	$CF_0 * (1+g)^2$	38.38
3	$CF_0 * (1+g)^3$	40.30
4	$CF_0 * (1+g)^4$	42.31
5	$CF_0 * (1+g)^5$	44.43
6 perpetual	$CF_5 * (1+l.t.g)$	45.96

Once country risk premiums have been estimated, the final question that we have to address relates to the exposure of individual companies to country risk. Should all companies in a country with substantial country risk be equally exposed to that risk? While intuition suggests that they should not, we will begin by looking at standard approaches that assume that they are.

We will follow up by scaling country risk exposure to established risk parameters such as betas, and complete the discussion with an argument that individual companies should be evaluated for exposure to country risk.

Summary

When investments in foreign territories bring additional exposure to risk, a supplementary risk premium should be added to the cost of capital. Our discount rate for the cash flows derived from such project should include compensation for all the risks of the cash flows of the project. If those risks are not reflected in the operating cash flows, they should be reflected in the financial cash flows.

A key issue is then how to quantify the additional risks, and how to incorporate these into the cash flow analysis of our expansionary project. Understanding country ratings is key to adjusting the cost of capital when necessary. Nonetheless, this might not be the only risk affecting the foreign market.

This chapter has presented a range of different approaches to adjusting the cost of capital to account for the additional risk of investing in markets other than the investor's home country. The list we have presented is by no means exhaustive as numerous authors and practitioners have contributed to this subject in an attempt to find refinements that work better in the various scenarios. However, we have discussed the approaches used more frequently and the most common problems managers and analysts encounter in using these methods. Analyzing why a range of models are used has helped us understand the complications and tradeoffs a financial manager has to face when determining the country risk premium, and more generally when assessing the cost of capital in multinational contexts.

6
The Optimal Capital Structure

Through time different theories have been proposed to explain the various ways corporations and individuals can fund capital asset projects and select the financial assets used as savings mechanisms. Frictions and transaction costs in the real economy mean that there are advantages in using each type of security. For example, the interest tax subsidy granted by some governments has conferred an advantage on debt financing. The evidence shows that, across sectors and at different periods of their lives, companies make choices that result in unique 'capital structures'. However, a few variables such as asset composition and expected future cash flow stability play a major role in a firm's ability to acquire debt. Hence, the belief is that an 'optimal structure' exists for each company at a specific point in time.

From the investors' point of view, this optimal structure will be the combination of financial assets that maximizes the utility of their consumption stream over time. From the corporation's point of view it will be the mix of debt and equity that optimizes the value of the corporation. Although the assumption is that such an optimal mix exists, determining this structure for specific firm has to be understood in the light of the different constraints each funding alternative imposes on the firm and the management of the corporations, as well as the consideration that this optimal structure might be a 'moving target'.

In this chapter we will swiftly review the theory of optimal capital structure. In addition to the characteristics of debt and equity, we bring into context the different strategic tradeoffs managers have to balance out when obtaining additional capital. These considerations include the evaluation of the consequences of increasing the size of the company's debt. We also provide a step-by-step example of the basic mechanism for changing a current, non optimal structure into an optimal capital structure.

The theory of optimal capital structure

Overall, the funds available to companies can be grouped into internal and external financial resources. In the first category are the funds the corporation generates through its operations or sales of assets. In simple terms, this is the net income that is retained in the company after all current costs within the financial period have been met. The second category includes funds that can be obtained in the financial markets, such as the issue of new equity or bonds, or the acquisition of bank loans.

Internal resources are constrained by the adequacy of their own existence. If we need more liquidity than can be currently obtained from this source, this option will not provide sufficient funds. In general, this is typical of firms in the first part of their life cycles, those in high-growth sectors, or others needing to raise capital for large new projects.

Using internal funds has a number of advantages. The first that comes to mind is the savings in transaction costs. To raise internal resources is less expensive than to acquire external resources because the firm does not incur any transaction costs such as fees or legal expenditure. From the managers' perspective, a second benefit might be that the firm will not undergo the discipline of the financial markets, which is cumbersome and expensive. Lastly, companies with high levels of cash flows are thought to have a greater tendency to be wasteful, providing excessive perks to employees and using resources on unprofitable investments. The market will reward consumption of these unused funds, whether via dividend payments or positive net present value investments financed with these excess resources.

However, there are also a number of reasons why firms might choose not to use internally generated funds, even if they were sufficient. For example, the firm might want to keep financial flexibility; it might wish to subject itself to the discipline of the markets; or it might want to convey information to perspective investors about the company's expectations of future growth.

Unlike internal resources, acquiring external debt or equity has the disadvantage that issuing costs will be incurred. In addition, the firm will have to undergo market scrutiny. Moreover, if the firm selects debt as a form of financing, this choice will impose further restrictions. From the firm's point of view, debt is characterized by the contractual requirements to make a series of fixed payments at specific points in time in the future. The advantage over the equity option is that these interest payments are tax-deductible. However, these outflows of interest and principal restrict the corporation's flexibility for embarking on additional projects, as a fixed portion of future cash flows are allocated to these obligations. Furthermore, should these payments not be met, the corporation could find itself in bankruptcy proceedings with management handing over control to the creditors. Consequently, it is often the case that, in order to protect the interests of the debt holders, restrictions are imposed on the amount of additional debt the firm can obtain as well as minimum levels of, for example, liquidity or debt to equity ratios the company needs to maintain. Accordingly, debt inflicts restraints on management, and the larger the amount of debt, the greater the discipline that is imposed.

Although additional debt results in greater financial discipline – an advantage – one cannot disregard the danger of financial insolvency. This results when debt payments are interrupted or only made irregularly by the borrower. This problem often arises as the result of holding excessive debt or some turn of events which changes the level of expected cash flows to be received by the corporation. As a consequence, the firm may have to seek bankruptcy protection to shelter it from its creditors in the case of temporary insolvency, or to shield the creditors when insolvency is final and the corporation has to be liquidated.

There is an 'optimal capital structure'. However, that structure might be a moving target because, in addition to balancing the advantages and disadvantages of each form of financing – internal versus external, debt versus equity or any number of hybrids – there is an intrinsic difficulty in forecasting the impact of each managerial action on the market and its feedback on the company. Announcing the acquisition of additional debt might have a negative impact on the market value of the corporation, decreasing the value of the equity, and increasing the debt to equity ratio beyond that for which it was planned. Additional decisions such as the terms and maturity structure of debt, and the allocation of voting control among different classes of equity holders, only complicate matters further.

To make funding decisions is a complex matter, so it is not easy to explain how management goes about making capital structure choices and how collective thinking on this subject has evolved through time. Nevertheless, various schools of thought have helped us think about this question. For example, there are frictionless market theories, where individuals and firms can buy and sell securities without incurring transaction costs. In addition, costly transaction theories explain choices in scenarios where transaction cost do exist.

The theories of capital structure that we can group under the heading of 'frictionless markets' use personal and corporate taxes to explain the marginal benefits and costs associated with debt financing. The conclusion of these proposals is that the optimal structure of a firm would be a function of those tax credits. In practice, however, companies with extremely high levels of debt in their capital structures are not that common. Even during leveraged buyouts it is difficult to find cases where debt approaches more than 80 or 90 per cent of the funding sources. It is therefore obvious that other factors, in addition to taxes, must be influencing the corporation's determination of its optimal capital structure. These other variables are considered under the 'frictions or costly transaction theories scenario' where, in addition to taxes, there are bankruptcy, asymmetric information and various types of agency costs.

In this chapter, all capital structure theories come together. However, our review will look at the subject from the point of view of decision-making. Here we will keep in mind that corporations are concerned with having quick access to adequate financing at a 'reasonable' cost, and with keeping financial flexibility to allow for future corporate growth. Furthermore, given that transaction costs and corporate and personal taxes currently exist, and that relations between corporations and their stakeholders are sensitive, management will have to pay attention to a myriad of variables, including the characteristics of the different financial instruments, their effect on governance issues, stakeholders' expectations, and the impact of the 'market's sentiment' in corporate value.

The classical theories of capital structure can be visualized in terms of the pie example used by Miller and Modigliani[1] (M&M). The overall question is to find the right proportions of debt and equity to fund a fixed amount of operating cash flow, or the corporate assets that supported it. In their 1958 work, M&M proposed that under certain conditions, the market value of any firm is independent of its capital structure. Intuitively, the idea is that the company's physical assets are the sole creators of value. Reshuffling the financing of these assets does not add value because it does not change the cash flows themselves. In this instance, the cash flows M&M are talking about are those available for distribution to the owners and creditors, that is, earnings after tax and interest expenses.

M&M's work is critical since it shows clearly that the relevance of the funding decision lies in the extent to which this decision affects corporate operations. Another decisive insight of their work was the recognition of the properties of perfect capital markets: no taxes, no transaction costs or frictions, value maximization as the common objective of all decision-makers, and perfect information. Relaxing these conditions was the first path optimal capital structure theory took as it began to develop.

Under the original assumptions of M&M's 1958 paper, the value of the corporation was found by capitalizing the expected return of the firm at the rate appropriate to its risk class: the method of financing was irrelevant. If the corporate tax rate is zero, the cost of capital is independent of capital structure.

However, if governments subsidize interest payments and corporate taxes exist, the cost of capital declines steadily as the proportion of new investment financed with debt increases. The value of the leveraged firm reaches a maximum when there is 100 per cent debt financing. If the firm is financed with both debt and equity, the cost of equity capital increases with higher proportions of debt. This makes sense because increasing financial leverage implies a riskier position for shareholders. As their residual claim on the firm becomes more variable they will require a higher rate of return to compensate them for the additional risk they take. This additional financial risk is incorporated in the cost of equity through the leveraged beta for different debt to equity ratios.

The introduction of personal as well as corporate taxes adds further complexity. Investors purchase financial assets with after-tax income. Therefore, they will compare the returns from their different investment options on an after-tax basis. If the personal income tax on stockholdings is less than the tax on income from bonds, then the before-tax return on bonds has to be high enough, other things being equal, to offset this disadvantage. Otherwise, no investor would want to hold bonds. That is, while it is true that owners of a leveraged corporation are subsidized by the interest deductibility of debt, this advantage can be counterbalanced by the fact that the required interest payments have been 'grossed up' by any differential that bondholders must pay on their interest income. Thus, in equilibrium, taxable debt must be supplied to the point where the before-tax cost of corporate debt equals the rate that would be paid by tax-free institutions, grossed up by the corporate tax rate.

The implications of personal income or capital gains tax differentials are that the gain to leverage may be much smaller than previously thought when focusing on corporate taxes alone. Consequently, the optimal capital structure might be better explained by the tradeoff between a small gain to leverage provided by government subsidies and relatively small costs, such as expected bankruptcy costs. Finally, it implies there is an equilibrium amount of aggregate debt outstanding in the economy that is determined by relative corporate and personal tax rates.

Under M&M's classical theory, different funding alternatives are presented as technical alternative instruments. For example, under certain conditions, debt and equity are equivalent choices. Under the 'relaxed assumptions', more modern view of the classical theory, the optimal mix of debt and equity is found by focusing on the tradeoffs of acquiring additional debt to take advantage of the tax subsidy, and the additional costs of financial distress as the amount of debt grows within the capital structure. This approach to optimal capital structure focuses on the cash flow aspects of debt and equity. However, it does not explore the impact that each form of funding has on the relations among the stakeholders who participate in the dynamics of the business, whether these are shareholders, directors, workers, bankers or customers. What matters most from this point of view is the market equilibrium price, rather than the subjective criteria of each individual investor which is relegated to the objective and impersonal expressed value of the equilibrium price.

Departing from this classical point of view, some researchers began to focus on relaxing the assumptions of perfect information and the common objective of value maximization. For example, Myers[2] (1984) and Williamson[3] (1988) suggest that each financial option affects governance issues differently. While the market is characterized by impersonal relations, inside the firm there are interactions that respond to principles different from those of the market. Williamson shows that debt and equity are aspects of governance. In his opinion they are not financial instruments but different governance structures. For example, the management of shares by businesses offers a greater degree of discretion than the management of debt. For him, agency and transaction cost theories are complementary, given that these costs and relations vary with the financing options. Issuing new equity requires agreement among shareholders, and is in general a process which is different to that of acquiring additional debt by, for example, obtaining a bank loan. If the conditions of a loan are not fulfilled, standard processes and laws regulate the associated economic and legal processes, and these are predefined and relatively homogeneous. However, interaction with shareholders does not follow such clear patterns. Shareholders might react in very different ways depending on how they perceive management performance. Hence, in this view, before opting for a specific form of financing the management team will evaluate the conditions of governance which follow from all the available options.

In 1984, Myers noted that firms prefer internal sources of funds to external, and that firms adapt their dividend payout policies to reflect anticipated investment opportunities. If a firm's internally generated cash flow is greater than its investment outlays, it first pays off debt, or invests in cash or marketable securities. If the surplus persists, the firm may gradually increase its target payout ratio. On the other hand, if internally generated cash flow is less than outgoings, the firm first draws down its cash balance and marketable securities portfolio. If external financing is required, firms issue the safest security first. They start with debt, then hybrids such as convertible bonds and then equity as the last resort. Myers (1984) called this view of firm's financing decision the 'pecking order theory'.

This theory suggests there is a hierarchic order in the financial selection made by firms wanting to embark on new capital projects. Some of the tenets of this theory are: (1) there is no target debt/equity mix, (2) there are two types of equity, internal and external, and (3) each firm's debt/equity financing mix reflects its cumulative requirements for external financing. The firm's financing mix is therefore a reflection of the company's profitability, dividend policy and investment opportunities through time. The pecking order theory describes observed corporate financing practice, but it does not explain why such policy is optimal or desirable. In this regard, two types of capital structure theories have been offered: 'managerial capitalism' and 'transaction costs'.

The managerial capitalism explanation is based on the idea that corporations are managed by professionals who work as the stockholders' agents. The theory suggests that there is a divergence of interest between the owners and these agents, who might not always act in accordance with the goal of maximizing shareholder wealth. For example, management might not use external financing, in order to avoid the discipline of the marketplace.

In this framework, Jensen and Meckling[4] (1976) introduced the concept of 'agency costs': a type of transaction cost associated with the corporate form of organization. Their paper provided support for the idea that firms prefer internal over external investment financing. Jensen and Meckling used the agency costs incurred in the corporate form of organization to argue for an optimal mix of internal and external financing. In a nutshell, their idea was that if the owner and manager are the same person, the decision to engage in on-the-job consumption of perks is consistent with owner utility maximization. If the firm is financed 50 per cent with debt and 50 per cent with equity (owner/manager), the owner-manager can consume perks, realizing 100 per cent of the benefits while bearing 50 per cent of the costs. The higher the proportion of external financing, the greater the manager's incentive to engage in perk consumption. Owners will try to monitor agents, but since this is costly, some perk consumption is inevitable. Based on this line of reasoning, there is a tradeoff between the benefits of utilizing external financing and the added costs of agency.

The preference for internal equity financing is also consistent with the asymmetric information hypothesis, because managers, in seeking to maximize the owner's wealth, will retain earnings only when doing so will further that goal. The point here is that the presence of asymmetric information, combined with a shareholder wealth-maximizing management team, establishes a preference for debt over equity financing, which completes the pecking order story: internal equity financing is preferred over external equity or debt, and debt is preferred to equity when external financing is utilized.

A second explanation for the pecking order theory is based on transaction costs. For example, earnings retention does not incur any transaction costs, unlike the issuing of debt and equity securities. One of the reasons proposed to explain these differences in issuing costs is the 'asymmetric information' hypothesis. This hypothesis assumes that insiders within the firm have superior information to outsiders, and therefore that if management is acting in the best interests of the firm's owners, they will offer to sell new equity shares only when they feel the market price is favourable to the present owners. If management feels the firm's shares are undervalued, they will not issue new stock. However, if investors sense that the firm's management is maximizing the owners' wealth, they will view the new stock issue as a signal that the firm's shares are overvalued in the marketplace. The case for the issuance of bonds is different, since a debt issue announcement could be interpreted as a sign that the firm believes its shares are undervalued. This signal mechanism can be exploited by management, who can use financial policy decisions to convey information to the market.

The first application of signalling in finance theory was presented in 1977 when Ross[5] constructed a capital structure theory based on the 'signalling of information' description of the manager's funding decision. The hypothesis proposes that implicit in M&M's irrelevancy proposition is the assumption that the market *knows* the return stream of the firm, and evaluates this stream to set the market value of the firm. Thus, what is valued in the marketplace is the *perceived* future stream of returns for the firm. This creates an opportunity to affect the market's perception by changes in capital structure. Managers, who have access to information about the firm's expected cash flows, will send out signals about the firm's future if they have the proper incentive to do so. Through these announcements, the firm alters its perceived risk class, though the actual risk class remains unchanged. However, to affect the market the signal has to be believable. Ross proposed that without some connection between management's compensation and the firm's true financial prospects, the signal would be weak and not valid.

In line with the ideas of Ross, Myers and Majluf[6] (1984) presented a signalling model that combines investment and financing decisions. Managers, better than anyone else, are in a position to know the 'true' value of the firm and of any future projects that it might undertake. When the firm has no new projects and the market knows it, issuing new equity is an unambiguous financial signal that the market could use to discover the insider information held by managers. When positive NPV projects are financed with equity issues, the signal becomes mixed.

Myers and Majluf noted that asymmetric information could result in firms passing up positive NPV projects. The reason is that the underpricing needed to get the project financed via a public security offering could outweigh its positive NPV. The loss of the positive NPV project is avoided if internally generated funds are used, but if the project's NPV is large enough to induce the firm to issue outside securities, debt will be the firm's choice. However, Myers and Majluf suggest that the information asymmetry problem is resolved if the firm uses its available liquid assets to finance positive NPV projects. This may therefore be a good reason for carrying excess liquid assets.

Managers will choose to send unambiguous signals about the firm's future if they have the proper incentive to do so. The incentive-signalling approach suggests that management might choose real financial variables, such as financial leverage, as the means of sending unambiguous signals to the public about the future performance of the firm. These signals cannot be mimicked by unsuccessful firms because such firms do not have sufficient cash flow to back them up, and because managers have incentives to tell the truth.

There are several 'debt capacity' theories that provide arguments for the limitation of debt issuance. The first and second have already been mentioned: the problem of information asymmetry, and the fact that partial ownership of the firm by the owner-manager can motivate him to seek an excessive number of perks. The third is the proposal that existence of debt financing under limited liability incites stockholders to accept suboptimal and high-risk projects. This will be done by transferring wealth from bondholders to stockholders. The idea is that management may stand to lose more than shareholders in the event of the firm's failure. To the extent that the firm's owners are unable to force their financial structure preferences on management policies, management may choose to use less financial leverage than the owners would desire and/or creditors supply. Some arguments supporting the limited use of debt financing have been built on the existence of the costs of financial distress. If debt financing increases, the risk of financial distress increases too, and if there are significant costs associated with financial distress and failure, the limited use of debt financing can be justified. The theory of debt capacity argues that at times this is the strongest constraint on a firm's borrowing, forcing owners to maintain a significant stake in its operations and thereby align their incentives with the creditors' interests. If the owners are the residual claimants on the firm's earnings but have little of their own funds invested, they will be motivated to make risky investments with the creditors' funds. Thus creditors have good reason to limit the company's use of debt funds.

Empirical evidence

In practice, firms do engage in active capital structure management. This can be seen by looking at cross-sectional differences in capital structures across firms and industries. Firms also differ in the maturity structure of their debt and use financial contracts involving call provisions, convertibility features, sinking funds and warrants.

Studies of firm's financial structures find a link between financial structure and industry class. While statistically significant, the explanatory power of these models is low, leaving much of the variation in financial structure unexplained by whatever variable (s) are being proxied by industry class. Also, pairwise comparisons of industry financial ratios have shown insignificant differences: that is, only some industry financial ratios differ. Furthermore, some studies have disclosed the fact that industry classification actually serves as a proxy for a number of fundamental factors related to the firm's size, earnings volatility, bankruptcy costs and asset growth.

There are two broad approaches to empirical tests of capital structure. The first one are cross-sectional studies that attempt to explain observed financial leverage as a function of, for example, the firm's tax rate, its non-debt tax shields, its potential for agency costs, its operating leverage, its systematic risk. The incremental impact of each of these variables on financial leverage can help to separate the competing theories of optimal capital structure. The second approach uses time series data, looking at the relationship between changes in leverage and simultaneous changes in the value of debt and equity on the announcement date of a leverage-changing event.

One recent cross-sectional study regressed leverage against earnings volatility as a proxy for bankruptcy risk, the ratio of depreciation plus investment tax credits to earnings as a proxy for non-debt tax shields, and the ratio of advertising plus research and development expenditures to net sales as a proxy for non-collateralizable assets. The first and third variables were significantly negative, suggesting that bankruptcy costs and collateral are important; but the second variable was significantly positive, seeming to be inconsistent with debt as a tax shield.

With respect to time series studies, generally speaking, leverage-increasing exchange offers have significant positive announcement effects. Exchanges of debt-for-debt have no significant effect on shareholders' wealth, and leverage-decreasing exchange offers have a significant negative effect. Seasoned equity issues are interpreted as bad news by the marketplace, with significantly negative announcement date effects on equity prices. Firms will resort to equity issues only as a last resort. Stock repurchases are at the opposite end of the spectrum. They increase leverage and they are interpreted as favourable signals about the future prospects of the firm.

All leverage-decreasing events have negative announcement effects, and all leverage-increasing events have positive announcement effects. The majority of events with no leverage change had insignificant announcement effects. Announcement with favourable (unfavourable) implications for the future cash flows of the firm such as investment increases (decreases) and dividend increases (decreases) were accompanied by significant positive (negative) effects on shareholders' wealth.

In 1980 DeAngelo and Masulis[7] devised a model to explain corporate leverage. Their hypothesis was that financial structures will be affected by changes in the costs of leverage (for example, reorganization), the corporate tax rate and the investment tax shield. Since there have been many changes in the tax code one would expect to see an equivalent pattern of volatility in corporate financing practice, but the empirical findings are not entirely clear.

With reference to their cross-sectional predictions, DeAngelo and Masulis also proposed that differential investment tax shields and marginal costs of leverage will induce firms to hold different optimal capital structures. Specifically, they point out evidence of differences in investment tax shields across industries proposing that, given the variation in available tax credits across industries, an inverse relationship between capital structure and investment tax credits should be expected. However, other studies contradict this idea. It does appear that tax shields and capital structures differ across industries, but the proposed negative association has not been found.

Other studies have made the following findings: 1) debt levels are negatively related to the uniqueness of a corporation's line of business, 2) transaction costs are a key determinant of the corporation's capital structure (for example, short-term debt ratios are inversely related to firm size), 3) support for an effect on debt ratios arising from non-debt tax shields, earnings volatility, collateral value, and future growth, and a negative correlation between insiders' holding of stock and the firm's debt ratio. Due to inconclusive findings with low explanatory power, the consensus is that the determinants of a firm's capital structure are still subject to debate and require further empirical investigation.

During 1958 and 1966 M&M studied the relationship between a firm's value and its capital structure. In the 1958 paper, M&M used a cross-sectional regression of the estimated cost of capital and the debt/total assets ratio for a sample of 42 oil companies and 43 electricity utilities. This analysis made no significant findings about the relationship between these variables. In a second paper, M&M analyzed the same question by breaking down the value of the firm into four components: the capitalized value of the firm's existing assets, its growth potential, its size, and its tax subsidy on debt. On this occasion M&M found that the existing assets accounted for 68 –75 per cent of the firm's value, growth potential for 22–4 per cent, firm size (inversely correlated with firm value) for 1–2 per cent, and the interest tax shield for 2–10 per cent. Overall this work supports the idea that debt financing creates value through the interest tax subsidy.

In 1983 Masulis[8] analyzed the impact of 133 corporate exchange offers on equity value. Corporate exchange offers involve the exchange of one type of security for another. The significance of such transactions lies in the fact that no cash changes hands, so they provide an opportunity to analyze the impact of a pure financial transaction on corporate value. Masulis showed that: 1) increases in leverage lead to increases in equity value, 2) the value of nonconvertible senior securities is inversely related to changes in financial leverage, 3) the magnitude of the change in value of nonconvertible senior securities is significant and substantially greater where the new issue is of equal or greater seniority, 4) the corporation's value changes with the amount of financial leverage used, and 5) estimates of the lower bound of the impact of a $1 change in the level of debt on firm value are between $0.23 and $0.45. The evidence presented by Masulis is consistent with the notions that taxes provide an incentive for debt financing, that there is a positive debt level information effect and that there is a leverage-induced wealth transfer across security classes.

Several authors have suggested that expected bankruptcy costs restrict corporate use of debt financing. For example, Haugen and Senbet[9] (1978) argued that as long as there are significant costs related to bankruptcy, there is an incentive for voluntary reorganization to avoid them. In addition, they also proposed that, although default on a debt obligation may not lead to formal bankruptcy or informal reorganization it may provide signals to prospective investors about the true financial condition of the firm, resulting in a devaluation of the firm's shares. Therefore, there may be a cost in the use of financial leverage in a world of asymmetric information, which may increase the likelihood that management will be forced to reveal 'unpleasant' information that would otherwise go unrecognized by investors.

How to estimate the optimal capital structure

In this section we provide a series of numerical examples to show the impact of taxes on capital structure decision-making. We also present a step-by-step example of how to estimate the optimal capital structure of a company under simplifying assumptions. Let us start by analyzing the adage 'debt has tax advantages'.

Throughout the first chapters of this book – particularly when talking about the company's beta – we explained the difference between operating risk and financial risk. To refresh our memories, we shall briefly recall that operating risk can be thought of as the risk of the assets of the company, that is, the risk arising from the firm's operations which can be measured by the ratio of changes in EBIT with respect to changes in revenues. Financial risk, in contrast, is associated with the use of leverage or, more generally, with any form of financing of the company that can be measured by calculating the change in net earnings with respect to changes in EBIT.

EBIT depends solely on the capacity of the company's assets to generate revenues, and the associated operational costs. On the other hand, net earnings reflect, in addition, the degree of leverage that the company carries. As debt is added to the capital structure, the differences between EBIT and net income are amplified. Hence, for any given level of operating risk, an increase in financial returns achieved by increasing leverage is always linked to an increased risk to those returns. This additional risk comes from the demands that debt repayment imposes on corporate cash flows that are sunk and fixed, independent of the level of operations the company is carrying out at any given time.

To illustrate these concepts let us assume we have two equal land-transportation companies. The first is solely financed with equity, while the second has debt in its capital structure. A general strike keeps the fleets of both firms inactive for a month. While both corporations may incur the same operational expenditures, the leveraged company will also have to attend to debt payments, subjecting itself to additional liquidity pressures. Hence, other things being equal, the second company will be at a greater risk of bankruptcy.

The graph below shows, for each level of EBIT, the earnings per share (EPS) that would need to be obtained depending on whether the funds were raised by issuing debt (dotted line) or equity (solid line). The unequal convenience of raising debt can be observed by looking at the bottom left-hand corner of the graph, where leveraging does not increase EPS beyond that which could be achieved through equity.

The situation we are discussing can be better analyzed by looking at the example shown in Table 6.1. The first column of the table shows six different EBIT levels. The second column shows earnings per share and return on equity information for each of the mentioned EBIT levels for the scenario where the company is financed with equity. The third column provides equivalent information for the scenario where the company chooses a mid of the debt and equity options the equity option. As we can see, 'all equity' financing is the superior choice for the lowest EBIT level and is also as good as the debt option for the second level. However, thereafter, the mixture of debt and equity provides superior earnings per share and return on equity numbers than the 'all equity' alternative.

In the light of the transportation company example, and Figure 6.1 and Table 6.1, we must wonder whether we should add debt to our capital structure. We realize that leveraging does not always have the same effect regardless of the EBIT the firm might be able to achieve. For example, if we expect that this figure will be above the threshold, shareholders are better off if the firm adds debt into their capital structure, but the opposite would be true if the firm did not reach the EBIT threshold. We might therefore want to consider how certain we are of our predictions before deciding which would be the better capital

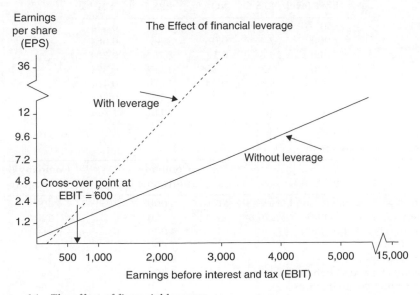

Figure 6.1   The effect of financial leverage

structure to use. If we are confident in our predictions, and if the predicted figure is above the threshold, debt would improve the shareholder's situation. However, if we are not that confident, the equity alternative might be the better choice.

Let us look at an example. Companies A and B run identical operations. The only difference between them is that company A is unleveraged, while company B is leveraged to the extent of $4,000, paying six per cent. The comparison of otherwise equal companies shows how the capital structure adds value to the firm that takes advantage of the tax deductability of interest payments.

Table 6.2 shows how both companies have the same EBIT. However, company B pays $96 less in taxes than company A, because B can deduct as a cost within the Income Statement $240 in interest payments. Other things being equal, and disregarding any serious probability of default, the implication of the example is that B is worth $96 more than A. If B keeps this capital structure though time, the cash flows generated by the firm's choice of capital structure could be discounted by the appropriate rate and treated as an annuity.

Table 6.3 presents an all-equity company that is analyzing the impact of acquiring $5,000 of additional funds, either in the form of debt or as additional equity. The assumptions are that the $4,000 EBIT does not change after the new funds are gathered, the interest paid on debt is 6 per cent, and the

Table 6.1   EPS and ROE

	Equity		Debt and equity	
EBIT level	EPS $	ROE %	EPS $	ROE %
500	1.2	0.03	0.96	0.024
1,000	2.4	0.06	3.36	0.084
2,000	4.8	0.12	8.16	0.204
3,000	7.2	0.18	12.96	0.324
4,000	9.6	0.24	17.76	0.444
5,000	12	0.3	22.56	0.564
15,000	36	0.9	70.56	1.764

Table 6.2   Tax savings

	Company A (unleveraged)	Company B (leveraged)
Earnings before interest and taxes EBIT ($)	4,000	4,000
Interest (zero in A, $4,000 @ 6% in B)	0	240
Earnings Before Tax (EBT)	4,000	3,760
Tax (40%)	1,600	1,504
Net Earnings	2,400	2,256
Bondholder and shareholder earnings	2,400	2,496
Tax savings due to interest	0	96

corporate tax rate is 40 per cent. The second column presents the current situation and the third and fourth the two alternative financing alternatives.

As shown in the table, prior to the new issue, the firm had an EPS of $9.60 and a ROE of 24 per cent. If the capital increase is done through equity, both these ratios are reduced because we have increased the number of shares and the equity investment. If debt is used, the decrease in both ratios is much smaller as the net earnings is reduced only by the increased interest payment. Compared to equity, additional debt has a positive impact in terms of EPS and ROE. In Table 6.4 we extend the example by assuming these monies will be generating a return of 15 per cent of the amount invested.

This example shows that both EPS and ROE are maximized when using debt instead of equity. However, as indicated earlier, this might not always be the case.

Table 6.3 EPS and ROE additional equity versus additional debt scenario

	Current	Option additional equity	Option additional debt
Equity	10,000	15,000	10,000
Debt	0	0	5,000
Number of shares	250	375	250
Share price	40	40	40
EBIT	4,000	4,000	4,000
Kd (6%)	0	0	300
EBT	4,000	4,000	3,700
Corporate tax (40%)	1,600	1,600	1,480
Net earnings	2,400	2,400	2,220
Earnings per share (EPS)	9.6	6.4	8.88
Return on equity (ROE)	0.24	0.16	0.222

Table 6.4 EPS and ROE additional equity versus additional debt scenario

	Current	Option additional equity	Option additional debt
Equity	10,000	15,000	10,000
Debt	0	0	5,000
Number of shares	250	375	250
Share price	40	40	40
EBIT	4,000	4600	4,600
Kd (6%)	0	0	300
EBT	4,000	4600	4,300
Corporate tax (40%)	1,600	1840	1,720
Net earnings	2,400	2760	2,580
Earnings per share (EPS)	9.6	7.36	10.32
Return on equity (ROE)	0.24	0.184	0.258

Estimating the optimal capital structure: Working through the process, step by step

We have examined how each source of financial capital constrains the corporations that acquire it. The optimal capital structure exists when the company is financed by the optimal mix of debt and equity. The mix can be calculated in numerical terms, but once this numerical optimum is found, its implications should be reviewed. The steps described below will help the reader to understand the process. We provide a detailed description of how to use the model in order to optimize the value of the company exclusively through changes in the capital structure. We therefore work through a static situation, in which the only variables that change are those pertaining to the cost of capital. This simplification allows us to focus on the effects and interactions that increases in debt have on the risk of the company through their effect on the cost of debt, equity and the effective tax rate. The steps are:

1. Estimate the current value of the company and expected future cash flows
2. Estimate the cost of debt for the various leverage scenarios
3. Estimate the cost of equity for the different leverage scenarios
4. Estimate the weighted average cost of capital for each leverage scenario
5. Estimate the value of the company for all leverage scenarios.

1. First step: estimate the current value of the company and expected future cash flows

The first step in this process is to gather the necessary data, and get a clear picture of the current financial statements and market values that we need in order to value the firm. In what follows, it helps to use a spreadsheet, which enables us to interconnect cells so that the impact of changes in the assumptions can be automatically evaluated without having to rework each part of the process manually. We provide examples of what these spreadsheets would look like throughout the exercise.

Our project begins by estimating the firm's free cash flows: this will enable us to evaluate the impact of the capital structure changes on the company's value. We are using the previously stated assumptions of a constant EBIT of $4,000, an annual amortization of fixed assets of $500 which is equal to the firm's new investments, and a tax rate of 40 per cent of the company's profits. In addition, the beta of the company is 1, the risk-free rate 5 per cent, and the market risk premium 7 per cent. With all these data we can easily follow the contents in each of the cells of the Table 6.5 below for the initial 'no debt' scenario.

2. Second step: estimate the cost of debt for the various levels of possible leverage in the capital structure

Table 6.7 is an example of the type of table we can use to assist us with the appropriate estimates in this step. In addition to the column headings we show

Table 6.5   Estimating the firm's free cash flow

EBIT	4,000
EBIT (1–t)	2,400
+ Amortization	500
– Capital investment	500
Free cash flow	2,400
Tax rate	0.4
Times interest earned	N/A (no debt)
Leveraged beta	N/A (no debt)
Unleveraged beta	1
Risk-free rate	0.05
Risk premium	0.07
Equity market value	20,000
Debt market value	0
Corporation market value	20,000
Debt rating	–
Kd before tax	Rf + Premium
Kd after tax	Kd (1–tax)
Ke, current	0.12
E/D+E	100%
WACC, current	12%

11 rows, one for each piece of data needed in the estimates. We have only provided three main columns: the first and last with the name and description of the variables required and the second split to show four different debt scenarios (zero, ten, forty and eighty per cent respectively). In this instance, to simplify matters we only show these leverage scenarios; in practice we would add an additional column for each level of debt that should be analyzed.

In the table, the first row shows the proportion of debt within the capital structure of the company. Note that D and E, the market values for the debt and equity of the company, must add up to the value of the company. If we are working with percentages, D and E must add up to 100.

The second row shows the value of the company at each of the specified levels of debt. This value is calculated as the result of the free cash flow available to the firm discounted by the weighted average cost of capital. For clarity, the estimate is done on a separate table and copied here.

The third row shows the debt to equity ratio. In the first scenario this would be 0/100 for zero per cent debt. As debt is added to the capital structure the ratio changes. For example, in the 40 per cent debt scenario the ratio would be 40/60 or 0.667.

The fourth row shows the market value of the corporate debt. If we know the value of the company we just need to multiply this value by the percentage of debt within the capital structure.

Table 6.6   Interest coverage ratio and rating

Interest coverage		Rating	Premium over risk-free rate (%)
from	to		
- ∞	0.499999	D	15.16
0.5	0.799999	C	12.66
0.8	0.999999	CC	10.66
1	1.249999	CCC	9.16
1.25	1.999999	B-	7.41
2	2.499999	B	7.16
2.5	2.999999	B+	5.16
3	3.499999	BB	4.16
3.5	4.499999	BBB	3.36
4.5	5.999999	A-	2.86
6	7.499999	A	2.36
7.5	9.499999	A+	2.06
9.5	14.499999	AA	1.76
14.5	+ ∞	AAA	1.36

Source: Standard & Poor's, June 1997.

The next row contains the EBIT. We have made the assumption that our revenues are not a function of the capital structure of the company. Hence this figure is constant through all levels of debt.

The sixth row shows the dollar value of the interest. This is estimated by multiplying the total amount of debt by its cost (four rows below).

The seventh row shows the interest coverage ratio. This ratio tells us how many times we can cover the interest expense with the EBIT shown two rows above, so this figure is given by dividing the EBIT by the interest expense.

The debt rating in the following row is obtained by comparing our interest coverage ratio with the ratings provided by different companies such as Standard and Poor's, Moody's, and Fitch. An example of data providing risk premiums on long-term bonds as a function of the interest coverage rate of large industrial firms published by Standard & Poor's in June 1997 is presented in Table 6.6. Remember that the rating is solely an assessment of the risk that the company will default on its payment obligations. Since in the first scenario of zero per cent debt we can cover our interest expense more than three hundred times in the original scenario, our rating for this level of debt (zero) is AAA. The rating changes as we move from the current zero-debt scenario through the different debt to equity mixes.

The interest rate charged would be the result of adding the risk-free rate and the risk premium assigned to each rating. In our example, we have assumed that a AAA company will be paying 1.36 per cent above the risk-free rate which we took as the bond market ten-year risk-free rate (5 per cent in the example). The increase in the firm's debt to equity ratio affects the its debt (along with its equity) risk, given the greater probability of default. When we add debt into our capital structure example, this increased risk will be shown in lower ratings and higher cost of debt (and also equity).

The last two rows show the effective tax rate and the cost of the debt after the tax savings are realized. If our earnings are negative, our effective tax rate will be below the stated 40 per cent. For example, if our EBIT is $4,000 and our interest expenses are $4,500, we will not be able to fully take advantage of the tax deductability of the interest expense. We therefore need to calculate the effective tax rate, which is the rate we should use in the estimate of the cost of debt.

Therefore, as long as our EBIT is equal to or greater than the interest expense, our fiscal savings will be 40 per cent. When our interest expenses are above our EBIT we can only deduct interest up to the EBIT. For example, assume that once we reach a capital structure where 90 per cent of the assets are financed by debt, our interest expenses reach $4,500. Given that we will only make fiscal savings up to the EBIT level, our savings will be less than 40 per cent and our cost of debt will increase. In our case, the EBIT is $4,000, and the interest expense is $4,500. Our new effective tax rate is no longer 40 per cent but 35.5 per cent. This is calculated by dividing the maximum fiscal savings we could obtain (EBIT*40 per cent) by the interest expense. Local tax norms might allow the company to recover this difference by charging retrospectively or sending it as a tax credit to future fiscal years.

In summary, the cost of debt can be determined as follows:

a. Prepare the financial statements of the company and calculate the main financial ratios, the WACC and the free cash flow.
b. Estimate the value of the company.
c. Determine the value of its debt for each level of leverage.
d. Determine the total interest payable and the financial ratios of the company for each of the new debt to equity ratios.
e. Use information from one of the rating agencies to determine the rating for each interest coverage ratio. Then associate this ratio with the interest rate premium that must be paid over the risk-free rate.
f. Be aware of negative income and its effect on the effective tax rate.
g. Estimate the cost of the debt after tax for each level of leverage.

Note that there are two circularities in the model. First, the interest rate is needed to calculate the interest coverage ratio and the interest coverage ratio is needed to calculate the interest rate. To solve this problem it is necessary to perform iterations until the interest rate and the interest coverage rate are consistent. Second, the value of the company is needed in order to estimate the value of the debt in currency, and in order to estimate the value of the company you need the value of the debt. This problem has also been solved by using iterations.

Table 6.7   Company value and leverage

	Level of debt				Explanation
Leverage scenario	0%	10%	40%	80%	D/D+E
Business value	20,000	20,199	20,397	18,638	For each level of debt
D/E	0.00	0.11	0.667	4	Debt to equity ratio
Market value of debt	0.00	2,020	8,158	14,911	[D/D+E] * Business value
EBIT	4,000	4,000	4,000	4,000	Independent of capital structure
Monetary interest value	0.00	128	600	1,515	Cost of debt * dollar amount of debt
Interest coverage ratio	–	31.14	6.66	2.64	EBIT/Interest expenditures
Debt rating	AAA	AAA	A	B+	For each coverage level
Interest rate	6.36%	6.36%	7.36%	10.16%	For each rating
Effective tax rate	40%	40%	40%	40%	Could change for various debt levels
Cost of debt after taxes	3.82%	3.82%	4.42%	6.10%	Kd (1- effective tax rate)

3. Third step: estimate the cost of equity for various levels of debt.

Again we provide a table to help us with our estimations through the example.

Table 6.8 has four columns. The first two show the percentage of debt within the capital structure and the debt to equity ratio. These have already been used in the second step, so we can just copy them. In the third and fourth columns we estimate the beta and the cost of equity for each level of debt. We have only included four rows, since this is enough for practising the estimates and observing the increasing impact of additional debt on the beta. The last column provides the cost of equity calculated using the CAPM. For this we have used the risk-free rate and the market risk premium provided at the top of the table. In summary, the steps for calculating the cost of equity with the CAPM for each level of debt are:

a. Estimate the leveraged beta of the firm for each level of debt. As described in earlier chapters, this estimate can be done in several ways. For example, the beta of an unlisted company can be estimated by finding the average of the unleveraged betas of similar listed companies and leveraging it again for the different levels of debt. If the company is listed we can use its own beta, again by unleveraging and leveraging it to obtain a number for each debt level. In this example, we have used the following formula:

$\beta_u = \beta_L /\{1+ (D/E)\}$
$\beta_L = \beta_u * \{1+ (D/E)\}$

Table 6.8 Estimate the cost of equity – CAPM

Risk-free rate 5%,
Market risk premium 7%

D/D+E	D/E	Beta	r_e
0%	0%	1.00	12.00%
10%	11.11%	1.11	12.78%
40%	66.67%	1.67	16.67%
...			
80%	400.00%	5.00	40.00%

Table 6.9 WACC and company value for different debt levels

D/(D+E) (%)	D/E (%)	r_e (%)	r_d (%)	WACC(r_a) (%)
0	0	12.00	0.00	12.00
10	11	12.78	3.82	11.88
40	67	16.67	4.24	11.77
80	400	40.00	6.10	12.88

The unleveraged beta of our example is 1. We use this beta to evaluate the next bracket where we have a ten per cent level of debt as follows: $\beta_L = \beta_u * \{1+ (D/E)\}$; $1.11 = 1.00 * \{1+ (10/90)\}$. If we are estimating the beta for 40 per cent leverage then: $\beta_L = \beta_u * \{1+ (D/E)\}$; $1.67 = 1.00 * \{1+ (40/60)\}$. As additional debt is added into the capital structure and the financial risk increases, the beta of the firm will rise, making the equity more expensive.

b. Lastly we estimate the CAPM using the given data and a different leveraged beta for each level of debt. As you recall, the CAPM formula requires the risk-free rate and the risk premium (RP) which are exogenous and fixed: Ke = Rf + β_L * RP. With the numbers in Table 6.8 in the first no-debt scenario, the current cost of equity will be: 5 per cent + 1.00 (7 per cent) = 12 per cent, and for the ten and 40 per cent level of debt: 5 per cent + 1.11(7 per cent) = 12.78 per cent and 5 per cent + 1.67 (7 per cent) = 16.67 per cent respectively.

4. Fourth step: estimate the weighted average cost of capital for various levels of debt.

Having estimated the cost of equity and the cost of debt for each scenario we can now estimate the weighted average cost of capital for each debt to equity ratio. The level of debt which minimizes the weighted average cost of capital is the optimal debt level and therefore that which maximizes the value of the firm (Table 6.9).

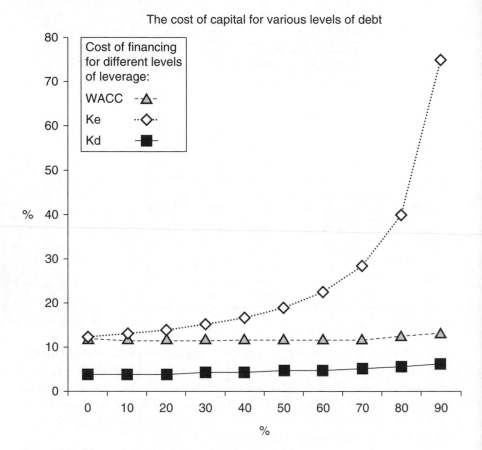

Figure 6.2   The cost of capital for various levels of debt

Applying the methods described in this note any company can judge whether it is possible to increase its value by modifying its capital structure or whether it has already reached its optimal capital structure.

5. Fifth step: estimate the value of the company for all debt levels.

This is accomplished by using the weighted average cost of capital calculated for each level of debt to discount the cash flows of the company. In our example, the cash flows are considered independently of the capital structure so they do not change with the different levels of debt.

Example for our company MACMA

The Income Statement of MACMA looks like this:

	(000)
Revenues	$14,100
-Operating expenses	$ 9,600
Gross earnings	**$4,500**
-Amortization	$ 500
EBIT	**$4,000**
-Interest expense	$0
EBT	**$4,000**

Next year's income statement and statements for the foreseeable future will resemble the above. In addition, capital expenditures are planned to reach $500 million per year. The market value of the company's equity is $20,000 million and the market value of its debt $0 million. Thus, since currently debt is not being used to finance long-term assets, the total value of the corporation is $20,000 million.

Based on MACMA's income statement we can estimate the current free cash flow:

EBIT *(1-t)	$2,400
+Amortization/deprecia-tion	$500
−Capital expenditures	−$500
FREE CASH FLOW	**$2,400**

If we assume that MACMA's free cash flow will not change in the future, we can estimate the implicit rate of growth using Gordon's formula. Recall that:

$$PV_{MACMA}= FCF * (1+g)$$

$$(WACC-g)$$

By replacing the variables by the known MACMA values (for example, the current value of MACMA is $20,000 million, the FCF $2,400), using the formula above the implicit growth g of MACMA is zero. This assumption simplifies our example, but this is not a very likely scenario. The growth rate would usually at least come near to the inflation rate.

Assuming that this rate of growth in free cash flow is maintained regardless of MACMA's capital structure, we can estimate its value for each level of debt. The optimal ratio of debt to equity is determined by taking on increasing amounts

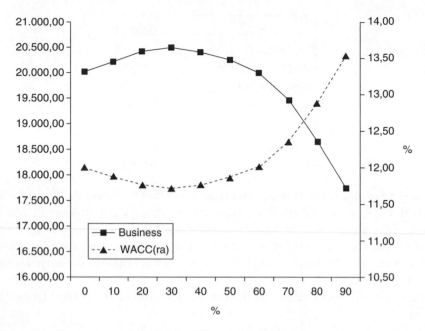

Figure 6.3   Firm value and WACC for different leverage levels

of debt until the marginal gain from leverage is equal to the marginal expected loss from bankruptcy costs. As the proportion of debt in the capital structure increases, the risks to shareholders and lenders also increase. This results in a U-shaped weighted average cost of capital and an optimal capital structure.

The optimal capital structure minimizes the weighted average cost of capital and maximizes the value of the firm. In Figure 6.3 we can see that this happens when the firm incorporates 30 per cent of debt into the capital structure. At this level the company would go from a value of $20,000 million to $20,483 million, the cost of equity would be 15 per cent, the cost of debt 4.06 per cent and the WACC 11.72 per cent.

Lastly, it is necessary to examine the impact of the new financial structure on the share price.

Let us assume that to effect the change in the capital structure from the initial scenario of zero per cent debt to the optimal of 30 per cent, the company issues bonds and buys back shares with the proceeds. The sequence of events is as follows:

- The company announces its intention to modify its long-term capital structure.
- The share price changes to reflect the new anticipated value of the company.
- The company issues debt and buys back shares at the new price.

Table 6.10   Optimal capital structure

	Current	Optimal
D/D+E	0%	30%
Beta	1	1.429
Cost of equity (Ke)	12.00%	15.00%
Interest rate (after tax)	3.82%	4.06%
WACC	12.00%	11.72%
Value of equity	$20,000	$14,338
Value of debt	–	$6,145
Value of company	$20,000	$20,483
Number of shares	20,000	14,000
Shares bought back	–	6,000
Price per share	$1.00	$1.024

As summarized in Table 6.10 currently MACMA has 20,000 million shares outstanding at a price of $1 per share. As a result of the change in financial structure the value of the company increases from $20,000 million to $20,483 million, and the share price rises from $1 to $1.024. These figures can be calculated by finding the difference between the current value of the firm and its value under the new structure. To this difference we add the old share value and divide the total amount by the number of shares originally outstanding (($1+$483) / 20,000).

If the value of the company with 30 per cent debt is $20,483 million, the value of its equity is $14,338 million, given that it issues $6,145 million in debt (the market value of the debt at this level). With these proceeds it repurchases 6,000 shares. After the operation, the number of shares outstanding will be 14,000 million.

How to effect changes in capital structure

The optimal capital structure of a corporation is determined by calculating the mix of debt and equity which maximizes its value. As we have just shown, this mix can be calculated numerically by simply calculating the tradeoffs which result from taking advantage of the tax deductability of the interest expense and the higher cost of this debt and the equity of the corporation as leverage is added to the structure. However, once this optimum is found, but before implementing any changes, the assumptions and considerations that lie behind the figure will have to be re-evaluated.

Given that each source of financial capital constrains corporations that acquire it, to understand the choices to be made we need to bring together the characteristics of each source of funds, the concepts proposed earlier, and the steps outlined for maximizing the firm's value. As became apparent in our numerical example, the use of debt should be maximized when tax benefits can be derived. If the company's effective tax rate is higher than the company's average, the firm may choose to increase the amount of debt so as to benefit from the tax shield it provides. However, at higher levels of leverage, the tax benefits might erode: the effective tax rate will diminish if interest expenditures are larger than disposable EBIT. Nonetheless, other things being equal, the higher the tax rate, the greater the tax benefits and the more likely the firm is to increase leverage. Debt also provides additional financial discipline. If the links between the company's shareholders and management are weak, the company could increase its level of debt as a means of effecting control. Furthermore, the effects of debt on the relationship among shareholders should also be analyzed.

If income volatility is high, future cash flows will be difficult to assess. Other things being equal, the more unpredictable the future cash flows, the greater the likelihood of insolvency. Two other instances in which lower levels of debt would be advisable are when company assets are intangible and when insolvency costs are high. Thus, when it is difficult to assess future cash flows, when our assets are intangible or when bankruptcy costs are high, we should aim for lower leverage levels.

Management needs to be aware of the impact that new sources of funds might have on the financial situation of the company before any serious proposal can be made and new strategy is implemented. It is therefore important to understand that 'maxims' such as those listed above cannot be our sole guidance in this maze of options.

'Pre-packaged' proposals targeting specific ratios might not work in every economic scenario and public announcements of capital structure changes might be received in various ways by the market, depending on a myriad of circumstances. Strategies which might be perfectly appropriate during a period of low inflation will strangle the firm if inflation is high. On occasions, money might be flooding the market and available to any debtor or, as we say in the period after 2008, funding might dry up to the point that even the most trustworthy firms have difficulty accessing credit. Furthermore, corporate needs and qualifications will be affected by the macro scenario. For example, in a high-inflation low-liquidity setting, it is more expensive to finance both working capital and capital investments, not only because the general level of prices is higher, but also because funding becomes more expensive. This will affect the right-hand side of the balance sheet more than you might think because, for example, when old debt matures it will have to be replaced at current higher rates. In this environment, it is possible that without any action on the part of the firm, ratios, including ratings, will change, making debt even more expensive, particularly short-term debt which is more liable to swing. It is not difficult to imagine that in these types of situations, conflicts can arise between product and operations managers who want to expand their lines, and finance directors, who might not be able to access sufficient capital, or any capital at competitive rates. Hence, once figure for the optimal capital structure is found, it is a good idea to think carefully about the hidden constraints that carrying high levels of leverage under different economic scenarios will impose on the firm.

For example, Piper and Weinhold[10] (1982) suggest that before acquiring high levels of debt, finance executives consider the following questions:

a. Determine the firm's short- and medium-term financial needs, considering both product lines and market strategies. Estimate the length of the needs and whether any projects can be delayed without major loss due to opportunity costs.
b. Enumerate the characteristics of the needs in terms of fixed versus variable rates, prepayment provisions, renegotiation possibilities, likely maturities, currency desirability and so on.
c. For each of the listed needs, verify the current market fund suppliers and re-assess the availability of funds under different economic scenarios.
d. Find out the criteria used by each lender and how these criteria would change under different economic scenarios.
e. Ensure sufficient funding for the most strategic projects, even under the worst conditions.
f. Assess how vulnerable the firm will become under different capital structure scenarios.
g. Gauge how the various capital mixes might affect the relationship between the firm, various lenders and stakeholders.
h. Ensure the strategy is implementable. Include fall-back plans.

When the capital structure is not optimal, answers have been given to all the questions above, and the decision to change the capital structure has been made, a plan must be drawn up in order to implement the restructuring. An example of the decisions to be made include: debt percentage target, speed and manner of the implementation, and vehicle for the exchange (for example, open-market repurchase versus fixed-price).

In our step-by-step example, the optimal debt target was calculated at 30 per cent. Our plan was to effect the change by selling debt and using the proceeds to repurchase equity. However, other options would be available, depending upon the specific firm's circumstances. In considering these alternative options, the first question the company needs to answer is whether the new target capital structure is going to be reached over a long period of time, or immediately.

Companies that can afford to increase their debt gradually could do so by borrowing funds to invest in new projects and slowly bring the capital structure closer to the optimum. If the company has a low level of debt, but does not have sufficiently attractive projects, it could increase its debt over time and use the new funds to buy back shares or pay dividends. Companies that are excessively leveraged and wish to gradually decrease their level of debt should also look for potentially attractive projects. If the company has positive NPV projects it should finance them from internal funds (retained earnings) or by issuing shares. If it does not have any attractive projects, it should use the internal funds it produces to repay its debt.

The method by which a company changes its leverage will depend upon the speed at which it needs to adjust its financial structure, and the existence of new projects that can be funded via debt or equity to alter the WACC. The firm's degree of confidence in the estimates, a comparison with sector standards, takeover risks, or the need to preserve financial flexibility might influence the firm one way or the other.

In the numerical example above, we assumed the firm will buy back shares in order to implement this change immediately. There are two ways this could be done: either by issuing debt and buying back shares or selling assets and buying back shares. The first option increases leverage in two ways simultaneously, as the debt issue increases the leverage and the share buyback reduces the level of equity. In the second case, the company can sell assets not needed for its core business and use the cash to reduce the equity by purchasing shares. This increases leverage by reducing the amount of equity.

When a company has too much debt, changing its capital structure might present some additional challenges. This is because being perceived as having a low level of solvency can make the acquisition of new funds more difficult. The difficulty lies in finding equity investors. In the best case scenario the firm could issue new shares and purchase the debt on the balance sheet. Two alternatives would be to either renegotiate its debt or sell assets. Under the first option the firm can either renegotiate its debt repayment schedule or offer equity in the company in exchange for part of the debt (debt-equity swap). Under the second option, it can use the funds to amortize part of the company's debt.

As suggested in our example, buybacks can be used to effect the change in the capital structure immediately. The number of shares to be repurchased will be a function of the firm's market value, its share price and the percentage of debt the firm is aiming for. Looking back at our numbers in Table 6.7, the total market value of the company is $20 million, and the stock price is $1. However, we need to change from zero to 30 per cent debt. Thus, as shown in our example, we sell debt for $6,145 million and use these funds to buy back six million shares.

Buybacks do not add value but they may affect value in two ways. First, the buyback announcement, its terms and the way it is implemented all convey signals about the company's prospects and plans. Second, when financed by a debt issue, buybacks change a company's capital structure. With regard to the first point, the action of announcing the purchase of the company's own shares sends information to the market, and this information is used by investors and analysts to attempt to understand what management really thinks about the company's prospects. Theoretically, the announcement of a share buyback indicates that management has such positive expectations they believe purchasing their own shares is the best investment they can make. If this signal is believed by the market, the announcement can boost the share price, but if that happens, the company will need to spend more money on purchasing shares to reach the desired debt target.

The price boost we assumed in the prior paragraphs is just one of the likely scenarios. However, a buyback announcement does not always have this effect, because the announcement and implementation have to be believable and, to a certain extent, how these signals are read is beyond corporate control. Nevertheless, some actions can be planned. For example, a buyback announcement can send a negative signal if it is contradicted or overshadowed by other information. This could happen if the firm overloads the market with a succession of unexpected or startling news releases, which would draw attention away from the repurchase announcement.

A similar effect can occur when the company is in a high-growth sector. A buyback announcement might be translated into a message saying 'we do not have any better positive NPV projects in mind'. Lastly, a third negative scenario is when there is a discrepancy between the corporate words, and its management's actions. This would happen if, for example, management sells its shareholding after the announcement. Actions speak louder than words, and the market will assume managers do not believe in their own value message. The estimating, planning, announcement and implementation all deserve the highest level of attention and coordination.

However, if after taking into account all the details it is decided that a share buyback is the best way to go, the exact method this will be done must be determined. There are three common ways in which repurchases can be made: open-market repurchases, fixed-price tender offers and auction base tender offers.

In open-market share repurchases companies make a repurchase announcement through the press. However, the only information they will publish is the total number of shares authorized for potential repurchase. The company will not commit to a price, timing or execution. This provides a lot of flexibility since the firm will just repurchase when convenient, at its own pace. A drawback of this method is that limits are set on a company's daily repurchases. For example, in order to prevent price manipulation the SEC sets this limit at 25 per cent of the average daily traded volume over the prior four weeks.

Open-market repurchase programs are convenient because the company controls, to a large extent, its buying patterns. Nevertheless, this 'lack of commitment' translates into this not being an effective way of signalling the market about undervalued shares. A second problem with this method is that, given the repurchase daily volume constraints, the process can drag on for a long time. Given that the company usually wants to complete the repurchase quickly, this method does not work especially well. It is therefore often thought that the best use for open-market repurchase programmes is as a means of distributing excess cash to shareholders in lieu of a dividend.

A second way to exercise the repurchase is through a fixed-price tender offer. In a fixed-price tender offer, the company will make an announcement inviting shareholders to tender their shares to the company. The period over which shares can be tendered is often set between three and four weeks, and the purchase price set with a typical premium between 15 and 20 per cent over the market price at the time of the announcement. Setting the right price is a key factor to ensure the operation's success. For example, if the price were to be too aggressive, the market might disagree with the company over its expectations and react by destroying value by, for example, transferring wealth from non-tendering to tendering shareholders.

A third method of effecting the repurchase is through auction-based tender offers. The most typical auction mechanism is the Dutch auction. The process starts with a company announcement of their willingness to seek tenders during a certain period of time for a proportion of the shares. For this purpose, a premium is offered. The shareholders are given a few weeks to tell the company how many shares they want to sell and the minimum price they will accept. The tender clearing price is set at the minimum needed to purchase the desired number of shares. All the shares will be purchased at the same time. An advantage of this method is that the system itself helps the company to price the deal correctly.

If done properly, a share buyback can be a good instrument for helping to effect a change in the firm's capital structure. However, management needs to be aware of the possible side-effects of each alternative. Given the number of variables that need to be aligned and the different sentiments the operation might awake in stakeholders, managers must exercise great care. Unless all the issues have been carefully considered, using a buyback can backfire and there are plenty of real-life cases to illustrate these instances.

Summary

In this chapter we have examined how each source of financial capital constrains the corporations that acquire it. The optimal capital structure is determined by calculating the mix of debt and equity that maximizes the value of the corporation. Through time, different groups of scholars have attempted to explain how managers select their capital structures. Currently, two schools of thought prevail. On the one hand, there are those who see the capital structure as the result of a tradeoff between the benefits and drawbacks of acquiring additional debt. On the other hand, there are those who believe there is a hierarchy of funding methods, starting with internal funding as the most preferred method, followed by debt and hybrid securities, and finally, external equity as the least preferred resource of additional funds. This hierarchy of preference is explained on the grounds of transaction and agency costs, as well as managerial needs to keep a certain degree of financial and operational flexibility.

There are advantages and disadvantages to the use of internal and external financial resources as well as to the use of debt or equity financing. Leverage is appropriate if servicing the debt does not impose a risk of financial distress for the firm and if there are profits which could be reduced by interest expense, in effect making the debt function as a shield from taxation. Companies whose cash flows can be predicted to a large extent will be better able to optimize their structures in this sense. However, companies in high-growth sectors will have to maintain their debt levels below the estimated optimum in order to retain the flexibility they need in order to take advantage of growth opportunities.

A second benefit of leveraging the capital structure is that debt imposes a certain type of financial discipline. This is because, unlike in the case of equity, interest and principal payments are contractually binding, thus forcing management to attend to the payout of future cash flows. It is argued that these cash outflow obligations prevent wasteful spending either on perks or on projects that earn returns below the company's cost of capital. As an extreme example, one can observe how in LBO situations, corporate operating performance (usually) improves considerably after its debt levels have risen.

It is clear that there is not a unique optimal capital structure strategy for all companies, not even for those in the same sector. The most advantageous capital mix will depend on the firm's assets, the part of the life cycle where the company stands, its investment opportunities, the specific company strategy, the firm's investor clientele, and management preferences. Finding an optimum requires a serious analysis of the tradeoffs given the characteristics of each source of funding, how these features can benefit the firm, and the competitive environment. Industry averages can give an indication of what might be reasonable, although adjustments for specific characteristics need to be performed. For example, attention ought to be paid to whether certain key variables such as tax rates, asset tangibility and variability of cash flows are equivalent. One would expect that if the company's effective tax rate is over the average, if the cash flow volatility is lower, and the company's tangible assets larger, then this company might carry more debt than the mean in the sector. Agency ratios and preoccupations about ownership dilution might also help explain divergence from the average.

To estimate the optimal capital structure can be purely a numerical exercise. However, once this numerical optimum is found, the listed consideration will have to be reviewed. It is appropriate to mention that 'pre-packaged' proposals targeting specific ratios might not work at all times. Strategies that might be perfectly appropriate during a period of low inflation will strangle the firm if inflation is high. Moreover, on occasions, money might be flooding the market or just as we can see in the present times, it might dry up, suddenly making it difficult to access funds. Hence it is a good idea to think twice about the hidden constraints of high levels of leverage.

To determine the desirable degree of leverage is a complicated matter, as debt has to facilitate rather than hinge on growth opportunities. Sufficient financial flexibility under different economic scenarios will have to be secured. This is essential in order to responding to unforeseen situations such as diminished cash inflows, or a competitor's new marketing strategy. Leverage reduces flexibility because it compromises future cash flows, as these will be tied to the repayment of prior loans. Thus, unless the company has other sources of financing (internal and/or external) this lack of additional resources can put the firm at a competitive disadvantage. Obviously, the specific situation would depend on a number of factors such as management's ability to negotiate with investors, the option of realizing liquid assets, and the receptivity of the market to new fundraising efforts by the firm. The greater the uncertainty about the firm's future cash inflows and outflows, the less likely it is to use debt. It is vital, then, to remember that the long-term growth of the firm rests more on its investments in capital projects and its operating strategy than on the funding aspects of these projects.

Conclusion

All businesses and investment projects need capital to operate. However, financial capital – the money tied up in the business, is not free. A project's cost of capital is the minimum expected rate of return the project needs to offer investors to attract money. Simply put, the cost of capital is the expected rate of return the market requires to commit capital to an investment. Thus, the cost of financial capital to a firm is the return the firm's investors (debt and equity holders) receive from lending their savings to be used by the firm's portfolio of investment projects.

But where does this minimum expected return come from? How do we estimate it? What are the expectations that the counterparties to the operation – lenders and borrowers – bring to the negotiation table? What constrains lenders' and borrowers' choices? Through its different chapters, this book has proposed answers to these and other questions. Below, as a summary and conclusion, we provide a very concise discussion.

Individuals, firms, and states need to determine how to make the best use of the financial capital required to create and operate businesses. In this pursuit corporations search for projects that earn returns larger than the projects' associated costs, investors seek securities that appreciate in value, financial institutions look for ways to reinvest deposits to earn profits, and states create policies that facilitate economic activities.

The cost of capital allows us to estimate the present value of the expected future cash flows associated with an investment opportunity. Setting the future cash flows of different projects on an equivalent value basis helps the investor make informed decisions when buying and selling assets and comparing alternative investment prospects. In this sense, the cost of capital is a criterion for choosing among potential uses of funds.

Because investors expect to be rewarded appropriately for lending their savings, the returns paid by the borrowers and obtained by the lenders is correlated to the risk of the cash flows of the investment projects. The riskier the investment, the higher the reward expected by the investor. Thus, independently of the source of funds, it is the risk of the investment opportunity that determines the cost of the financial capital of the project under review. The cost of capital is tied to the risk of the investment project.

The return investors expect to earn on the average market risk of the firm's investments is the firm's weighted average cost of capital (WACC). When the risk of a project deviates from this average, adjustments are made and a premium is added to or deducted from the WACC to reflect the risk of the specific project.

For example, when investments in foreign territories bring additional exposure to risk, a supplementary risk premium should be added to the WACC of a firm. A key issue is then how to quantify the additional risks, and how to incorporate this estimate into the cash flow analysis of our expansionary foreign project.

The cost and proportions of each of a firm's sources of funding at any given point in time make up its WACC. To identify the components of the capital structure of a firm one can consider all existing sources of capital used for the long-term financing of its operations and, in addition, any significant amounts of short-term funding which de facto are a permanent part of the capital structure of the company. However, this exercise only provides information about historical sources of funds: those that are already in the books. Management looking to start new projects will be concerned with future funding, and will have to evaluate whether the same or a different capital structure is appropriate for facing the managerial challenges the future might bring.

Depending upon its risks, each component of an entity's capital structure has its own cost. For measuring the cost of equity, the capital asset pricing model (CAPM) is the technique management use most often. However, given that no one model, including the CAPM, is the best suited for all circumstances, other methods are also common. Furthermore, in practice, the use of any one of the approaches introduced within the pages of this book requires some problem-solving on the part of the manager.

For instance, a common predicament is that we are trying to determine the right return for risks that evolve through time and cannot be measured precisely at the start of a projects. Future risks can only be approximated and often these assessments are done by assuming that the future will resemble the past. Insofar as the future does resemble the past, expectations derived from historical data will approximate the true future outcomes. However, when this is not the case, using historical information such as a beta to assess future outcomes will lead to the wrong predictions. In these circumstances management will have to use the information at hand to see if some fine-tuning will help them improve their estimates.

In addition, a series of caveats affect our cost of capital estimations. For example, inflation affects our assessment of the value of the assets of a company, and inflation changes over time. A related consideration is that the nominal cost of capital that derives from market interest rates and the expected returns on equity is a function of anticipated inflation. Thus, we need to consider the impact of inflation when dealing with projects that generate cash flows over multiple periods.

A second example arises when a firm is not publicly traded. In such a situation we need to bear in mind a few issues that affect the cost of capital. For instance, the liquidity of the ownership stake in the privately held company is less than that of publicly held stock, and we cannot observe the privately held firm's equity market value. Furthermore, often the owner is key to the successful development of the business. These and other characteristics of privately owned firms call for specific adjustments to the cost of capital, such as liquidity and key person discounts, and control premiums, among others.

Through time, different explanations have been proposed of how managers choose their capital structures. Currently, the main split of opinion is between those who think the capital structure is the result of a trade-off between the benefits and constraints of acquiring additional debt and those who believe there is a hierarchical order of preference in funding, which starts with internal funding as the most preferred method, followed by debt and hybrid securities, and finally, external equity as the least preferred source of additional funds. This hierarchy is explained on the grounds of transaction and agency costs, as well as managerial needs to keep a certain degree of financial and operational flexibility.

Given that there are advantages and disadvantages to the use of internal and external financial resources, as well as to the use of debt, equity or hybrid financing, throughout the pages of this book we have examined how each source of financial capital constrains the corporations that acquire it.

For example, leverage is appropriate if servicing the debt does not impose a risk of financial distress for the firm and if there are profits which could be reduced by interest expense, leverage can act as a shield from taxation. Companies whose cash flows can be predicted to a large extent will be better able to optimize their structures in this sense. However, corporations in high growth sectors might have to maintain their debt levels low in order to keep the flexibility they need to take advantage of growth opportunities.

Industry averages can give an indication as to what type of capital structure might be reasonable for firms in different sectors. Nevertheless, adjustments for characteristics of the specific company must be made. For instance, attention ought to be paid as to whether certain key variables such as tax rates, asset tangibility and variability of cash flows are equivalent across firms in a given sector.

The optimal capital structure for an entity is found when the mix of debt and equity which maximizes the value of the corporation is determined.

Nonetheless, it is clear that the optimal capital structure strategy is not the same for all companies, not even for those within the same sector. The most advantageous capital mix will depend on the firm's assets, the point in the life cycle where the company currently stands, its investment opportunities, the specific company strategy, the firm's investor clientele, management preferences and capital availability, and the market's conditions at each point in time. Finding an optimum requires a serious analysis of the tradeoffs given the characteristics of each source of funding, how these features can benefit the firm, and the competitive environment.

To determine the optimal capital structure can be done on a purely numerical basis, and we have shown how to do the calculation. However, once this numerical optimum is found, the assumptions used in the estimate will have to be revisited. It is appropriate to mention that pre-packaged proposals targeting specific ratios, for example, debt to equity, might not always work. Strategies which might be perfectly appropriate during a period of low inflation will strangle the firm if inflation is high. On occasions, money might be flooding the market and available to any debtor or, as we say in the period after 2008, funding might dry up to the point that even the most trustworthy firms have difficulty accessing credit. Hence it is a good idea to think twice about issues such as the hidden constraints imposed by high levels of leverage or the fact that the selected strategies have to be sustainable through time.

To determine the desirable degree of leverage is a complicated matter as debt has to facilitate rather than hinge on growth opportunities. For instance, sufficient financial flexibility under different economic scenarios will have to be secured. This is essential in order to respond to unforeseen situations such as diminished cash inflows, or a competitor's new marketing strategy.

Leverage reduces flexibility because a potion of the future cash flows will be tied to the repayment of prior loans. Thus, unless the company in question has other sources of funds this lack of financial flexibility can put the firm at a competitive disadvantage. Obviously, the specific situation would depend on a number of factors such as management's ability to negotiate with investors, the option of realizing liquid assets, and the receptivity of the market to new fundraising efforts by the firm. It is vital, then, to remember that the long-term growth of the firm rests more on its investments in capital projects and its operating strategy than on the funding aspects of those projects. Having said that, it is also worth remembering that a business opportunity such as investing in a new capital project can only be afforded under specific circumstances.

It can help to understand the overall situation if we look at it simultaneously from the point of view of both the parties involved: the borrower and the lender.

Once the manager or entrepreneur has identified an investment opportunity that enriches the corporation, she will be concerned with financing her idea. In doing this, she will have to find a balance between different sources of funds, considering both the cost of the funds needed for the project, and the preservation of her managerial freedom. Thus, as far as possible our entrepreneur will seek funding from lenders and/or equity holders while at the same time attempting to safeguard her collateral and flexibility. On the other side of the negotiating table, the lender and/or shareholder will seek to protect her investment by limiting her exposure and demanding the appropriate return. This will be achieved by requesting sufficient collateral in terms of assets, including cash flows, and negotiating covenants over such matters as the preservation of certain ratios (e.g. liquidity), and the acquisition of further debt. In exchange, the cost of the funds will be linked to market benchmarks which will include the necessary premiums to encourage the equity or debt holder to accept the risks of the project.

Finding the adequate financial structure for a project requires a comprehensive understanding of the standpoints of entrepreneur and lender. Only if each party understands the objectives and needs of the other will the negotiation produce a sustainable result that will last for the duration of the project. This book has therefore addressed both parties' points of view. In addition, determining the optimal weighted average cost of capital for a corporation requires strategizing the comprehensive financial needs of the overall firm over time, in such a way that the financial manager becomes a facilitator of corporate growth and does so at the optimal financial cost.

Notes

1 A General Introduction to Risk, Return, and the Cost of Capital

1. The return on an investment can be expressed as an absolute amount, for example, $300, or as a percentage of the total amount invested, such as eight per cent. The formula used to calculate the percentage return of an investment is: (Selling price of the asset – Purchase price of the asset + Dividends or any other distributions which have been paid during the time the financial asset was held) / Purchase price of the asset. If the investor wants to know her return after taxes, these would have to be deducted.

2. A share is a certificate representing one unit of ownership in a corporation, mutual fund or limited partnership. A bond is a debt instrument issued for a period of more than one year with the purpose of raising capital by borrowing.

3. In order to determine whether an investment in a specific project should be made, firms first need to estimate if undertaking the said project increases the value of the company. That is, firms need to calculate whether by accepting the project the company is worth more than without it. For this purpose, all cash flows generated as a consequence of accepting the proposed project should be considered. These include the negative cash flows (for example, the investments required), and positive cash flows (such as the monies generated by the project). Since these cash flows happen at different points in time, they must be adjusted for the 'time value of money', the fact that a dollar, pound, yen or euro today is worth more than in five years. This adjustment is done by discounting (dividing) the future cash flows by a rate which reflects the return desired by the firm if undertaking the project under scrutiny.

4. Equity is the capital raised from owners, such as common stock shareholders.

5. The overall general upward price movement of goods and services in an economy, usually measured by the Consumer Price Index and the Producer Price Index. As the cost of goods and services increases over time, the value of a currency falls, since the purchasing power of individuals decreases. That is, with the same amount of money a person cannot buy as much as she could previously.

6. A note is a short-term debt security, usually with a maturity of five years or less.

7. Liquidity refers to the possibility of converting the asset (house, painting, share of stock, etc.) into cash quickly and with no loss of value. For example, if cash is needed in a hurry, the homeowner might not have time to find the best possible buyer for her house and some value will be lost during the transaction. On the other hand, common stocks traded in big markets are very liquid as they can be converted into cash fast and without any loss.

8. http://nihoncassandra.blogspot.com

9. A statistical measure of volatility. More generally, it measures the extent to which a series of values are spread around their average.

10. We could rank women attending a conference by height. Most of the population would group between 5' 2" to 5' 7", while those taller or shorter would only be a small percentage of the population. Hence the probability that any one attendee

230

would fall under this range is larger than the probability that anyone would be 6′ 3″ or 4′ 8″, for example.

11. Preferred stock is a hybrid security which combines the characteristics of debt and equity.

2 The Components of the Cost of Capital and Alternative Models

1. For their work on this, William Sharpe, Harry Markowitz and Merton Miller jointly received the Nobel Memorial Prize in Economic Sciences.
2. Black, F. and Scholes, M. (1973). The pricing of options and corporate liabilities. *Journal of Political Economy,* 81 (May/June 1973), 637–54.
3. Copeland, T. E. and Weston, J. F. (1988). Financial theory and corporate policy. (3rd edition) Reading, MA: Addison-Wesley, 468–71.
4. Hsia, C. (1991). Estimating a firm's cost of capital: An option pricing approach. *Journal of Business Finance and Accounting,* 18(2), 281–7.
5. Stephen A. Ross (1976). The arbitrage theory of capital asset pricing. *Journal of Economic Theory* (December), 241–60.
6. Chen, N., Roll, R. and Ross, S. A. (1986). Economic forces and the stock market. *Journal of Business* (1986), 383–403.
7. Fama, F. and French, K. (1992). The cross-section of expected stock returns, *Journal of Finance* (1992), 427–86.

3 Problems in Using the Models

1. A more in-depth discussion on the CAPM is provided in the Appendix.
2. Robert C. Merton (2003). *Continuous-Time Finance.* (Revised edition) Blackwell Publishing, 97–119 and 446–520.
3. F. Macaulay (1938). *Some Theoretical Problems Suggested by the Movements of Interest Rates, Bond Yields and Stock Prices in the United States since 1856.* New York: National Bureau of Economic Research. Cited in Bodie, Z. A. Kane and Marcus, A. J. *Investments.* (3rd edition) Irwin.
4. The right risk free rate to use in asset pricing models: A note. September 1998, www.stern.nyu.edu/~adamodar
5. The most widely used database, from Ibbotson Associates, has returns going back to 1926. Jeremy Siegel, at Wharton, recently presented data going back to the early 1800s.
6. Booth (1999) examines both nominal and real equity risk premiums from 1871 to 1997. While the nominal equity returns have clearly changed over time, he concludes that the real equity return average has been around 9 per cent over that period. He suggests adding the expected inflation rate to this number to estimate the expected return on equity.
7. Adapted from 'Best Practices' in Estimating the Cost of Capital: Survey and Synthesis' (R. Bruner, K. Eades, R. Harris, and R. Higgins), *Financial Practice and Education* (Spring/Summer 1998). This reference was taken from the note prepared by Professor Robert Harris, and draws, in part, directly from 'Best Practices' in Estimating the Cost of Capital: Survey and Synthesis,' and thanks go to the authors for their permission to reproduce these results. Copyright © 2004 by the University of Virginia Darden School Foundation, Charlottesville, VA. All rights reserved.

4   Caveats

1. Most flotation expenses are fixed, so the total cost of selling bonds and stocks is proportionally lower for large issues than for small ones. This may explain why firms prefer to raise large amounts of external funds infrequently rather than small amounts often. For issues of the same size, it has been shown that the cost of raising equity is higher than the cost of raising debt.
2. Fisher, I. (1930) The theory of interest. Library of Economics and Liberty. Retrieved March 21, 2010 from www.econlib.org/library/YPDBooks/Fisher/fshToI.html.
3. Amihud, Y. and Mendelson, H. (1989). Liquidity and cost of capital: Implications for corporate management. *Journal of Applied Corporate Finance* (Fall), 65–73.
4. The median is the numeric value splitting the upper and lower part of a distribution in half. To find this value we need to order all observations from the lowest value to the highest (or vice versa) and choose the one in the middle.
5. Kraus, A. and Litzenberger, R. (1976). Skewness preference and the valuation of risky assets. *Journal of Finance* (September), 1085–1100.
6. Black, F. and Scholes, M. (1973). The pricing of options and corporate liabilities. *Journal of Political Economy*, 81, 637–54.
7. Several academic studies show that option-based compensation leads to a greater likelihood of earnings restatements and outright fraud. See Agrawal, A. and Chadha, S.(2006). Corporate governance and accounting scandals. *Journal of Law and Economics*, 371–406; Burns, N. and Kedia, S. (2006). The impact of performance-based compensation on misreporting. *Journal of Financial Economics*, 35–67; and Denis, D. J., Hanouna, P. and Sarin, A. (2006). Is there a dark side to incentive compensation? *Journal of Corporate Finance* (June), 467–88.

5   Country Risk

1. http://www.standardandpoors.com, http://www.moodys.com, http://www.fitchratings.com
2. This column follows Moody's descriptions.
3. Moody's adds numeric modifiers 1, 2 and 3 to each generic classification for ratings Aa to Caa. Modifier 1 indicates that the instrument is of the highest quality within its category, modifier 2 indicates an average qualification and modifier 3 positions the instrument in the bottom bracket of the generic category.
4. Godfrey, S. and Espinosa, R. (1996). A practical approach to calculating costs of equity for investment in emerging markets. *Journal of Applied Corporate Finance*, 9(3), 80–90.
5. Erb, C., Harvey, C. and Viskanta, T. (1995). Country risk and global equity selection. *The Journal of Portfolio Management* (Winter), 74–83.
6. See note 5.
7. Estrada, J. (2000). The cost of equity in emerging markets: A downside risk approach. *Emerging Markets Quarterly*, 4 (Fall), 19–30 and Estrada, J. (2001). The cost of equity in emerging markets: A downside risk approach, II. *Emerging Markets Quarterly* (Spring), 63–72.

6   The Optimal Capital Structure

1. Modigliani, F. and Miller, M. H. (1958). The cost of capital, corporation finance and the theory of investment. *American Economic Review*, 48(3), 261–97.

2. Myers, S. C. (1984). The capital structure puzzle. *Journal of Finance*, 39(3), 575–92.
3. Williamson, O. (1983). Corporate finance and corporate governance. *The Journal of Finance*, 43(3), 567–91.
4. Jensen, M. and Meckling, W. (1976) Theory of the firm: Managerial behaviour, agency costs and capital structure. *Journal of Financial Economics*, 3, 305–60.
5. Ross, S. A. (1977). The determination of financial structure: The incentive-signalling approach. *The Bell Journal of Economics*, 8(1), 23–40.
6. Myers, S. C. and Majluf, N. S. (1984). Corporate financing and investment decisions when firms have information that investors do not have. *Journal of Financial Economics*, 13, 187–221.
7. DeAngelo, H. and Masulis, R. W.(1980). Optimal capital structure under corporate and personal taxation. *Journal of Financial Economics*, 8, 3–29.
8. Masulis, R. W. (1983). The impact of capital structure change on firm value: Some estimates. *Journal of Finance*, 38(1), 107–26.
9. Haugen, R. and Senbet, L. (1978). The insignificance of bankruptcy costs to the theory of optimal capital structure. *Journal of Finance*, 33(2), 283–393.
10. Piper, T. R. and Weinhold, W. A. (1982). How much debt is right for your company? *Harvard Business Review*, 60(4), 106–14.

References

Agrawal, A. and Chadha, S. (2005). Corporate governance and accounting scandals. *Journal of Law and Economics*, 48(2), 371–406.

Amihud, Y. and Mendelson, H. (1989). Liquidity and cost of capital: Implications for corporate management. *Journal of Applied Corporate Finance,* 2(3) (Fall), 65–73.

Bhandari, L. C. (1988). Debt/equity ratio and expected common stock returns: Empirical evidence. *The Journal of Finance,* 43(2), 507–28.

Black, F., Michael, C. J. and Scholes, M. (1972). The Capital Asset Pricing Model: Some Empirical Tests, in Michael C. Jensen (ed.), *Studies in the Theory of Capital Markets*, New York: Praeger, 79–121.

Black, F. and Scholes, M. (1973). The pricing of options and corporate liabilities. *Journal of Political Economy*, 81 (May/June), 637–54.

Booth, L. (1999). Estimating the equity risk premium and equity costs: New ways of looking at old data. *Journal of Applied Corporate Finance*, 12(1), 100–12.

Brown, S. J. and Weinstein, M. I. (1983). A new approach to testing asset pricing models: The bilinear paradigm. *The Journal of Finance,* 38(3) (June), 711–43.

Bruner, R., Eades, K., Harris, R. and Higgins, R. (1998). 'Best practices' in estimating the cost of capital: Survey and synthesis'. *Financial Practice and Education*. Spring/Summer, 13–28.

Burns, N. and Kedia, S. (2006). The impact of performance-based compensation on misreporting. *Journal of Financial Economics*, 79, 35–67.

Chen, N. F. (1983). Some empirical tests of the arbitrage pricing theory. *The Journal of Finance,* 38(6), 1393–414.

Chen, N., Roll, R. and Ross, S. A. (1986). Economic forces and the stock market. *Journal of Business* (July), 383–403.

Copeland, T. E. and Weston, J. F. (1988). *Financial Theory and Corporate Policy*. (3rd edition) Reading, MA: Addison-Wesley, 468–71.

Conway, D. A. and Reinganum, M. R. (1980). Stable factors in security returns: Identification using cross-validation. *Journal of Business and Economic Statistics, 6,* 1–15.

DeAngelo, H. and Masulis, R. W. (1980). Optimal capital structure under corporate and personal taxation. *Journal of Financial Economics*, 8, 3–29.

DeBondt, W. F. and Thaler, R. H. (1985). Does the stock market overreact? in R. H. Thaler (ed.), *Advances in Behavioral Finance*, 249–264.

Denis, D. J., Hanouna, P. and Sarin, A. (2006). Is there a dark side to incentive compensation? *Journal of Corporate Finance*, 12(3) (June), 467–88.

Dhrymes, P., Friend, I. and Gultekin, M. (1984). A critical re-examination of the empirical evidence on the arbitrage pricing theory. *The Journal of Finance,* 39 (2), 323–46.

Erb, C., Harvey, C. and Viskanta, T. (1995). Country risk and global equity selection. *The Journal of Portfolio Management* (Winter), 74–83.

Estrada, J. (2000). The cost of equity in emerging markets: A downside risk approach. *Emerging Markets Quarterly* (Fall), 19–30.

Estrada, J. (2001). The cost of equity in emerging markets: A downside risk approach, II. *Emerging Markets Quarterly* (Spring), 63–72.

Fama, E. F. (1970). Efficient capital markets: A review of theory and empirical work. *The Journal of Finance*, 25(2), 383–417.

Fama, E. F. and French, K. R. (1992). The cross-section of expected stock returns. *The Journal of Finance*, 47(2), 427–66.

Fama, E. F. and French, K. R. (1993). Common risk factors in the returns on stocks and bonds. *Journal of Financial Economics*, 33, 3–56.

French, K. R. (1980). Stock returns and the weekend effect. *Journal of Financial Economics*, 8(1) (March), 55–69.

Godfrey, S. and Espinosa, R. (1996). A practical approach to calculating costs of equity for investment in emerging markets. *Journal of Applied Corporate Finance*, 9(3) (Fall), 80–90.

Haugen, R. and Senbet, L. (1978). The insignificance of bankruptcy costs to the theory of optimal capital structure. *The Journal of Finance*, 33(2), 283–393.

Hsia, C. (1991). Estimating a firm's cost of capital: An option pricing approach. *Journal of Business Finance and Accounting*, 18(2), 281–7.

Ibbotson, R. G. and Sinquefield, R. A. (1976). Stocks, bonds, bills, and inflation: Simulations of the future (1976–2000). *Journal of Business*, 49(3) (July).

Jegadeesh, N. and Titman, S. (1993). Returns to buying winners and selling losers: Implications for stock market efficiency. *The Journal of Finance*, 48(1), 65–91.

Jensen, M. C. (1969). Risk, the pricing of capital assets, and the evaluation of investment portfolios. *Journal of Business*, 2, 167–247.

Jensen, M. and Meckling, W. (1976).Theory of the firm: Managerial behavior, agency costs and capital structure. *Journal of Financial Economics*, 3, 305–60.

Kraus, A. and Litzenberger, R. (1976). Skewness preference and the valuation of risky assets. *The Journal of Finance*, 31 (4) (September), 1085–1100.

Levy, H. (1972). Portfolio performance and the investment horizon. *Management Science*, 36, 645–53.

Macaulay, F. (1938). *Some Theoretical Problems Suggested by the Movements of the Interest Rates, Bond Yields, and Stock Prices in the United States since 1856*. New York: National Bureau of Economic Research. Cited in *Investments*, Bodie, Z., Kane, A. and Marcus, A. J. (3rd edition), Chicago, IL: Irwin.

Markowitz, H. M. (1952). Portfolio selection. *The Journal of Finance*, 12(7), 77–91.

Markowitz, H. M. (1983). Nonnegative or not nonnegative: A question about CAPMs, *The Journal of Finance*, 38(2) (May), Papers and proceedings Forty-First Annual Meeting of the American Finance Association, New York. December 28–30, 1982, 283–95.

Masulis, R. W. (1983). The impact of capital structure change on firm value: Some estimates. *The Journal of Finance*, 38(1) (March), 107–26.

Merton, R. C. (1971). Optimum consumption and portfolio rules in a continuous-time model. *Journal of Economic Theory*, 3, 373–413.

Merton, R. C. (2003). *Continuous-Time Finance*. (Revised Edition) Blackwell Publishing, 97–119 and 446–520.

Modigliani, F. and Miller, M. H. (1958). The cost of capital, corporation finance and the theory of investment. *American Economic Review*, 48(3), 261–97.

Modigliani, F. and Miller, M. (1966). Some estimates of the cost of capital to the electric utility industry, 1954–57. *American Economic Review*, 56(3) (June), 333–91.

Myers, S. C. and Majluf, N. S. (1984). Corporate financing and investment decisions when firms have information that investors do not have. *Journal of Financial Economics*, 13, 187–221.

Piper, T. R. and Weinhold, W. A. (1982). How much debt is right for your company? *Harvard Business Review*, 60(4) (July/August), 106–14.

Reinganum, M. R. (1981). Misspecification of capital asset pricing: Empirical anomalies. *Journal of Financial Economics, 9,* 19–46.

Reinganum, M. R. (1983). The anomalous stock market behavior of small firms in January: Empirical tests for tax-loss selling effects. *Journal of Financial Economics, 12,* 89–104.

Roll, R. (1977). A critique of the asset pricing theory's tests. *Journal of Financial Economics,* 4, 129–76.

Roll, R. (1978). Ambiguity when performance is measured by the securities market line. *The Journal of Finance, 33*(4) (September), 1051–69.

Roll, R. (1983). Vas ist das? The turn-of-the-year effect and the return premia of small firms. *The Journal of Portfolio Management, 9,* 18–28.

Roll, R. and Ross, S. A. (1980). An empirical investigation of the arbitrage pricing theory. *The Journal of Finance, 35*(5), 1073–103.

Ross, S. A. (1976). The arbitrage theory of capital asset pricing. *Journal of Economic Theory,* December, 241–60.

Ross, S. A. (1977). The determination of financial structure: The incentive-signaling approach. *The Bell Journal of Economics,* 8(1) (Spring), 23–40.

Ross, S. A., Westerfield R. W. and Jordan, B. D. (1995). *Fundamentals of Corporate Finance.* (3rd edition), Chicago, IL: Irwin.

Trzcinka, C. A. (1986). On the number of factors in the arbitrage pricing model. *The Journal of Finance, 41*(2), 347–368.

Williamson, O. (1988). Corporate finance and corporate governance. *The Journal of Finance, 43*(3), 567–91.

Worthington, A. C. and Higgs, H. (2006). Efficiency in the Australian stock market, 1875–2006: A note on extreme long-run random walk behavior. *Faculty of Commerce – Accounting & Finance Working Papers,* Paper 21.

Websites

Beta estimates from stock exchanges. Retrieved from http://www.valueline.com

Beta estimates from stock exchanges, and Treasury Bills or Government Bonds for the USA. Rating Risk premiums in basis points. Retrieved from http://www.standardand-poors.com/home/en/us

Beta estimates from stock exchanges. Retrieved from http://es.finance.yahoo.com

Beta estimates from stock exchanges. Retrieved from http://www.bloomberg.com

Beta estimates from stock exchanges. Retrieved from http://www.ml.com

Beta estimates from stock exchanges.Retrieved from http://www.mscibarra.com

Damodaran, A. The right risk-free rate to use in asset pricing models: A note, September 1998. Retrieved from http://pages.stern.nyu.edu/~adamodar/

Fisher, I. (1930). *The Theory of Interest.* Library of Economics and Liberty. Retrieved 21 March 2010 from http://www.econlib.org/library/YPDBooks/Fisher/fshToI.html

Markowitz, H. M., Miller, M. H., Sharpe, W. F. (1990) The Sveriges Riksbank Prize in Economic Sciences in Memory of Alfred Nobel. Retrieved from http://nobelprize.org/nobel_prizes/economics/laureates/1990/sharpe-autobio.html

My favorite bloggers. Retrieved from http://nihoncassandra.blogspot.com/

Rating Risk premiums in basis points. Retrieved from http://v3.moodys.com

Rating Risk premiums in basis points. Retrieved from http://www.fitchratings.com

US and Colombian bonds. Retrieved from http://www.tradingeconomics.com/

Further reading

Allen, D. E. (1993). The pecking order hypothesis: Australian evidence. *Applied Financial Economics*, 3, 101–12.

Andrés, P., Azofra, V. and Rodríguez, J. (2000). Endeudamiento, oportunidades de crecimiento y estructura contractual: un contraste empírico para el caso español. *Investigaciones Económicas*, 24(3).

Armitage, S. (2005). *The Cost of Capital: Intermediate Theory*. Cambridge: Cambridge University Press.

Baskin, J. (1989). An empirical investigation of the pecking order hypothesis. *Financial Management*, 18(1) (Spring), 26–35.

Bernstein, P. L. (2005). *Capital Ideas: The Improbable Origins of Modern Wall Street*. Hoboken, NJ: John Wiley & Sons, Inc.

Bernstein, P. L. (2007). *Capital Ideas Evolving*. Hoboken,NJ: John Wiley & Sons, Inc.

Bevan, A. A. and Danbolt, J. (2002). Capital structure and its determinants in the UK: A decompositional analysis. *Applied Financial Economics*, 12, 159–70.

Bodie, Z. and Merton, R. C. (2001). *Finance*. Upper Saddle River, NJ: Prentice Hall.

Damodaran, A. (1999). *Applied Corporate Finance: A User's Manual*. Hoboken, NJ: John Wiley & Sons, Inc.

DeAngelo, H. and Masulis, R. W. (1980). Optimal capital structure under corporate and personal taxation. *Journal of Financial Economics*, 8(1) (March), 3–29.

Ehrhardt, M. C. (1994). *The Search for Value: Measuring the Company's Cost of Capital*. Boston, MA: Harvard Business School Press.

Fama, E. F. and French, K. R. (2002). Testing trade-off and pecking order predictions about dividends and debt. *The Review of Financial Studies*, 15(1) (Spring), 1–33.

Frank, M. Z. and Goyal, V. K. (2003). Testing the pecking order theory of capital structure. *Journal of Financial Economics*, 67, 217–48.

Goetzmann, W. N. and Ibbotson R. G. (2006). *The Equity Risk Premium: Essays and Explorations*. New York: Oxford University Press, Inc.

Hamada, R. S. (1972). The effect of the firm's capital structure on the systematic risk of common stocks. *The Journal of Finance*, 27(2), 435–52.

Harris, M. and Raviv, A. (1991). The theory of capital structure. *The Journal of Finance*, 46(1) (March), 297–355.

Heinkel, R. (1985). A theory of capital structure relevance under imperfect information. *The Journal of Finance*, 35(5) (December), 1141–50.

Ibbotson Associates (2006). *Stocks, Bonds, Bills, and Inflation 2006 Yearbook*. Chicago, IL.

Kim, E. H., Lewellen, W. G. and McConnell, J. J. (1979). Financial leverage clienteles: Theory and evidence. *Journal of Financial Economics*, 7, 83–109.

Kraus, A. and Litzenberger, R. H. (1973). A state-preference model of optimal financial leverage. *The Journal of Finance*, 28(4) (September), 911–27.

Myers, S. C. (1993). Still searching for optimal capital structure. *Journal of Applied Corporate Finance*, 6(1) (Spring), 4–14.

Ogier, T., Rugman, J. and Spicer, L. (2004). *The Real Cost of Capital: A Business Field Guide to Better Financial Decisions*. Harlow: FT Prentice Hall.

Pratt, S. P. and Grabowski, R. J. (2008). *Cost of Capital: Applications and Examples*. (3rd edition) Hoboken, NJ: John Wiley & Sons, Inc.

Poitevin, M. (1989). Financial signaling and the 'deep-pocket' argument. *RAND Journal of Economics*, 20(1) (Spring), 26–40.

Rajan, R. and Zingales, L. (1995). What do we know about capital structure? Some evidence from international data. *The Journal of Finance*, 50(5), 1421–60.

Robicheck, A. A. and Myers, S. C. (1996). Problems in the theory of optimal capital structure. *Journal of Financial and Quantitative Analysis*, 1(2) (June), 1–35.

Shyam-Sunder, L. and Myers, S. C. (1999). Testing static tradeoff against pecking order. *Journal of Financial Economics*, 51, 219–44.

Smith, C. W. and Warner, J. B. (1979). On financial contracting: An analysis of bond covenants. *Journal of Financial Economics*, 7, 117–61.

Index